ROUTLEDGE LIBRARY EDITIONS:
INDUSTRIAL RELATIONS

Volume 38

WHITE-COLLAR PROLETARIAT

WHITE-COLLAR PROLETARIAT

The Industrial Behaviour of British Civil Servants

MICHAEL P. KELLY

Routledge
Taylor & Francis Group

LONDON AND NEW YORK

First published in 1980 by Routledge & Kegan Paul Ltd

This edition first published in 2025
by Routledge
4 Park Square, Milton Park, Abingdon, Oxon OX14 4RN

and by Routledge
605 Third Avenue, New York, NY 10158

Routledge is an imprint of the Taylor & Francis Group, an informa business

British Library Cataloguing in Publication Data
A catalogue record for this book is available from the British Library

ISBN: 978-1-032-81770-5 (Set)
ISBN: 978-1-032-81393-6 (Volume 38) (hbk)
ISBN: 978-1-032-81399-8 (Volume 38) (pbk)
ISBN: 978-1-003-49962-6 (Volume 38) (ebk)

DOI: 10.4324/9781003499626

Publisher's Note
The publisher has gone to great lengths to ensure the quality of this reprint but points out that some imperfections in the original copies may be apparent.

Disclaimer
The publisher has made every effort to trace copyright holders and would welcome correspondence from those they have been unable to trace.

WHITE-COLLAR PROLETARIAT
The industrial behaviour of British Civil Servants

Michael P. Kelly

ROUTLEDGE DIRECT EDITIONS

ROUTLEDGE & KEGAN PAUL
London, Boston and Henley

First published in 1980
by Routledge & Kegan Paul Ltd
39 Store Street,
London WC1E 7DD,
9 Park Street,
Boston, Mass. 02108, USA and
Broadway House,
Newtown Road,
Henley-on-Thames,
Oxon RG9 1EN
Set in IBM Adjutant
and printed in Great Britain by
M. and A. Thomson Litho Ltd, East Kilbride
© Michael P. Kelly 1980

British Library Cataloguing in Publication Data

Kelly, Michael P.
White-collar proletariat.
1. Civil service - Great Britain
I. Title
301.5'5   JN425
ISBN 0 7100 0623 3

CONTENTS

FIGURES

PREFACE

This book is concerned with the industrial behaviour of a group of
white-collar workers in Britain - Civil Servants. I test whether
changes in the industrial behaviour of these workers can be explained with reference to the sociological concept of proletarianization. I proceed by delimiting the concept of proletarianization, by an examination of some of the work of Marx where the
concept originates, then by specifying the way in which the concept has been used by subsequent writers. I draw attention to a
number of key variables which sociologists have taken as critical
in the study of proletarianization. These are level and source of
income, social origins and the organization of work. I argue that
most of the formulations of the concept of proletarianization are
inadequate from an empirical or theoretical point of view. I
examine the variables in the context of white-collar workers in
the Civil Service. My empirical focus is the Civil Service,
because within that organization there are a variety of white-
collar occupations which may be compared and there is much available material on the Civil Service, including evidence presented
to Royal Commissions, government statistics, autobiographies of
retired or serving Civil Servants and trade unionists, minutes of
union conferences and the trades union journals.

I have found in the Civil Service a degree of change in the
pattern of industrial behaviour (such as resort to strike action
and other forms of militancy) but I argue that this cannot be explained by the concept of proletarianization. I suggest a number
of reasons for this and in my conclusion suggest alternative modes
of explanation for white-collar militancy. These findings are
then placed in the general context of mainstream sociology.

Michael P. Kelly

ACKNOWLEDGMENTS

The research on which this book is based was carried out with the aid of a postgraduate grant from the Social Science Research Council and a grant in aid of research from the Research Board of the University of Leicester.

I owe a large debt to David Field, who read earlier drafts of this manuscript and made many detailed and constructive criticisms, and to Professor Ilya Neustadt who gave me the time and encouragement to complete this work. I would also like to thank the Civil Service Pay Research Unit and the Society of Civil and Public Servants who allowed me access to their records and where individual Civil Servants and union officials discussed with me some of the issues raised in this work. Many other individuals and organizations have helped in various ways. In particular I would like to thank Professor Keith Kelsall, Professor Olive Banks, Mr Norman Ashton, Mr Steve Crook, Mr Stuart Miller, Ms Debbie Hardy, Mrs Doreen Butler, Mr Joseph Leveson and the Research Committee of Dundee College of Technology.

The table from 'The Civil Service Volume 4: Factual, Statistical and Explanatory Papers (Fulton Report) 1968', and the extract from 'Civil Service Statistics 1975' are reproduced with the permission of the Controller of Her Majesty's Stationery Office.

Finally I would like to thank my wife Tessa Kelly who typed the final draft of the manuscript and provided much needed encouragement to get this project finished.

In spite of all the generous help I have received, I alone am responsible for the errors and problems that remain.

ABBREVIATIONS

A Level	General Certificate of Education: Advanced Level
ACA	Assistant Clerks Association
APEX	Association of Professional, Executive, Clerical and Computer Staff
ASTMS	Association of Scientific, Technical and Managerial Staffs
CPSA	Civil and Public Services Association
CSCA	Civil Service Clerical Association
CSD	Civil Service Department
DHSS	Department of Health and Social Security
DTI	Department of Trade and Industry
HMSO	Her Majesty's Stationery Office
HNC	Higher National Certificate
HSC	Higher School Certificate
IPCS	Institution of Professional Civil Servants
LTR	London Telecommunications Region
NALGO	National Association of Local Government Officers
NEDCS	National Economic Development Councils
O Level	General Certificate of Education: Ordinary Level
RAF	Royal Air Force
SCPS	Society of Civil and Public Servants
SCS	Society of Civil Servants
TMO	Telephone Managers Office
TUC	Trades Union Congress
VAT	Value Added Tax

Part One

BACKGROUND TO THE STUDY

Chapter 1

INTRODUCTION

In the 1960s and early 1970s it was fashionable for pundits to draw
attention to the so-called crisis of modern industrial society.(1)
Spectators of the contemporary scene observed diverse phenomena
which some thought marked a turning point in the history of modern
society. Generally these writers focused on such things as student
protest,(2) civil disorder,(3) and even urban guerrilla warfare.(4)
It seemed to some authors that significant new social movements had
emerged which constituted a serious threat to established society,
and depending upon their political persuasion this was viewed either
optimistically or pessimistically. Above all one series of events
stood out; this was the so-called 'French Revolution' of 1968.(5)
    The 'Revolution' had its origin in localized student protest in
France. From March 1967 onwards the university campus at Nanterre,
a satellite university of the Sorbonne, was the scene of constant
minor incidents which led finally to its closure.(6) This dispute
overspilled to the Sorbonne and when the rector there summoned the
police to clear the courtyard of demonstrators many students were
arrested. This in its turn appears to have provoked a demonstration
of a large number of hitherto uncommitted students and when this
was viciously broken up by the police the university authorities had
a large student revolt on their hands.(7) The disturbances gathered
momentum and the students won a number of 'victories' in the
streets, with the worst fighting taking place on the night of 10-11
May.(8) By 15 May the movement had spread throughout France and in
many places students had occupied their faculties. By 17 May the
dispute had widened and some young workers (many of whom were not
union members) joined with the students. On 17 May all the Renault
factories in France were occupied by workers who proclaimed an in-
definite strike. A wave of other stoppages spread throughout the
country, and included the textile industry, railways, shipyards,
the metro, buses, and banks, until by 20 May two million workers
were on strike with 250 factories occupied.(9) Sporadic and sometimes very violent clashes between police and demonstrators
occurred during May and June and attempted negotiation between the
students and strikers and the government failed to reach a settlement. The strike continued until the middle of June when amidst a
highly charged emotional campaign the government of De Gaulle was
reaffirmed in power.

For some observers the 1968 Revolution was symptomatic of an all-pervasive crisis in capitalist societies.(10) It was thought particularly significant that workers and students had co-operated with one another, and this was interpreted as heralding a new phase in revolutionary politics.(11) Particular significance was attached to the fact that many workers who participated were not traditional members of the working class, but were young, highly skilled technologists and scientists who did not normally engage in industrial action of this sort. This atypical form of protest was thought to imply some process of proletarianization of the middle ranks of French society.

On the whole the significance of the French strike seems to have been over-stressed at the time. Certainly the practical consequences were less than extensive. The students succeeded in the sense that there were some institutional and structural changes within the French universities, but in the main similar demands from the workers were not met. Instead some workers received pay increases and other financial improvements but no institutional changes took place in the factories.

A number of serious questions for analysis are raised by these events for the sociologist. Was the strike of May/June 1968 merely an internal French phenomenon, or did the strike have wider significance in relation to other advanced societies? A number of authors have argued that the French case was significant because student-worker co-operation, and especially the militancy of the technologists and scientists, was allegedly prototypical of what would occur in other modern industrial societies. This is important sociologically, since if this is the case it implies far-reaching changes in the class structure of modern societies. This book takes up this issue, but examines the British case. Thus I am concerned with the industrial behaviour of a group of white-collar workers in Britain - Civil Servants. I am particularly interested in three types of white-collar workers in the Civil Service, namely middle managers, clerks, and scientists. I focus on these because in both continental Europe and the USA there was in the 1960s an apparent radicalization of these and similar occupational groups that has supposedly led to their politicization and their participation in militant industrial action.(12) On a smaller scale the same process appears to have been happening in Britain although not in as dramatically evident a form. The aim of this book is to shed light on these general issues which may be specified as follows: first, has any radicalization or politicization taken place in Britain?; second, if so to what degree is the phenomenon similar to that observed in continental Europe and the USA?; and finally, are the explanations given for the American and European cases relevant to the British case?

The rationale behind the choice of the British Civil Service as the 'test case' for this investigation was that I wanted to study an occupational group that could be easily compared to the European and American groups which other writers had studied; that was typical of the non-manual sector of the British occupational structure; and that had a recorded history. This last feature was particularly important because the ahistorical nature of the European and American analyses poses major problems for the validity of the explanations offered therein.

A number of other factors made the Civil Service an ideal focus
for the study. Until quite recently the Civil Service was regarded
as having a 'good' record of industrial relations in the sense that
fiercely contested disputes were rare. Indeed the Civil Service
publicly congratulates itself on its fine record of industrial
relations.(13) Moreover the popular stereotype of the British Civil
Servant belies any notion of industrial militancy. But behind this
peaceful and harmonious exterior a number of other features are evident which challenge this conventional point of view. In the 1970s
the unions of both the middle managers and the scientists became
affiliated to the TUC; something that both the memberships had
rejected in earlier periods. Also in recent years the unions within the Civil Service have come to concern themselves more with
broader national and international political matters, whereas
twenty years ago interests focused mainly on internal Civil Service
issues like pay, promotion and superannuation. Today, although
these are still important, other issues such as national pay policy,
industrial democracy, civil rights and apartheid are more common.
Perhaps the most significant change is that Civil Servants resorted
to official strike action in 1973 and 1979 for the first time in
their history. Furthermore, a number of Civil Servants voiced the
opinion that their pay and conditions seriously lagged behind the
private sector of British industry and the unions began to question
the effectiveness of their bargaining and negotiating machinery.(14)
Thus in the late 1960s and 1970s the Civil Service appeared to be
entering a new phase of industrial relations and therefore seemed
to be extremely suitable as a case study.
    This book is divided into three sections. In the first I specify
the rationale for this study and identify the main concerns of the
work. I do this with reference to the origins of the problem in
the work of Marx and then consider the ways in which these issues
have been developed by more recent theorists. This enables me to
specify the main issues with which I will be concerned. The second
part of the book contains my main empirical findings. Here I examine the history of industrial relations in the Civil Service; the
organization of the Civil Service, with particular reference to the
application of scientific management principles and the use of
advanced technology; the demographic and social backgrounds of
Civil Servants; and their rates of remuneration. This part of the
book concludes with an examination of the way which these factors
have affected the industrial behaviour of Civil Servants. In Part
three I link the main empirical findings to the theoretical questions raised in Part one and draw out the main implications of my
work both for the study of white-collar workers in particular and
for Sociology in general.

Chapter 2

THE MIDDLE CLASS IN INDUSTRIAL SOCIETY: A CASE OF PROLETARIANIZATION

THE ORIGINS OF THE PROBLEM

This chapter identifies the various theoretical and empirical studies which have posited major changes in the middle levels of the class structure of modern industrial societies, and therefore expands the idea of politicization and radicalization discussed in the previous chapter.

An examination of the literature reveals that predictions concerning the political activity of the middle classes have been a fairly constant feature of sociological writing through the twentieth century.(1) The debate is much older than the May Movement of 1968, and the French writers were merely the latest in a long line of thinkers who had concerned themselves with the middle classes. The debate has its origins in the work of Marx, and indeed certain of the ambiguities found in his work repeat themselves in the contemporary literature. This chapter will demarcate the various positions which have emerged in relation to the class position of the middle levels of industrial society.

I will begin by considering three important elements in Marx's analysis: class position, consciousness of class position; and industrial and political behaviour.

Class position (2)

Marx argued that there were certain underlying social laws which were important in determining both the structure and the dynamics of society. One means of ascertaining these laws was to study the divisions in society, particularly those divisions he termed classes, and indeed the comprehension of the nature of class would make clear the social laws.(3) Marx argues for the logical and empirical necessity of understanding the material conditions which underlie human existence.(4) Consequently the relationships which develop between men in the course of producing the material necessities of life are of great importance. The relationships which develop in this process form the basis of the structure of inequalities in all societies. Marx then posits that by studying the conflicts between

6

groups of men we can understand the process of social change, since social change is the inevitable result of these conflicts.

The crucial problem for subsequent analysis was the identification of these competing groups, and it is at this point that ambiguities arise in attempting to operationalize the Marxian scheme. Marx never systematically laid down precisely what he meant by classes or how to identify them and indeed his final manuscript breaks off at the point where he looks as if he is about to provide a systematic definition.(5) He argued in 'Capital' that there were three great social classes in nineteenth-century capitalist society, namely wage labourers, capitalists, and landowners.(6) These divisions were not necessarily empirically absolute and some transient and intermediary groups could be encompassed in this scheme. Thus in this instance the class structure is not viewed as static but as something dynamic and changing. Consistent with this, Marx thought that the intermediate strata would gradually disappear because he thought there was an overall tendency for the gradual polarization of the class structure to occur until only two basic classes remained, the proletariat and the bourgeoisie. This conception implies a process of class formation with an inbuilt tendency for members of society eventually to settle into one or other of the two great classes. At an economic level the class position can be determined by the relationship of society's members to the means of production.(7)

For Marx, history consists of the long-term struggles between competing classes of men.(8) This has important implications for the understanding of the middle strata of society, since in this process of change intermediate groups must eventually join one or other of the competing groups. This process is described as class polarization. In Marx's scheme the group polarizing around the proletariat will be the larger and hence most of the movement from the middle strata of society will be into this group. This process is known as proletarianization. There are various groups of workers who will be affected in this way including clerks and some members of the professions. Marx provided an explanation of this in 'Capital', with reference to the related concepts of labour power and surplus value. Marx first distinguishes between labour, which is a physical act, and labour power, which is the potential for work and is what the labourer actually sells to his employer in return for wages. Labour power is a commodity which can be exchanged for money. However the proletarian according to Marx has only this commodity to sell, unlike the property-owning capitalist who has many assets. In the course of working the labourer produces value, but only receives a proportion of this back in the form of wages. Surplus value is defined as the difference between the value of what the worker produces and the wage he receives for doing it. This surplus value is expropriated by the capitalist and provides for his profits and superior wealth.(9) This is absolutely crucial for Marx in explaining the polarization of society because it is through the process of the expropriation of surplus value and its accumulation by the capitalist that the gradual pauperization of the other sectors of society takes place.

Marx argued that clerical workers do not produce surplus value directly (10) but in spite of this the price of clerical labour,

and hence the wages of clerical workers, is determined by the value
of the clerk's labour power in the same way as a manual worker.
Thus what the clerical worker costs the capitalist and what he
brings in for him are different things.(11) The clerical worker
does not create surplus value as such but adds to the capitalist's
income by helping him to reduce the cost of realizing surplus value
from others. In other words, although the clerical worker is only
an employee his function is primarily to help in the exploitation
of other sectors of the work force. Marx believed that this function placed the clerk in the ranks of the better-paid class of
skilled wage workers; but the clerk was undeniably proletarian and
it was, therefore, only a matter of time until recognizable class
polarization occurred, and proletarianization could be said to have
taken place. This would happen as the clerk's skill was devalued,
the rate for doing clerical labour fell, as capitalism became more
sophisticated, the specialized division of labour increased, and
general education which provided for clerical skills was made available to all.(12)
    Marx therefore clearly argued that the middle strata of society
would become proletarianized as part of the overall process of
social change. Proletarianization is the conditioning factor in
the polarization of society into two opposing and hostile camps.
These groups in their turn provide through a dialectical relationship the dynamic forces that will lead society to its next developmental stage. Much of the debate with Marx has focused on the
middle strata of society to determine the extent to which this prediction has come true. The debate about proletarianization is
central to this. The fact of proletarianization, if it can be
observed, implies that far-reaching changes in the social structure
of society are either taking place or about to take place which
following the Marxian prescription will be readily observable among
non-manual labour. This issue has subsequently been taken up by
many writers and in this chapter I will examine the various ways in
which these writers have attempted to understand the class position
of clerical labour.

Class consciousness

Marx provided a theory of the consciousness of class as an integral
feature of his ideas about class. He argued that nineteenth-century
industry had given rise to the factory system in which workers were
organized like an army. This caused resentfulness among the workers
about their subjection, both to the system as a whole and to the
machines.(13) The relationship between the employer and employee
was held to be fundamentally antagonistic and this antagonism had a
number of results. Conflict would develop which at first would be
purely localized and individual: gradually, however, through the
chaos of amorphous protest, social movements based on common economic conditions and experiences would develop.(14) With the increasing concentration of workers in larger factories and a gradual
homogenizing of experience, class movements such as trades unions
would be formed.(15)
    In this sense Marx views class consciousness as the inevitable

result of industrialization. Yet elsewhere Marx questions this
determinism and points out that there is a difference between the
mere existence of a group of workers sharing common experiences of
exploitation and their willingness to do something about it:
> Economic conditions had first transformed the mass of the people
> of the country into workers. The combination of capital has
> created for this mass a common situation, common interests. The
> mass is thus already a class as against capital, but not yet for
> itself. In the struggle ... this mass becomes united, and con-
> stitutes itself as a class for itself.(16)

Thus although Marx sees a clear relationship between economic conditions and class consciousness the two things must be conceptually
distinguished.

The concept of class consciousness has a number of implications
for the study of the middle levels of society. The crucial question
for subsequent writers is that while the white-collar workers are
on the whole propertyless, and therefore in terms of class position
proletarian, their class consciousness remained underdeveloped and
their political and industrial behaviour was very often antithetical
to such things as trade unionism.(17) The charge of 'false consciousness' is therefore levelled at the white-collar worker. This
is an extremely problematic idea because the term 'false' is a
logical category and implies its opposite, 'true'; and 'consciousness' is a psychological or physiological term. People's beliefs
and sentiments exist and can therefore be neither true nor false;
only statements about their beliefs and sentiments can be true or
false.(18) What is usually meant by the term 'false consciousness'
is that a particular group's beliefs and sentiments about their
class position do not correspond to their actual class position.
Much of the literature on white-collar workers has taken false consciousness as its central problem. In other words, an examination
is made of why the propertyless clerks have not become a class for
themselves. But class consciousness presents a number of significant difficulties. Again these difficulties have their roots in
Marx's own work. Marx uses the term 'class consciousness' in three
distinct ways:(19) first, where a class shares a set of beliefs and
values regardless of their content; second, where members of a
class are aware of their membership and hence have consciousness of
class; and third, where a small number of members of a class are
aware of their class interests and actively pursue them. But even
if this latter group do pursue these interests out of a sense of
exploitation there is no a priori reason to assume that their class
consciousness will be revolutionary.(20) Following Marx, authors
have taken one or other of these three types as the key problem,
and yet each position is only partial. Similarly there has been a
tendency to study consciousness of class as distinct from class
position and political action. To study proletarianization these
three things must be considered together.

Industrial and political action

Class-based political action would be the result of the emergence
of class consciousness, and Marx thought that this might be mediated

through the trades unions and antagonisms in the workplace. Thus
in studying political action of a class-conscious kind Marx was
particularly interested in the growing labour movement of the
nineteenth century. The conflicts which developed in the workplace
were particularly important for Marx by virtue of his materialist
position, and since trades unions appeared to be important institutions in this respect Marx considered their role.

    Some of the difficulties that bedevil the study of trades unions
and class consciousness today were present in Marx's writings; his
attitude to trades unions and trade unionism seems to have had
essentially two aspects. On the one hand Marx urged trade union
activity because it supposedly created the nuclei for social, other-
directed behaviour in the worker and thus encouraged class consciousness. But it can also be argued that he thought that trade union
activity alone could not itself restructure society.(21) This
latter position seems to have stemmed from the fact that towards
the end of his life he realized that trades unions were not fully
representative of the working class but merely the more highly
skilled elements of it, that trade union leadership was corrupt, or
that some form of embourgeoisement of the working class was taking
place.(22) Subsequently other writers have been even more scathing
about the possibility of trades unions helping to generate class
consciousness. Lenin observed a form of instrumental economism in
trades unions, meaning that purely economic issues established
locally in the workplace (for example wages, hours and conditions)
dominated trade union affairs, and that these issues detracted from
the generation of class consciousness.(23) Michels saw trades
unions as necessarily oligarchic and bureaucratic and that either
institutional inertia or displacement of goals would mean that
trades unions could never have a revolutionary role.(24) Trotsky
observed that as capitalism became more advanced and hence more
prone to crisis, capital would either destroy working-class movements altogether or would treat trades unions as the junior partners in the administration of capital in return for reasonable or
moderate demands.(25)

    Empirically not all trade union behaviour is class-based politi-
cal action. Some writers on proletarianization seem to make the
assumption however that it is. It is mistaken to take an increased
level of trade union activity as indicative of the growth of class
consciousness. However in spite of the difficulties, the phenomena
of class, class consciousness and political action must be considered together. Writers who have concentrated on one or other of
these dimensions have produced narrow definitions of such concepts
as proletarianization.

Summary

Any attempt to understand the relationship between class position,
consciousness of class position, and class-based political and
industrial behaviour is difficult. Studies of the industrial behaviour of manual workers reveal some of the likely pitfalls, summarized as follows. First, as we have just seen, class consciousness

and false consciousness are problematic terms.(26)   Second, class
consciousness may mean a number of different things, and revolutionary consciousness as described by Marx is rare indeed.(27)
Third, trade union behaviour may manifest all, some, or none of the
following characteristics: desire for control over the work situation,(28) instrumental economism,(29) occupational consciousness,(30)
or even class consciousness.(31)   Fourth, in certain circumstances,
desire for control, instrumentalism or particularism may give way
to or even generate class consciousness,(32) but this relationship
is variable and depends on a number of other conditioning factors
such as tradition, the rate of economic growth, the date of the
first period of industrialization, the rate of technical change,
employer and union attitudes.(33)   Fifth, to infer changes in class
consciousness from changes in union behaviour is at best naive and
simplistic and most often fallacious.(34)   Thus it is most important to avoid an over-deterministic theory of the working environment conditioning industrial behaviour.   Although in most writings
on manual workers such a gross determinism is rare, in some of the
material on white-collar workers it is more common.

POST-MARXIAN THEORIES OF PROLETARIANIZATION (35)

Introduction

I have distinguished several different phenomenal levels, class
position, consciousness of class and political action.   These are
significantly different and must be treated as such.   In the writ-
tings I consider below this is not always done which is a serious
defect.   I argue that proletarianization can only be understood
with reference to the three dimensions of class position, consciousness of class, and industrial and political behaviour.(36)
This seems to be clear enough reading the relevant sections in
Marx's work, and although Marx does not define proletarianization
in this way it is implied in his writings.   The extent to which
this implication has been ignored by many subsequent authors has
led to much confusion in the use of the term 'proletarianization'.
I will use my definition to criticize post-Marxian theorists as
well as to construct my own study.
    When reviewing the post-Marxian literature on proletarianiz;tion
one is confronted with an alarming number of different discussions
about what proletarianization is.   In fact what most writers refer
to are indicators of the concept of proletarianization.   The concept is itself derived from implicit definitions of class, which do
not always conform to a Marxian definition.   In addition, the
mediation of the operationalizing of the concept into indicators is
problematic, first in a logical sense in terms of the relationship
between the definition of proletarianization and the indicators of
proletarianization, and second in terms of empirical accuracy.
There is a tendency to define proletarianization in a number of
different ways which I argue are inconsistent with Marx's usage,
and are only partial reflections of the concept.   Some indicator of
the definition is propounded, for example income level or social
origin, and observed changes in the indicator are taken as evidence

of proletarianization. This generally stems from a failure to distinguish between the separate dimensions of class position, consciousness of class and industrial and political action. In addition the alleged changes in the indicators can be questioned on
simple empirical grounds of accuracy.

   Writers on this topic have tended to concentrate on two types of
indicators; those which refer to the market situation of workers
and those which refer to the work situations. Those writers who
concentrate on market situation concern themselves with two kinds
of question; first about the level and source of income and second
about social origins of the work force. Those writers who observe
work situations concern themselves with two related aspects; the
nature and content of work and the conditions under which it is
carried out.(37)

Market situation

Income
(a) Level of income It has become something of a sociological
truism to assert that the levels of incomes of white-collar workers
have fallen, relative to those of manual workers. This is then taken
as evidence of proletarianization. Here the indicator is level of
income and the concept of proletarianization hinges on a definition
of class based on income levels. With varying degrees of force this
is applied either selectively to different types of white-collar
workers or sometimes to them all. Proletarianization usually
however in this context refers only to class membership (as defined
by income), and predictions about consciousness or political action
are not normally applied.(38) There are a number of problems with
this position, of evidence and interpretation. First, it is not
always clear which non-manual workers are being considered and this
distorts the method of computation. Thus if we simply refer to
routine clerical workers, possibly their salaries relative to manual
workers have fallen, but this is not necessarily the case with
higher and middle management. But even if there do exist average
differences in weekly earnings of manual and non-manual workers
there will be an intrinsic distortion because manual workers generally work longer hours than non-manual workers and absolute figures
ignore fringe benefits etc. which accrue to white-collar workers.
(39) Even the assumption that clerical salaries have fallen can be
questioned on a number of other grounds. First, the median income
figures which are usually referred to are in part the result of
factors which relate to sex. Generally women have earned less than
men and therefore if women are excluded for computational reasons
from the white-collar sector and only the incomes of male workers
are compared then there is no, or only a slight, fall in the differential.(40) Second, the gross figures used to calculate the income
statistics are in part derived from the census of occupations and
this greatly masks differences in the career structure of skilled
and white-collar workers. Thus what is usually called the white-
collar median is actually the base or starting-point salary for many
white-collar occupations, whereas the figures quoted for skilled
workers refer to the top level of the working-class career.(41)

Furthermore, the alleged extent of the depreciation of the white-
collar salary depends on where the base line of the index is drawn.
The assertion that white-collar salaries have fallen is usually
based on a figure with the base line either before 1918 or 1918-39.
If however the base line is fixed after 1945 then the extent of the
decline is far less dramatic.(42)

But a more serious theoretical problem emerges. First, to
allege that the incomes of the middle strata in society have fallen
relative to other groups, and then to argue that this is prima
facie evidence of proletarianization begs the question as to the
definition of class being used, and highlights the logical problem
of the relationship between the indicator and the definition. Marx
very clearly states that class is not determined by level of income.
(43) Moreover since proletarianization implies a relationship to
class position, to use as an indicator something which is not
itself the only criterion of class is suspect. There is a connection between class and income but it is not necessarily direct, and
level of income cannot be taken as the absolute indicator of class.
In sum, then, to allege proletarianization by using as an indicator
falling income levels fails on empirical grounds, since the evidence
of falling incomes is contentious anyway, and on logical grounds
because of a suspect definition of class.

(b) Source of income In these writings attention is focused on the
source of income of the middle strata of society.(44) In particular, attention is directed towards the labour power of the middle
strata and the concept of the production of surplus value. It is
held that since the nineteenth century non-manual occupations have
largely drawn their salaries from the surplus value produced by
manual labour.(45) However with changing technology and increased
bureaucratization, white-collar workers are increasingly concerned
with tasks which do themselves produce surplus value. Thus the
salary of the white-collar worker is made up of two elements; his
wage for productive work and a portion of surplus value produced by
other workers as he helps the capitalist expropriate surplus value.
Proletarianization is said to occur when the source of income for
the worker is determined increasingly by his own labour power and
less by the surplus value of others. A narrowly defined concept of
class is being discussed.

This is a very interesting application of Marx's theory, but
because it is at such a high level of abstraction it cannot be
tested empirically and remains therefore largely speculative. Moreover, even if as a theory it was verifiable it could still not
account for political or ideological change among groups of workers
who are supposedly proletarianized since the theory only operates
at the narrowest of economic levels. The proponents of this point
of view would not necessarily regard that as a serious defect since
its status is heuristic rather than descriptive. The main difficulty confronting this position, however, is its foundation in
Marxian economics. In fact the theory adheres quite closely to its
Marxian antecedents, but the Marxian antecedents are themselves
suspect. Classical Political Economy from which Marx developed the
labour theory of value has long been abandoned by economists. It
is more than problematic therefore, when sociologists choose to
erect a theory on such a foundation. However, proponents of this

particular type of Marxian analysis would refute the criticism, arguing that a redefined labour theory of value provides a vivid demonstration of the exploitation of workers in modern society.

But in my view more significant still are two serious questions in relation to the theory of class embedded in such writings. First, it is extremely problematic as to whether Marx saw source of income as the sole determinant of class. The section in 'Capital' is ambiguous on this and sociologists dispute the matter among themselves.(46) But more importantly the definition of class used by Carchedi derives directly from Lenin, and Lenin's notion of class differs significantly from that of Marx.(47) At the logical level there are problems relating the definition to the indicator, and no means exist to test the proposition empirically.

Social origins of the workforce
Some authors bring the social origins of the workforce under scrutiny as an attempt is made to discern proletarianization. It is asserted that for various reasons (technological changes, expansion of numbers of employees, the growth of new occupations, etc.) the workforce in the white-collar world is today measurably different to that which existed in the nineteenth century. This is indicated by the changing social origins of the workforce. These general social factors can be delimited and specified into two broad categories, social class of origin and sex.

(a) Class of origin It is argued that since the nineteenth century clerical occupations of all kinds have tended to be filled increasingly by individuals who originated in the working class.(48) This simple notion of intergenerational upward mobility has long been known to observers of western society.(49) The argument appears to be a kind of proletarianization by default; that is, recruitment from the proletariat equals proletarianization. Although there is abundant evidence that clerical and other lower white-collar jobs are no longer as socially exclusive as they once were, it is something of a redefinition of proletarianization to consider this qua proletarianization in terms of Marx's original notion. Children of manual workers who become non-manual workers tend to take up fairly modest white-collar positions and mobility into professional positions requiring long periods of training is less common.(50) In general it can then be established that the lower reaches of the clerical world are becoming increasingly proletarian in origin, but this is scarcely the same thing as proletarianization as part of overall class polarization. Upward social mobility for the children of manual workers can conceivably be taken as the contradiction of proletarianization and polarization. In this case the definition of proletarianization is altered out of all recognition from the original Marxian scheme.

Sometimes this 'proletarianization' of clerical occupations is taken a step further and changes in the levels of political activities are predicted. It is argued that as clerical occupations become more proletarian a change in a clerk's industrial behaviour takes place. Thus he will join trades unions and go on strike. I examine the evidence of this below but generally one can state that this is a very dubious assertion.

(b) Feminization The most significant other change in the

demographic profile of this sector of the workforce has been its feminization (51) and this in its turn has been suggested as evidence of proletarianization.(52) This interpretation is in contrast to the usual sociological convention which takes feminization as a significant reason for the deradicalization of the clerical workforce, where feminization is taken to be one of the reasons why trades unions have had difficulty in organizing white-collar workers on a large scale.(53)

Concentration on feminization as an indicator of proletarianization presents a number of problems.(54) In terms of a definition of class the position of women is problematic. The sociological convention is to regard women as appendages of either their fathers or husbands and to define their class position in that way. Such a form of sexism is difficult to sustain empirically where in modern industrial society women constitute an important element of the working population in their own right.(55) In terms of a definition of proletarianization and the use of feminization as an indicator of it, it is extremely difficult to unravel the implicit link between proletarianization and feminization. This implicit logical relationship is further confounded by the open question of the definition of class being used and the position of women in the class structure. These dual sets of problems have generally been sidestepped by arguing that a characteristic of the wage-salary structure of western societies is that women receive less than men at nearly every level. Thus the increase in feminization in the clerical sector has artificially kept down the salaries of all clerical workers. The definition of proletarianization used here is therefore based on a definition of class determined by income. As I argued above, this position is untenable. A second method of circumventing the problem has been to argue that social mobility is short-range. One of the most common sorts of short-range upward social mobility was when the daughter of a skilled manual worker moved into a clerical occupation. This immediately fails on logical grounds because a dual set of criteria are being used to define class; a woman's class is defined by her father's occupation when determining where she came from, but by her own occupation when determining where she arrived. Another problem emerges in relation to political-industrial behaviour. Traditionally sociologists have argued that highly feminized workforces are unlikely to be militant. This does not mesh with a definition of proletarianization which also encompasses the class-consciousness and political-behaviour dimension of the concept.

Work situation: technological changes in the organization of work

In the material on this area of study a number of different things are emphasized.(56) Along with changes in the composition, size and function of the middle strata of workers in industrial society, technological change has occurred which has supposedly had profound effects on the workers involved. These changes are readily observable and it is held that they have had an important influence on the class position of workers involved. This in its turn is alleged to affect political behaviour. Little heed is paid to the mediation of class position and consciousness of class, the assumption seemingly being that some general deterministic relationship exists. Various writers have chosen to discuss different sections of the middle strata. Essentially two basic emphases are discernible, one concentrating on the higher echelons (managers, administrators and specialists), and one looking at the lower echelons (routine clerks, machine operators).

At this point I wish to introduce a typology of white-collar occupations (see Fig.2.1). The purpose of this typology is heuristic not descriptive. My aim is to introduce an element of conceptual clarification to the discussion which follows.(57) Such a typology is necessary because it would be mistaken to view non-manual occupations as homogeneous.(58) One of the problems which has pervaded the literature is precisely this failure.

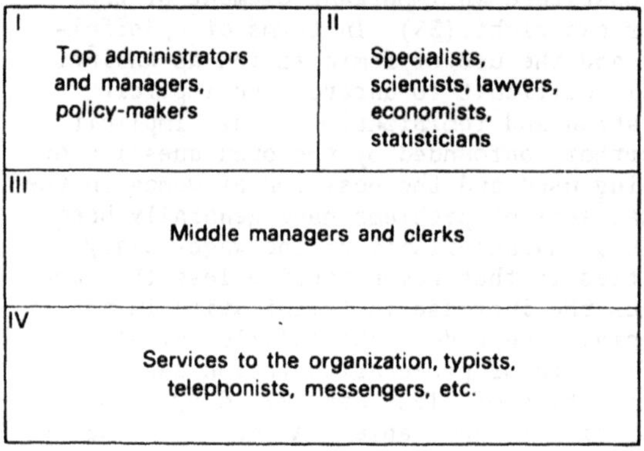

I	II
Top administrators and managers, policy-makers	Specialists, scientists, lawyers, economists, statisticians
III Middle managers and clerks	
IV Services to the organization, typists, telephonists, messengers, etc.	

FIGURE 2.1　Typology of occupations in a bureaucratic organization

Perhaps the most striking thing about the middle level of industrial society is that since the nineteenth century it has become increasingly complex. The typology is designed to account for this. The complexity is most noticeable in the industrial and/or commercial enterprise itself. The clerks in the nineteenth century were a small group of men who although generally found in subservient positions within small offices stood a good chance of being promoted or even of becoming full partners in the enterprise. The functions of the clerk were many and various with his being something of a 'Jack of all trades' within the office.(59) However the size of the enterprise has expanded and functions within it have become differentiated until it is now possible to distinguish four types of worker. These are as follows: first, managers and chief executives who may or may not be shareholders in the enterprise and who basically control the bureaucratic machine; second, the group of specialists and technicians who advise on certain specific matters (for example planning, legal matters, technical matters) and who execute specialized functions (for example research);(60) third, and distinct from these two groups, are the middle and lower levels of the enterprise which carry out varying degrees of routine functions, processing information and so on. Finally another group exists at the bottom of the hierarchy who carry out the routine servicing of

the organization. It is possible to separate analytically these
functions, although in the empirical world there would be many
instances of overlap. Significantly in the nineteenth century such
functional distinctions would not have been the norm. Fitting the
typology to the empirical world presents a number of problems.
First, some occupations are not easily encompassed in it and second,
whereas this typology is very rigid in practice it is likely that
the categories would not necessarily be mutually exclusive. However
the object of the typology is to help comprehend the empirical
world and this can be done very conveniently using the typology, if
we consider each group in isolation. For the most part this book
does not discuss the routine-servicing group of workers.

The higher echelons
(a) The technocrats Writers concentrating on this group of workers
have produced some of the most provocative and startling discussions,
yet ultimately they are perhaps the most disappointing. I outline
here a schema which is not representative of any particular writer
but which tries ideal-typically to encapsulate the basic propositions.(61) Primarily the argument is that modern capitalism is
characterized by the growth of new occupations because of changes
and advances in technology. A new type of worker emerges in response to the technological and bureaucratic impulses of modern
society. This group of 'technocrats' consists of a cadre of experts
and technicians whose knowledge, which is highly esoteric, is the
most vital part of modern industrial society (or post-industrial
society to use their preferred term).(62)
    The technocrats are regarded as particularly interesting because,
in spite of their esoteric knowledge which is allegedly so important and although this group are to be found close to the very
heart of modern enterprises, they are apparently effectively divorced from control. Their position in the hierarchy is formally
that of employees but allegedly their real and potential power is
greater than that of ordinary employees.(63) This is crucial for
the technocratic theorists, because the level of concentration of
the technocrats coupled with their subservient position in the
hierarchy (after having stressed the importance of their power!)
results in plainly visible 'contradictions' for the workers. This
'contradiction' leads the writers then to predict that this group
is likely to become, or is in the process of becoming, the 'vanguard of the proletariat' because both radicalization and proletarianization are said to have taken place. It is argued thus that
the power position, subservience and education are sufficient to
bring about, among other things, changes in class consciousness.
Evidence of French technicians supporting the Paris students in
1968 is produced in support of this notion.
    Apart from blatant redefinition of certain important Marxian
concepts and then the attempt to fit the redefined ideas on to a
procrustean neo-Marxian perspective, a number of other serious
objections can be made against this position. A primary problem
is its failure to distinguish empirical description from theoretical prescription.(64) In other words, the writers who discuss
this group both describe (though only partially) certain dramatic
but commonplace phenomena (the arrival of computers and other

advanced technological hardware), and then go on to predict the course which advanced societies will follow. The theoretical position is thus at once teleological and unidimensional: teleological in the sense that the important phenomena are selected and focused upon with the desired end state in mind (usually some radical transformation of society) and unidimensional by concentrating on advanced society, particularly the USA and France. This unidimensionality fails to take account of developmental patterns in other parts of the world and at the same time masks important differences within the social structures of the advanced western societies,(65) while making ethnocentric assumptions about the rest of the world. Indeed technocratic theories are quite attractive since they include and make reference to some of the most striking features of the contemporary world; but merely to add on the new category of post-industrial society or technocratic society is to adhere to a narrow developmental view of social change. Furthermore, to assert the primacy of knowledge on a crude index of numbers involved is to assert its importance, not to explain it.(66)

But in the final analysis the assumptions made about political behaviour are the most unsatisfactory. First of all the writers ask us to accept that they have explained the emergence of a new important stratum of society. This is a highly problematic starting-point because in spite of all the references to knowledge and power, the new stratum's emergence is really not explained at all. However, even if this new stratum can be identified (if not explained) mere identification does not explain its political orientation. This is most important because on the whole the technocratic writers hold an implicit and deterministic theory of political action based on a neo-Marxian theory of class consciousness. The assumed determinism operates in the direction of work position to class consciousness and action. This contradicts much of the known empirical material on class and class consciousness. But it is of vital importance to separate analytically the realm of work and politics. This the technocratic theorists do not do because they do not adequately explain first the emergence of the new stratum, nor second the structure of the 'post industrial society' in which the new stratum is important - in fact emergence and structure are often conflated. Third, the assumption is made that the political orientation will be left wing or radical, yet no reason is established as to why this should be the case; instead the questionable evidence of French technicians in 1968 is cited or vague reference to power and subservience is made.

At the empirical level there is very little support for the technocratic theorists.(67) It has been found that in modern industrial organizations the *financially* important cadres (as opposed to a technocratic elite) are not only still vitally important but moreover are still ascendant. Empirically then the fit between the theory and empirical world is not good and there is a conceptual failure to distinguish between analysis, prediction, prescription and description. In terms of the specific theory of proletarianization, to start from a position of observing political action which is in some sense unusual and then to provide theories which purport to explain it and call this proletarianization is to take political change as evidence of change in class

position. This is not a particularly valid method of proceeding
in the light of the distinctions which must be made between class
position, consciousness of class and political action.
(b) *The senior bureaucrats, professionals, top administrators and
higher management* This position takes as its starting point the
separation of ownership and control in the commercial enterprise.
Thus it is argued that with the rise of the joint stock company
whose shareholders are not necessarily the same as the managers
and executives, the managers are in a nominal position of employee.
The second major premise underlying these writings is that the
professionals have suffered a gradual loss of independence since
the nineteenth century and now find themselves in the position of
employees. Both phenomena are well known in the sociological literature.(68) But the writers in this area sometimes make a conceptual leap from describing loss of autonomy and independence,
nominal employee status and erosion of privilege, to predicting
that these changes will in themselves produce a politicized workforce and that this politicization is to be taken as evidence of
proletarianization.(69) The writers assume that the move to
employee status is experienced as 'bad'. This is not necessarily
so; for example, in law and medicine a move to group practice is
partly a result of the attractions offered (such as sharing
expensive equipment and ancillary staff and being able to take
holidays and have weekends off duty).
   This idea of proletarianization has a number of important weaknesses. First, one can hardly sensibly describe professionals
as occupying a proletarian position simply because they are now
often employed in large enterprises and are therefore nominally
employees, and because managers no longer conform to the classic
entrepreneurial style of nineteenth-century capitalism and are also
nominally employees. The nominal employee status ignores completely the very important social configurations impinging on the
professional and manager. Life-style and salaries are still
sufficiently different from the mass of the population to mark off
such individuals from the rest of the population. Second, in terms
of alleged political outlook there is very little evidence to find
support for this conception of proletarianization. Thus although
the conditions of work for this type of worker are different from
that of the nineteenth century the mere fact of difference is
insufficient to demonstrate a causal relation with political
behaviour. Dubious evidence from France and elsewhere is more
speculative than sociological. This idea of proletarianization
flies in the face of the evidence to the contrary which shows that
on the whole professionals and managers have a very different view
of the class structure of society from that traditionally held to
be a radical or a class-conscious one.(70) Traditionally it was
argued that professionals and administrators orientated themselves
toward professional associations rather than trades unions. This
idea has been challenged to some extent in recent years. It has
been noted that there has been a tendency for professional workers
either to change over to trades unions or else to change the
policy of their professional association so they exhibit seemingly
trade union characteristics. In Britain the actions of hospital
consultants (71) and junior hospital doctors (72) in working to

contract and generally adopting traditional trade union methods
are held to be particularly significant. But several points must
be noted. Militant action cannot itself be taken as an example of
proletarianization since the purpose of such militant professionals may be the very opposite of proletarianization, i.e. they may
wish to protect themselves from competition and maintain or even
increase the differential between themselves and other groups of
workers. Indeed professional action of this kind may be protective and aggressive but this is not necessarily anything to do with
class feeling.

However, the major problem with this perspective is the nature
of the comparison involved. What the writers do is to compare the
situation of an ideally represented model of the professional in
the nineteenth century (a model usually derived from the paragon
professions of law and medicine) with the 'professionals' found
working in the mid-twentieth century in large corporations. The
loss of professional autonomy occurs over a one-hundred-year period
and is therefore unlikely to be a serious consideration in the
minds of contemporary professionals. Furthermore, serious doubts
can be laid on the empirical accuracy of the ideal model of the
nineteenth-century independent practitioner being compared with
that of today.

This type of writing which posits proletarianization of the
professional suffers from the same logical deficiencies as the
technocratic theorists, in that a conflation takes place between
politico-industrial behaviour and work situation; when these
elements are separated and the supposed causality is demonstrated
then the implicit determinism does not stand up to a rigorous test.

The lower echelons: routine clerical workers and bureaucratic
services
This variant of proletarianization concentrates on persons involved
in the routine functions of white-collar work, e.g. clerks, shop
assistants and so on. A number of very important studies have
been carried out on this group of workers but when attention is
diverted to the idea of proletarianization a number of weaknesses
emerge. Usually the writers concentrate on the modern office.
It is argued that along with changes in the division of labour and
levels of technology several fundamental things have happened in
the office. First it has become much larger, and gradually mechanization (the introduction of typewriters and adding machines)
and later automation (computers) have changed the relations of
production. Thus machines allegedly carry out tasks which hitherto were done by clerks.(73) This is said to have had several
important effects. Increasingly the clerical worker has a smaller
portion of the unit of work to do and contemporaneously his task
has become more repetitive. The clerk has thus become a kind of
machine minder who is easily replaceable. In addition the once
esoteric skills such as the ability to read, write and do elemen-
tary calculations (once an undeniably middle-class prerogative)
have been extended through universal education to the population
at large.(74)

The argument usually stops at this point, positing simply that
these features are in themselves evidence of proletarianization;

sometimes however the argument is carried one step further and it is suggested that since the mass of clerical work has come to resemble factory work, clerks will increasingly adopt workers' traditional responses (e.g. trade unionism) to their condition. Examples of increased white-collar trade unionism are then cited as proof and sometimes this is taken to indicate changes in consciousness of class.

At a theoretical level, a number of reservations must be made about this position. Certainly one can argue that such workers doing repetitive tasks in large 'clerical factories' do resemble a white-collar proletariat since they fulfil the criteria of non-ownership of the means of production and in addition non-control of the work situation. Thus using a narrow definition this group might be termed proletarian. This however is not a great theoretical advance nor a phenomenon on which most writers in the subject would disagree.(75) The major puzzle however was originally the clerical workers' insistence on maintaining social distance from manual workers and their reluctance to join the trade union movement.(76) In recent years there has been an apparent increase in the numbers of white-collar workers joining unions. For some writers this is taken as proof that the predictions concerning the concentration of clerks in clerical factories and their political response are being borne out, and that perhaps at last clerks are realizing their 'true class consciousness' and as such can be said to be becoming proletarianized.

This contention is however open to a number of serious challenges. In the first place white-collar unionization is not a new phenomenon; there are societies in the west where white-collar workers have long been unionized and militant, for example France. (77) Second, there are societies where although white-collar workers do not have such a tradition, some sections of the clerical workforce have been unionized to a great extent for as long as the manual workforce.(78) Thus to emphasize overall patterns of change in union membership as a new radical phenomenon is an over-simplification.

An analysis of the figures on white-collar union membership is revealing in itself. It can be demonstrated that the figures on union membership of white-collar workers only just keep pace with the increasing numbers of white-collar workers in the workforce anyway with large sectors still unorganized.(79) Certainly one can admit that by joining trades unions clerical workers are behaving in ways which would have been atypical, though not unheard of, in the nineteenth century, but this in itself is not evidence of proletarianization. Furthermore mechanization, per se should not be taken as evidence of proletarianization. If correlations are made with the rising numbers of white-collar workers in unions and increased mechanization no clear relationship can be discerned.

But primarily the notion of proletarianization in this instance falls down at the level of causation between observed changes in organizations and predicted political results. First, it makes the assumption that it is possible to theorize inductively from the particular to the general in respect of political behaviour, i.e. small-scale political phenomena (clerks joining unions) are

interpreted as indicators of class-wide attitude changes in respect
of the middle class without sufficient evidence. Second, the three
variables of industrial behaviour, voting behaviour and political
behaviour are correlated. Indeed these things are often related
together but the exact relationship remains speculative.(80) In
addition, by hypothesizing that attitude changes are brought about
directly by a tangible alteration to work situations the writers
are indulging in a form of behavioural-psychological explanation.
It is not particularly sophisticated to claim that by making
clerical work situations come to resemble factory situations,
white-collar workers will begin to behave like manual workers and
that changes in consciousness of class will take place. This
narrow determinism tends to render the outside office experience
unimportant in spite of the fact that there is much evidence which
stresses the importance of the outside work experience.(81)

Summary: The problem of internal and external validity in the
thesis of proletarianization (82)

Two sets of problems impinge on the literature I have considered
in this section; namely problems of internal and external validity.
By internal validity I refer to the logical relationship between
the indicator and the definition, and by external validity I refer
to the empirical relationship between the indicator and the world.
At a logical level the relationship between the indicators of
proletarianization and the definitions of class was found to be
problematic in nearly all the writings considered. A clear distinction was not maintained in the literature between the measured
change in such things as income levels, social origins, organizational change, and in the three aspects of class identified by
Marx, namely class position, class consciousness and political
action. At the empirical level, because the data-gathering process
was often little more than speculative, grave doubts can be cast on
some of the findings. Moreover since some, though not all, of the
writings use an inductive form of reasoning to argue for large-
scale change in the class structure from small-scale changes in
the organization of work, then doubts can be also cast on this.
     At a more basic level there are a number of other weaknesses.
First, the cavalier treatment of data by these writers is coupled
with an absence of rigorously defined concepts.(83) Second, it is
often unclear as to whether proletarianization is a descriptive
category, an hypothesis, or a prediction. Problems of validity
and technological determinism apart, however, the most important
criticism is the assumption that given the technological changes
the political response will be of a left wing kind by the white-
collar workforce. However, no evidence is produced to say why it
will be left wing and equally one could imagine a situation where
the response of the workers would be romantic, reactionary or even
fascistic.(84) The potential of a swing to the right is scarcely
a characteristic of class consciousness required in a Marxian
model of proletarianization.

THE IMPLICATIONS FOR THIS STUDY

In the previous sections I showed that the theoretical and empirical writings on proletarianization could be reduced to a series of indicators. These were of two types concerned with the market and work situation of white-collar workers. Systematically these types can be broken down into a series of propositions about the empirical world which can then be tested.

The propositions and their implications for the Civil Service

Market situation
(a) *Income proletarianization* The proposition is that the incomes of white-collar workers have fallen relatively or absolutely to, those of manual workers: the implication is that the pay of Civil Servants has fallen also, and the pay of the British Civil Service will thus be examined over time.
(b) *Different sources of income* The proposition is that the incomes of non-manual workers are derived increasingly from their own productive labour and less from the productive labour of others: the implication for this study is that the sources of incomes of Civil Servants should be examined.
(c) *Feminization* The proposition is that the white-collar workforce is becoming increasingly feminine in character: thus the manpower and sex composition of the labour force in the Civil Service will be analyzed historically.
(d) *Social origin* The proposition is that the white-collar labour force is becoming increasingly 'proletarian' in origin as children of manual workers move into non-manual occupations: thus I will undertake to study the demographic profile of the labour force in the Civil Service historically, and the social class of origin, the geographical origin and educational backgrounds of Civil Servants will be analysed.

Work situation
(a) *Bureaucratization* The proposition is that as large-scale organizations become increasingly big they become increasingly bureaucratic and the employee loses his identity as a specialist or professional. This study will therefore examine the extent of bureaucratization in the Civil Service, and such things as hierarchical relations, the role of management, discipline and conditions of service will be analysed.
(b) *Mechanization and automation* The proposition is that with changes in the division of labour brought about by technological advances the functions and nature of clerical work have changed, producing routinization and repetitiveness: therefore this study will examine the extent and type of mechanization and automation in the Civil Service.
    In each case the crucial point of reference will be the relationship between the different aspects of class position, class consciousness and industrial behaviour, and accordingly I attempt to relate the various indicators of proletarianization to these aspects. A further important referent for this study lies within

the debate about the post-industrial society. Some of the writers
under consideration in this chapter went a step further than the
simple political results of the phenomena they studied. They
posited no less than a radical transformation of the very structure
of advanced industrial society. In general they worked at a micro-
level, by documenting changes there and then predicting changes in
the macro-structure of society. Two basic themes can be discerned
- a strong version of the thesis and a weak version. In the strong
version the authors posit that an important change is taking place
within the ranks of the middle classes in industrial societies. It
is argued that certain sectors of the middle classes are beginning
to recognize two things. First that their 'true' class position is
as the non-owners of capital, and second that their revolutionary
potential is enormous. The implication of this is, then, that
western society is going to move, is moving or has already moved
into a new stage where the capitalist order will very likely be
overthrown or replaced and a new type of society will emerge. The
weak version merely states that some kind of politicization of the
middle class is occurring and that this politicization can be
explained with reference to broad social changes. I will pursue
these issues in the conclusion of this book.

SUMMARY

This chapter began with a consideration of the Marxian theory of
class, class consciousness and social change, and examined the
importance of proletarianization in such a theory. I distinguished
several distinct concepts which are important in this literature,
viz. class position, class consciousness, and political behaviour,
and I pointed out that some authors failed to separate these analytically; this, it was argued, was particularly significant when
talking about the proletarianization of the middle levels of
society. I argued that because of the confusion of these three
concepts writers had used the notion of proletarianization in a
number of different ways and that this was further confounded by a
failure to define rigorously the relationship between definitions
of proletarianization and class and indicators of them. I then
argued that broadly speaking two major schools of thought existed
in relation to proletarianization; those concerned with market
situations and those concerned with work situations. I was able,
by representing the situations ideal-typically and schematically,
to illustrate the various positions and critically examine them
from a logical, sociological, theoretical and empirical point of
view. They were all found to be wanting in some respect. On the
whole, failure to distinguish between class position, consciousness of class and political action was found to be the most serious
omission. This indicates what the important areas of my own empirical study will be.

Chapter 3

OVERVIEW: THE GROWTH
OF THE CIVIL SERVICE

THE EARLIEST CIVIL SERVICE

The British Civil Service is one of the largest employers of labour
in Britain. Its activities affect everyone to a greater or lesser
extent. This has not however always been the case either in relation to its size or to its functions and until the nineteenth
century the Civil Service, as that term is contemporarily understood, did not exist. The earliest recorded indigenous civil
service existed in Anglo-Saxon England when among the ruling elite
administration emerged as a distinct activity and writers were
employed on a full-time basis.(2) Throughout the Feudal Period
little advance was made beyond a very rudimentary division of
labour, but this system gave way to a more centralized form of
administration, and by Tudor times an embryonic civil service had
emerged which performed the basic functions of the state, viz.
collection of revenue, maintenance of law and order, defence and
the conduct of external relations.(3) By the beginning of the
eighteenth century appointments to the government service were
made by the political party in power and a patronage system had
developed. The administrator's job was freehold and very often
the property of the occupant who could accordingly dispose of it
as he chose.(4) No centralized universalistic organization or
appointment system existed.
    Even in the first part of the nineteenth century most of the
nominations for posts were in the hands of ministers and some of
the better positions went to politicians who had lost their parlia-
mentary seats.(5) Patronage led to a certain amount of inefficiency and dishonesty but in spite of this successive governments
continued to raise revenue and carry out various limited functions.
(6) There were some complaints about the low calibre of the clerks
although at this time the public was unaccustomed to think of the
Civil Service as an entity, but rather as the constituent departments; the 'ill-assorted series of more or less independent
Government Offices.'(7) Distinct white-collar groups could be
discerned at this time in the form of managers and clerical func-
tionaries. This division of labour was formalized later in the
nineteenth century, first in the Northcote-Trevelyan report and

25

later in subsequent government reports, commissions and enquiries which hastened the processes of rationalization and bureaucratization in the service.(8)

THE GROWTH OF CENTRAL GOVERNMENT IN THE LATE NINETEENTH AND EARLY TWENTIETH CENTURIES

A number of developments altered the Civil Service and changed it from the ill-organized series of departments to its present-day bureaucratic structure. First there were shifts in government policy from the non-interventionism and laissez faire strategy of the emergent nineteenth-century bourgeois state to full-scale intervention in the economy, welfare, health, education, housing and employment which characterizes twentieth-century government in Britain.(9) In the social, education and welfare fields after 1834 the role of central government was mainly the supervision of local or voluntary activities such as the administration of the Poor Law and the Boards of Health.(10) Gradually through the nineteenth century these activities became increasingly centralized until by the early twentieth century the central government had responsibility for the provision of limited educational, health and welfare services, old-age pensions and so on. The state largely abstained from overt economic and scientific activity with the notable exceptions of its operations in the Post Office and the Admiralty.(11)
By 1914 central government had critical control over the four functions of raising revenue, maintenance of law and order, defence and external relations; whereas activities relating to provision of social services were still peripheral and small-scale. At that time the Civil Service was 270,000 strong, the largest part of which was the Post Office (209,000). Of the remainder, 20,000 were concerned with the collection of taxes; 10,000 involved in defence (excluding the armed forces); 7,000 with internal law and order; 9,000 in various economic departments (for example the Board of Trade); 5,000 in social services; and less than 1,000 concerned with external affairs.(12) The impact of the First World War was enormous with regard to the functions which the central government took over during the hostilities. Some of the functions were relinquished after the war, for example those concerned with rationing, while others were maintained. New ministries appeared at this time, such as the Ministry of Pensions to deal with disabled servicemen, and the Air Ministry to deal with the newly formed RAF. The Ministry of Health was established in 1919 containing the old Local Government Board and the Insurance Commission for England and Wales. Following financial troubles in the railway industry and industrial unrest in the mines the Board of Trade extended its jurisdiction and in 1919 the Ministry of Transport was established.(13)
The second major change impinging on the central government was that it became the largest single consumer of science in the United Kingdom. In 1915-16 the Department of Scientific and Industrial Research was set up as a direct result of the exigencies of war. This marked an important turning-point because it was the

beginning of direct central government interest in applied scientific research and concomitantly the birth of the scientific Civil Service which today accounts for a large number of Civil Service employees.(14)

This era of rapid expansion was followed by one of stability and steady growth during the next two decades. In 1934 the Unemployment Assistance Board was set up to take over from the Ministry of Labour and local authorities the responsibilities for the able-bodied unemployed. By 1935 there were some 303,000 non-industrial Civil Servants, of whom 166,000 were employed in the Post Office; thus the proportion employed in central administration had risen 225 per cent since 1914.(15)

The Second World War marked a watershed in the development of the Civil Service and greatly speeded up the processes of central government's expansion into the social, economic and scientific spheres. In the post-Second World War era the government maintained many of the functions it had assumed during the war and conceived of certain social policies, such as the maintenance of full employment, as desirable. In 1948 the National Health Service was set up with its scheme of comprehensive social insurance. Some ministries did not survive the war (for example those of Home Security, Economic Warfare, and Information) but others like Supply, Fuel and Power, and Food did.(16) Extensions of the Social Services led to other changes, such as the establishment of Town and Country Planning and later the Ministry of Local Government. The changes brought about by the war and its aftermath have had a lasting effect on the size of the Civil Service and by 1956 the numbers of Civil Servants outside the Post Office was over 358,000, six times as many as in 1914.(17) Since that time the numbers of Civil Servants have expanded gradually although in the 1960s and 1970s the growth levelled out somewhat. In 1977 the total number of Civil Servants in Britain was 745,161.(18) The present figure would be much higher but for the fact that in 1969 the Post Office became a public corporation (nationalized industry) and the official statistics no longer compute postal employees with other Civil Servants.

THE PRESENT DAY CIVIL SERVICE

Civil Servants are conventionally defined as 'servants of the Crown, other than holders of political or judicial offices, who are employed in a Civil capacity whose remuneration is paid wholly and directly out of monies voted by Parliament'.(19) The term 'Civil Servant' is not therefore synonymous with the idea of a state employee because such workers as members of the armed forces, the judiciary, employees of the nationalized industries, local government and the police are not included. The Civil Service is a fairly arbitrary concept because some groups of workers are sometimes included and sometimes not; thus since 1969 the Post Office is no longer considered as part of the Civil Service. This book is however not concerned with state employees or even with Civil Servants, but with types of white-collar workers who happen to be defined as Civil Servants.

These types of white-collar workers are employed in central
government. Central government is itself divided into a number
of departments or ministries whose functions include the regula-
tion of the economy (the Treasury and the Department of Trade),
raising revenue (Customs and Excise and the Inland Revenue),
defence (Ministry of Defence), and social welfare (the Department
of Health and Social Security).(20)
    These central government departments are staffed nearly exclus-
ively by Civil Servants of two kinds; those concerned with administration and clerical duties, and those concerned with the execution of some specialized activity (such as scientific research).
Within the two basic categories of Civil Servants a bureaucratic
division of labour is found, with clearly defined lines of authority and specified competences. Until 1970 Civil Servants concerned
with administration and clerical duties were divided into three
separate hierarchies, namely the administrative class (equivalent
to top management in industry), the executive class (equivalent to
middle management), and the clerical class (which carried out the
routine clerical activities in the organization). In 1970 following the implementation of the Fulton proposals the three hierarchies were merged into one.(21)

THE GROWTH OF THE CIVIL SERVICE

The overall growth of the Civil Service has been 176.4 per cent in
the twentieth century but types of Civil Service work have
increased at different rates in the same period (see Table 3.1).
Top management in the Service has shown an increase of 1,280 per
cent during the period 1929-77. This huge increase is somewhat
misleading because the methods of computing the absolute numbers
in this category were different in 1929 and 1977, and the latter
figure includes some grades of Civil Servants who would not previously have been included. As a proportion of the total Civil
Service the top management sector has increased since the mid-
1930s from 0.4 per cent to 2 per cent. In the same period top
scientists within the Civil Service have increased 924 per cent
while middle management and the clerical grades have increased
342 per cent and 154 per cent respectively (see Table 3.2). There
are however regional differences in the spread of Civil Servants,
as growth patterns have varied from region to region. There is a
pattern of metropolitan concentration of Civil Servants but this
is tempered by several factors. London draws higher rather than
subordinate classes, the administrative and clerical classes rather
than technicians and scientists, and women as against men.(22)
    Of the most senior positions a majority are found almost exclus-
ively in London with a minority in Edinburgh. Most scientists
work in the South and Midlands, and it is only middle management
and clerks who are evenly distributed over the regions with over
one-third working in Scotland and Northern England.(23) In the
case of low grades there is some evidence of localized recruitment.
    There have been some changes in the distribution of Civil
Servants regionally (see Table 3.3). All regions except Inner
London and East Anglia have had increases in the total number of

TABLE 3.1 The growth of the Civil Service, 1914-77

Date	Number of Civil Servants	% increase on 1914
1914	270,000	
1935	303,000	12.2
1964	629,000	132.9
1975	693,921	157.0
1977	746,161	176.4

Sources: F.M.G. Willson, 'The Organization of British Central Government 1914-1964', 1963, pp.22-30, 345; 'Civil Service Statistics 1977', p.21.

TABLE 3.2 The growth of the Civil Service by types of occupation, 1929-77

	1929	1937	1950	1956	1966	1977	% increase
I Administrators and top managers	1,100	1,300	3,000	2,500	2,500	15,181	1,280
II Scientists (top scientists only)	700	-	3,300	3,400	4,100	7,167	924
III(a) Middle management (executive officers)	15,400	17,700	68,300	68,200	83,600	68,135	342
III(b) Routine clerks (clerical officers, clerical assistants)	66,100	94,900	226,700	184,400	212,300	168,034	154

Sources: The Treasury, Numbers of Civil Servants in Various Departments and Classes 1929 to 1966. Memorandum Number 4 submitted, 'The Civil Service Volume 4: Factual, Statistical and Explanatory Papers', HMSO, London, 1968, p.271; A. Halsey and I. Crewe, 'Social Survey of the Civil Service', HMSO, London, 1969, p.302; and 'Civil Service Statistics 1977', pp.22-4.

TABLE 3.3 The distribution of non-industrial civil servants by region, 1970-77

Regions	Nos 1.1.70 000s	% of total	Nos 1.4.74 000s	% of total	Nos 1.1.77 000s	% of total	% change 1970-7
Scotland	39.1	8.3	45.0	9.0	51.5	9.3	31
Northern Ireland	3.5	0.7	4.0	0.8	4.5	0.8	29
North	30.1	6.4	31.0	6.2	35.5	6.4	18
North West	43.1	9.1	46.0	9.2	55.5	10.0	29
Yorkshire and Humberside	22.9	4.8	24.0	4.8	30.0	5.4	31
Wales and Monmouth	18.8	4.0	24.0	4.8	31.0	5.6	65
West Midlands	22.9	4.8	24.0	4.8	29.0	5.2	27
East Midlands	16.7	3.5	18.0	3.6	21.0	3.8	25
East Anglia	10.5	2.2	10.0	2.0	11.0	2.0	5
South West	38.9	8.2	42.0	8.4	51.5	9.3	32
South East (excluding London)	76.7	16.2	84.0	16.7			
Outer London	45.8	9.7	58.0	11.6	236.0	42.0	4
Inner London	104.2	22.0	92.0	18.3			
Total	473.2	100.0	502.0	100.0	556.5	99.8	17.6

Sources: 'Civil Servants and Change', The Wider Issues Review Team, Civil Service Department, 1975, p.42; 'Civil Service Opinion', vol.49, 1971, p.143; 'Civil Service Statistics 1977', p.10.

Civil Servants, but region by region the relative concentrations have altered slightly with all except the North and East Anglia tending to increase. The most rapid growth area has been Wales, but in spite of large-scale dispersal London and the South East retain the largest concentration of Civil Servants with a little over 40 per cent working there.

In many important respects the Civil Service shows similar trends to the white-collar workforce as a whole. It has rapidly increased in the twentieth century while different sectors of it have grown at different rates. The scientific sector has seen the most dramatic increase, while middle management and routine clerical work has steadily increased. These latter functions have been absorbed largely outside the metropolitan South.

The Civil Service is very large, its functions extremely varied, and it contains a variety of types of workers the study of which is pertinent to a discussion of proletarianization. These types of workers are top managers, scientists, middle managers, and clerks. The Civil Service therefore presents an ideal focus of study. The organization has itself evolved over a number of years and I have only sketched in here a very brief discussion of its growth. My main focus in this book is not the evolution of a bureaucratic organization but changes in the industrial and

political behaviour of a group of white-collar workers. Therefore
I refer back to the structure of the organization of the Civil
Service only where this impinges directly on my discussion of
proletarianization.

Part Two

THE EMPIRICAL STUDY

Chapter 4

THE MARKET SITUATION OF CIVIL SERVANTS I: INCOME

INTRODUCTION

The purpose and plan of the chapter

In chapter 2 I derived two propositions relating to income proletarianization from the literature on the subject; first that the
incomes of white-collar workers had fallen relative to that of
manual workers, and second that the income of white-collar workers
is increasingly derived from their own productive labour and less
from the surplus value produced by others. In this chapter I shall
examine evidence bearing on the first proposition by inspecting
data on wages and salaries of Civil Servants in the United Kingdom.
I was unable to test the second proposition because my data relate
to income levels and not to source of income. This is not necessarily a serious problem since the writer formulating this position
did not intend it to be tested.
    I will briefly outline some of the methodological problems in
dealing with the data. I will then analyse wages and salaries of
a cross-section of the working population of Britain and of Civil
Servants. Finally, I will relate these findings to the main· issues
of the study.

Methodological problems

The main sources I have used for comparative purposes are the
studies by Bowley, Routh and the Department of Employment.(1)
Between them these three give an approximate picture of historical
changes. The most up-to-date figures are contained in 'The New
Earnings Survey'. They are also the most comprehensive and therefore I have tended to concentrate on recent changes rather than
earlier ones. Hence my conclusions in relation to the period
1968-78 are the most reliable while those for the period before
1955 are more speculative. On the whole the figures for the Civil
Service are more comprehensive than for the population at large
although they go back in a continuous series only as far as the
mid-1950s.(2) Again the information for the period 1960-78 is

quite comprehensive and thus facilitates easy comparison with
figures for the rest of the working population. This is doubly
fortuitous since the main focus of my study of the industrial
behaviour of Civil Servants is on precisely this period.
    There are a number of problems to be faced in using the data on
wages and salaries of the British workforce and their relative
changes over time. First, no single series of data exists. Second,
the data which do exist use an alarming number of different census
categories, definitions and statistical techniques. This is particularly problematic when, as here, making comparisons over time.
Another complication is that some of the figures refer to average
calculations, e.g. mean salary levels, while others are specified
in terms of median or modal calculations. It was not therefore
always possible to provide a series of figures where the type of
average was constant. Moreover, the Civil Service salary figures
I have used are not averages but salary scales. To circumvent
this problem I have picked out various points on the salary scale
for comparative purposes as well as examining the span of the
scale.

GENERAL TRENDS IN WAGES AND SALARIES IN THE UNITED KINGDOM
IN THE TWENTIETH CENTURY

Despite the deficiencies noted above it is possible to use the
information available in a way which can throw light on my problem. I showed in chapter 2 that it has become something of a
commonplace to state that non-manual incomes have fallen relative
to manual earnings. Some writers take this as evidence of proletarianization,(3) and I argued that the definition of class involved
in such a formulation was suspect.(4) However, at an empirical
level in the United Kingdom further problems arise. In the United
Kingdom the evidence for the decline in the differential is scat-
tered and incomplete, and the studies which have pursued the issue
are largely based on American data.(5) With reference to Britain
we know with some certainty that between 1914 and 1920 there was
a general narrowing of the extant differential between wages and
salaries as the money earnings of manual workers increased rapidly
in relation to non-manual workers, while non-manual earnings lagged
behind. In the years 1920-3 wage rates and manual earnings fell
while non-manual earnings were much more stable. Over the next
ten years (1924-34) there was a downward drift of money earnings
which was more pronounced among manual rather than non-manual
workers, and was more pronounced among the unskilled than the
skilled. Between 1934 and 1944 manual earnings moved upwards at
an accelerating pace, with the maximum rises between 1938 and 1940,
while salaries increased rather more slowly at first and after
1940 did not increase very much. In the period immediately after
the Second World War all money earnings rose while the differential
between manual and non-manual remained largely unaltered, but
after 1951 the differential began to narrow again until around
1956 when it began widening as semi-skilled and unskilled manual
workers began to lose most in relative terms.(6) (See Table 4.1,
and Fig. 4.1.)

TABLE 4.1   Changes in relative earnings of main occupational
groups, 1913/14-60 (male earners only)

	Indices of earnings - occupational group average expressed as a percentage of average for all men in the same period				
	1913/14	1922/4	1935/6	1955/6	1960
Higher professions	357	326	341	244	253
Managers and administrators	217	269	237	234	230
Lower professions	169	179	165	97	105
Foremen	123	150	147	124	126
Clerks	108	102	103	82	85
Skilled manual workers	108	101	105	98	99
Semi-skilled manual workers	75	70	72	74	72
Unskilled manual workers	69	72	70	69	67
All non-manual workers	142	158	152	144	145
All manual workers	88	83	85	83	82
All men	100	100	100	100	100

Source: Westergaard, J. and Resler, H., 'Class in a Capitalist
Society: A Study of Contemporary Britain', Penguin, London, 1976,
p.74.

   Table 4.1 reveals several important trends which impinge directly on the problem. First, all categories except managers,
administrators and foremen have lost out in real terms in the
period 1913-60. Second, the differential between the extreme
categories of higher professionals and unskilled manual workers
has decreased, although this does not include various fringe benefits which accrue to higher salary grades in management and elsewhere. Third, in general terms the differential between all non-
manual workers and all manual workers has not altered noticeably.
Thus the statement that the incomes of white-collar workers are
falling relative to those of manual workers must be viewed with
some scepticism. It follows then that when a general case for
income proletarianization is argued it is based on two income
groups at the extreme ends of the wage-salary structure, rather
than on the middle levels of the class structure. In the Marxian
formulation it is the changes in the middle levels which are held
to be the most significant.
   Table 4.2 shows that within the clerical and administrative
field there have been changes within that occupational group.
There have also been variations between this group and manual
workers. The salaries of administrators, managers and senior
clerks have been considerably above those of manual workers, but
in the period 1935-78 the differential has decreased. Lower

TABLE 4.2 Money earnings of manual, non-manual and specific other male occupations, per annum (averages)*

Occupation Year	Manual men	Non-manual men	Managers & administrators	Clerks with considerable responsibility	Clerks with some responsibility	Clerks (routine)
1931	109.46					
1935	159.00		634.00	440.00		192.00
1940	149.06					
1952	309.18					
1954	325.58					
1955	527.00		1541.00	1480.00		523.00
1959	663.00					
1960			2034.00	1850.00	1071.20	682.00
1968	1164.80	1445.60	1809.60	1346.80	1248.00	904.80
1970	1362.40	1856.40	2532.40	1622.40	1357.20	1050.40
1971	1497.60	2022.80	2693.60	1768.00	1528.80	1159.60
1972	1669.20	2256.80	2938.00	1970.80	1814.80	1258.40
1973	1924.00	2485.60		2168.40	2368.80	1596.40
1974	2199.60	2813.20	3447.60	2589.60	2756.00	1882.40
1975	2808.00	3530.80	4128.80	3120.00	3302.00	2350.40
1976	3291.60	4212.00	4862.00	3780.40	3499.60	2943.20
1977	3614.00	4596.80	5371.60	3988.40	4128.80	3192.80
1978	4076.80	5194.80	6073.60	4383.60		3510.00

* See Appendices 1, 2 and 3 where I distinguish which are mean and which are median calculations. Categories derived from source material, although in certain instances I have had to telescope various groups.

Sources: The Department of Employment, 'The New Earnings Survey 1968-78', HMSO, London 1970-78; Routh, G., 'Occupation and Pay in Great Britain 1906-1960', Cambridge University Press, Cambridge, 1965, pp.78,104; and Bain, G.S., 'The Growth of the White Collar Unionism', Clarendon Press, Oxford, 1970, p.52.

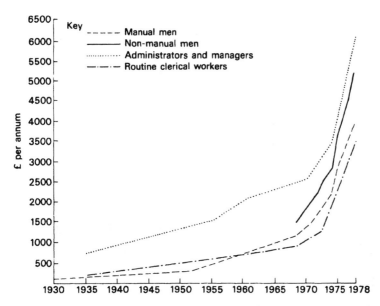

FIGURE 4.1   Graphical representation of general changes in the
relative earnings of men (omitting extreme scores(a)) in selected
occupations, 1930-78 (b)
(a) Extreme scores omitted to give a better general representation
    of the trends. Extreme scores arise where different sources
    have used different categories.
(b) Categories derived from source material (see Table 4.2).

clerical positions show a decline in the differential only when
the base line is drawn in the 1930s. Comparisons of post-war
figures only show that the average for manual men is above the
routine clerical average. A decline in the differential is only
observable when making comparisons before 1939.

   This type of broad comparison reveals very little, because the
averages are calculated in such a way that subtle differences in
types of occupations are masked. Thus the generic term 'non-
manual' includes both the chairman of ICI and his secretary. This
illuminates the difficulties associated with discussions of proletarianization based on broad comparisons of manual and non-manual
rates.

   An examination of the figures in recent years shows that the
earnings of non-manual males kept ahead of the earnings of manual
male workers and that by 1978, if anything, the differential was
actually increasing. Thus at first sight, it appears that the
evidence contradicts the sociological conventional wisdom. However when the figures for non-manual workers are broken down into
types of occupation different trends can be observed. Thus the
earnings of managers and administrators outstrip the annual earnings of manual workers, and in recent years the differential has
increased. This tendency is under-represented in the chart (Fig.
4.1) in real terms because figures on average incomes do not take

TABLE 4.3 The per-annum salaries of selected grades of senior civil servants compared with national average, 1939-78

Occupation / Year and salary in £	National administrators	Higher executive officer	Senior executive officer	Principal	Senior Principal or senior chief executive officer	Assistant Secretary	Administrative Trainee/ Assistant Principal
1939		650 (T)	860 (T)	1100 (T)		1500 (T)	
1950		865 (T)	1075 (T)	1375 (T)		2000 (T)	
1955	1541	1090 (T)	1325 (T)	1595 (T)		2600 (T) / 2300 (M) / 2000 (B)	743 (M)
1956		1225 (T) / 1055 (B)	1530 (T) / 1285 (B)	1950 (T) / 1650 (M) / 1375 (B)	2000	2700 (T) / 2400 (M) / 2100 (B)	815 (M) / 605 (B)
1957		1285 (T) / 1110 (B)	1605 (T) / 1350 (B)	2050 (T) / 1730 (M) / 1450 (B)	2200	2700 (T) / 2400 (M) / 2200 (B)	855 (M) / 635 (B)
1958		1290 (T) / 1120 (B)	1610 (T) / 1355 (B)	2070 (T) / 1740 (M) / 1460 (B)	2240		860 (M) / 635 (B)
1961		1430 (T) / 1222 (B)	1872 (T) / 1508 (B)	2418 (T) / 2106 (M) / 1716 (B)	2564		1004 (M) / 738 (B)

Year	(M)	(B)	(T)	(M)	(B)		(T)	(M)	(B)	(T)	(B)	(T)	(B)	
1962	1044	768				2715	2569	2244	1837	1947	1568	1487	1271	
1963	1075	791	3500	3150	2800	2743	2646	2311	1894			1532	1309	
1964	1107	815	4300	3800	3300	2929	2725	2330	1951	2250	1845			
1965	1274	895	4500	4000	3500	3500	3002	2629	2174	2329	1910	1811	1521	
1966	1291	926				3500	3107	2721	2250	2411	1977	1874	1574	
1968	1381	991	4815	4280	3745	3745	3324	2911	2408	2580	2115	2005	1684	
1969	1430	1020	4950	4400	3850	3850	3425	2990	2475	2710	2220	2100	1740	
1970	1630	1162	5640	5015	4390	4390	3902	3407	2820	3099	2529	2392	1982	2532
1971	1740	1260	6300	5620	5000	5000	4400	3940	3250	3400	2775	2625	2150	2693

Occupation Year and salary in £	National administrators	Higher executive officer	Senior executive officer	Principal	Senior Principal or senior chief executive officer	Assistant Secretary	Administrative Trainee/ Assistant Principal
1972	2938	2890 (T) 2301 (B)	3638 (T) 2969 (B)	4708 (T) 4216 (M) 3878 (B)	5350	7276 (T) 6260 (M) 5350 (B)	1871 (M) 1355 (B)
1973		2961 (T) 2445 (B)	3796 (T) 3129 (B)	4908 (T) 4397 (M) 3635 (B)	5550	7476 (T) 6460 (M) 5550 (B)	1998 (M) 1467 (B)
1974	3448	3585 (T) 2953 (B)	4542 (T) 3756 (B)	5775 (T) 5216 (M) 4360 (B)	6300	7988 (T) 7141 (M) 6300 (B)	2782 (M) 1819 (B)
1975	4129	4477 (T) 3711 (B)	5628 (T) 4671 (B)	7115 (T) 6543 (M) 5416 (B)	8340	10570 (T) 9870 (M) 8260 (B)	3492 (M) 2280 (B)
1978	6074	5718 (T) 4842 (B)	7032 (T) 5937 (B)	8729 (T) 7552 (M) 6791 (B)	10151	12273 (T) 11302 (M) 10043 (B)	4062 (M) 3713 (B)

Sources: The Civil Service Pay Research Unit, see Appendix 1, 'The Royal Commission on the Civil Service 1953-55' (The Priestley Commission), HMSO, London 1955 (1966 reprint), p.78; 'The Royal Commission on the Civil Service 1953-55; Minutes of Evidence taken before the Royal Commission', HMSO, London, 1955, p.238; and Halsey, A. and Crewe, I., 'Social Survey of the Civil Service: The Civil Service Vol.3 (1) Surveys and Investigations: Evidence Submitted to the Committee under the Chairmanship of Lord Fulton, 1966-68', HMSO, London, 1969, p.113.

Key: T = Top of grade;   M = Middle of grade;   B = Bottom of grade

account of either the fringe benefits which accrue to management
nor the longer hours worked by manual workers. Moving on to the
clerical sector proper it can be seen that senior clerks have
actually lost an absolute pecuniary advantage in the inter-war
period and now only just hold their own against the averages for
manual workers. Clerks involved in routine duties have lost not
only an erstwhile differential advantage, but now significantly
lag behind the average for manual workers (Table 4.2 presents a
summary picture of this).
    My general conclusion from this albeit limited data is that
there is limited support for the notion that non-manual workers'
earnings have fallen relative to manual workers in the lowest
region of the clerical domain, *but this does not apply to those
non-manual workers in middle management and above.*

THE SALARIES OF CIVIL SERVANTS (7)

I will take examples of Civil Servants from each category I outlined in the typology contained in chapter 2.

Category I: Administrators and managers

In this section I concentrate on the group of Civil Servants who
are situated in the upper reaches of the bureaucratic hierarchy and
who are concerned with the management and administration of the
Civil Service. Their responsibilities and functions vary from
major policy-making and advice to ministers, through the heading of
large establishments, personal assistance to ministers, to the
ordinary middle and upper middle management in the Civil Service.
Most of the members of this category are career Civil Servants who
entered the service in their early twenties as young graduates.(8)
They constitute a social and educational elite within the Civil
Service and it is from their ranks that the so-called Whitehall
Mandarins are drawn. In terms of Civil Service grades they are:
higher executive officers, senior executive officers, principals,
senior principals, and assistant secretaries. Their earnings are
set out in Table 4.3 and Fig.4.2.

Higher executive officers, senior executive officers and principals
By treating grades separately a number of different trends can be
observed which enable us to comment on the proposition that the
salaries of these white-collar workers have fallen relative both
to their own pre-war levels and in relation to manual wages, and
that therefore income proletarianization has occurred. At the
higher executive officer level the scale lagged behind the national
average for administrators and managers for a long period from the
mid-1930s to the early 1970s. In the mid-1970s the higher executive officer scale gained rapidly but this trend has been reversed
in the most recent past. The acceleration in the scale is most
pronounced after the period of major Civil Service reorganization
in the early 1970s (see Fig.4.2.A). At the senior executive
officer level the evidence shows that this grade as a whole lagged

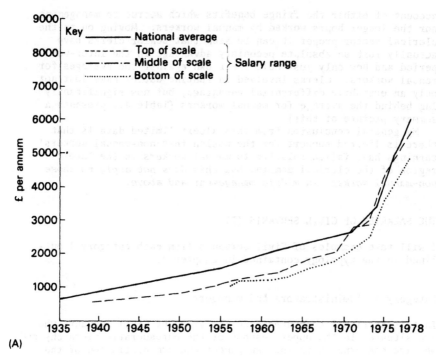

(A)

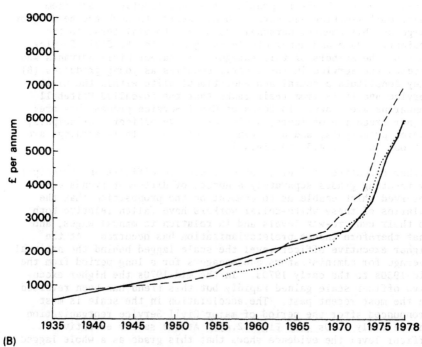

(B)

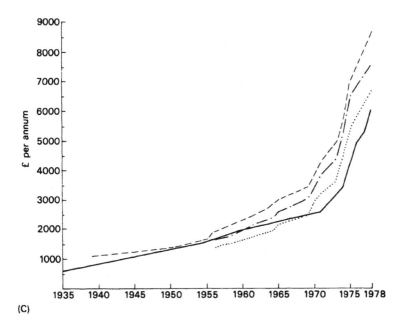

(C)

FIGURE 4.2 Graphical representation of changes in the salary
scales of higher executive officers (A), senior executive officers
(B) and principals (C), relative to changes in the national average for administrators and managers

Sources: As in Tables 4.2 and 4.3.

behind the national average for managerial salaries well into the
1960s at both extremes of the scale (see Fig.4.2.B), but the early
1960s saw the whole grade advancing vis à vis national averages
until by the mid-1970s the senior executive officer scale was in
advance of the national average. This trend tailed off in the years
1977 and 1978. There is little evidence over the period 1935-78 of
a decline in average terms in this grade. Among principals the
earliest figures show that people at the top of this grade were consistently better off than the national average and by the mid-1950s
the midpoint on the principal scale was above the national mean.
But this must be measured against the systematic bias built into
the principal scale. This grade operates a regular promotion system both into and out of it; the grade itself is pyramid-shaped and
thus a majority of the grade are concentrated in the lower parts of
it. Therefore there will be a tendency for the average (mean)
salary of principals to fall below the midpoint on the salary
scale. In the late 1960s and 1970s there has been a tendency for
the rate of increase in the salaries of principals to be greater
than the rate of increase of the national average (see Fig.4.2.C).
Within this grade there is no evidence of income proletarianization.

Senior principals and assistant secretaries
Of the other grades being here considered (senior principal and

assistant secretary) there is little meaningful point in comparing
them with national average figures for administrators and managers.
More realistically top Civil Service salaries of this kind ought to
be compared with senior posts in industry, although these latter
figures are usually quite unreliable. Two points can however be
observed. First, compared with before the Second World War, top
Civil Service posts are less well remunerated in real money terms
than they were, although even at the present time their earnings
are considerably above national averages. Compared with some
equivalent occupations top Civil Servants are better off (e.g. when
compared with university teachers), but compared with top posts in
industry they do not do particularly well. Thus on balance there
is evidence of a decline in real money terms for top Civil Servants
while absolute advantages over a large majority of the rest of the
population have been maintained.

Training grades for senior Civil Service posts (assistant principals,
administration trainees)
On the whole the salaries of this group are low compared with the
rest of category I which they ultimately join, but this is due to
their lowly position in the hierarchy. The salaries of administration trainees, and before them assistant principals, have held
their own in relation to the existing levels since the mid-1950s,
although by the mid-1970s the very bottom of the scale was a good
deal lower than the national average. There is however no evidence
of income proletarianization among this group. In view of the fact
that nearly all members of this grade eventually join the top
administrators it would be naive to regard the salaries of a training position as truly indicative of anything other than the salary
of a training grade. Socially and educationally members of this
grade share most of the characteristics of top administrators and
managers and have shown reluctance to use militant action to
further their aims.

Summary
Within category I we observe that individual grades have been
affected differently by changes in the overall pay structure of
Britain. There has been an overall tendency for all the salaries
to decline in real money terms vis à vis the pre-war figures because
purchasing power has declined as the rate of inflation has increased. But there is also a marked tendency for this category to
do better than the rest of the population in absolute terms. The
decline in relation to the pre-war position is a very slow one over
a long period of time, and although it is a decline it would be
naive to term it proletarianization. Indeed in relative terms the
incomes of this group have fallen in relation to manual workers,
but this relative narrowing of the differential has not reduced
category I to the level of the majority of the population. Thus
realistically the evidence on this category belies any notion of
proletarianization. Indeed of all the variants of proletarianization, given the social milieu in which these Civil Servants live
and work, this is sociologically the least likely.(9) The evidence
on income is tenuous and it would be naive to read it as
proletarianization.

Category II: scientists and other specialists

In this section I examine the salaries of Civil Service scientists
in particular and compare them with the salaries of scientists and
technicians outside government establishments (see Table 4.4). The
findings also apply inter alia to other Civil Service specialists
though I do not consider them here in detail. The generic term
Civil Service scientist is an all-embracing one and includes, for
example, the heads of major research establishments (Royal Greenwich
Observatory, Porton Down) and the members of individual research
teams, as well as laboratory technicians and assistants. Therefore
several different grades of Civil Service scientist will be distinguished as well as different types of non-government scientific
workers for comparative purposes.

Top government scientists (chief scientific officers, deputy chief
scientific officers, and senior principal scientific officers)
These men are concerned in part with the administration of government science as well as science research proper. They head the
scientific establishments or head research divisions in the larger
establishments. In their case it is fairly meaningless to compare
their salaries with the national average figures for all scientific
workers. Since 1958 chief scientific officers, deputy chief
scientific officers and senior principal scientific officers have
all enjoyed fairly rapid salary increases. This is however in part
due to a catching-up effect as an attempt was made to bring top
scientists' salaries into line with Civil Service administrators'
salaries. The salaries of top Civil Service scientists have two
characteristics in relation to other wages and salaries. First they
are considerably above the norm of the national averages, and
second they are consistently above the average for other scientists
and technologists. Moreover there has been a long-term trend for
top Civil Service scientists' salaries to increase faster than
those outside. This is partly because there were very few government scientists originally and therefore there was no unified
salary scale.(10) Scientists' salaries were individually assessed
and the level at which they were assessed was not particularly high.
With these biases in mind there seems to be no evidence of income
proletarianization because among these scientists there has not
even been a relative decline since before the Second World War.

Intermediate scientific grades
When considering the intermediate government scientific grades
(principal scientific officer, chief experimental officer, senior
scientific officer, senior experimental officer and higher scientific officer/experimental officer) a rather different picture
emerges. First, any consideration of the salary scales over time
is complicated by the structural changes in the Civil Service which
took place in the early 1970s.(11) Certain grades have had their
character radically transformed and the pay structures altered.
Therefore time series data ought to be considered in this light.
The highest intermediate grade (principal scientific officer) has a
salary scale consistently above all levels of the national average
compared to all scientists, with the top of the grade showing a

TABLE 4.4 The salary scales of selected grades of scientific Civil

Occupation Year Salaries £ p.a.	National average all scientists	Chief scientific officers	Deputy chief scientific officer	Senior principal scientific officer	Principal scientific officer
1958		3100-3350	2450- 2750	2050- 2350	1410-2000
1961					1716-2418
1962					1785-2515
1963		3863-4050	3275- 3600	2800- 3150	1839-2590
1964		4625-4700	3975- 4300	3300- 3800	2100-2900
1965		5000-5250	4175- 4625	3500- 4000	2174-3002
1966		5000-5250	4175- 4625	3745- 4286	2250-3107
1967					
1968	1976	5150	4465- 4950		2408-3324
1969		5240-5500	4600- 5000	3850- 4400	2475-3425
1970	2054	5880-6000	5240- 5700	4390- 5015	2820-3902
1971	2283	6600-6750	5830- 6380	5000- 5620	3100-4100
1972	2569	7930-8250	6607- 7450	5350- 6260	3317-4387
1973	2616	8180-8500	6807- 7700	5550- 6460	3472-4575
1974	2912	8780-9000	7629- 8457	6300- 7280	4227-5550
1975	3749	10950	9764-10840	8260- 9388	5257-6874
1978	5486	13047	11718-12492	10043-11300	6609-8461

Sources: Appendices 1 and 2.

three-fold increase in salary in the years 1968-78. The national
average for all scientists increased at about the same rate in the
period 1968-78. The bottom of the intermediate grades (chief
experimental officer, senior scientific officer, senior experimental
officer and the higher scientific officers) are around the national
average for scientists although the length of some of the scales
makes comparison less than exact. The science grades on the whole
have the characteristic that the majority of members of a grade are
concentrated in the lower levels and one can therefore assume that
the average (mean) salary of Civil Service scientists in this group
will actually fall below the national average.

The bottom scientific grades
Of the lowest scientific grades in the Civil Service (senior scientific assistant/scientific officer, scientific assistant/assistant
scientific officer, and assistant experimental officer) the most

Servants compared with national averages for scientists, 1958-78

Senior scientific officer	Higher scientific officer/ experimental officer	National average laboratory technicians	Scientific officer/ senior scientific assistant	Assistant scientific officer/ scientific assistant
1160-1370	945-1160		753-1007	630- 670
1342-1654	1087-1336		811-1082	650- 788
1396-1720	1130-1389		843-1125	676- 811
1438-1722	1164-1431		868-1159	696- 855
1481-1825	1199-1474		894-1269	750- 920
1635-2082	1319-1675			
1744-2155	1365-1734		1031-1359	803- 985
				803- 985
1866-2306	1461-1855	1222	1103-1454	859-1054
1925-2327	1514-1910		1200-1560	910-1100
2193-2703	1725-2177	1424	1367-1777	1037-1253
2303-3255	1810-2350	1643	1120-1900	1235-1359
2464-3483	1946-2515	1809	1206-2043	1328-1500
2615-3640	2076-2667	2007	1318-2177	1440-1612
2798-3895	2221-2854	2168	1435-2329	1547-1899
3979-5511	3095-4237	2948	2038-3357	1950-2428
5154-6898	4104-5448	4248	2839-4415	2731-3303

useful comparison that can be made is not with the national average for all scientists but rather the national averages for all laboratory technicians and the like. On balance the further one looks back at the relative scales of this group of scientists and national averages the better off the Civil Servants were. Thus in the late 1950s at all levels this group of Civil Service scientists was above the national average. This trend continued until the 1960s when gradually the bottom of these scales began to lose their relative advantage, and continued until all low scientific grades were by the mid-1970s relatively worse off than the national average. Thus over time this group of scientists has not enjoyed as high a percentage increase as others in equivalent occupations. In comparison with the working population as a whole these Civil Service scientists are worse off now than the national average for manual occupations. At this level, then, there appears to have been a relative decline in the earnings of this group - a trend which has

been particularly marked in recent years - and so we might argue
that in this group some income proletarianization has taken place.

Summary
Treating Civil Service scientists as a homogeneous category for the
purposes of a test of income proletarianization would be fruitless
in view of the important differences in their salary trends. Comparison made between types of scientific Civil Servants and non-
scientific personnel in the population at large reveals some interesting trends, all of which call into question any simple assertion
of income proletarianization. First, top and intermediate scient-
tists have a consistent advantage over manual and clerical workers
as well as over the national average for managers. Technicians on
the other hand do worse than all three categories of workers here
compared. The only case for proletarianization of scientists by
income therefore appears among the lowest grades of scientists.
This group is also heavily recruited from working-class backgrounds.
(12) However, both top scientists and technicians are represented
by the same trade union which has not exhibited a very great tendency towards militancy. It is not clear whether the impetus for
the lowly technicians to take militant action, particularly on pay,
is swamped by the more senior scientists; or whether some other
factor is at work which acts as an intervening variable. (This
variable might be the fact that many scientists work in isolated
research stations and that isolation does not produce a shared
experience of grievance.) The scientists provide a crucial test
for the technocratic theorists examined in chapter 2 (13) where it
was argued by some writers that the scientific elite was a likely
source of militancy. In spite of the trends in their wages and
salaries the scientists were the least militant of the workers
studied.

Category III: middle management and routine clerical occupations

When considering this sector a number of things must be noted.
First, the material on this and on comparative groups is more plen-
tiful so that a fuller picture can be obtained. Second, the figures
on non-Civil Service occupations, particularly in relation to the
early period, may not be exactly comparable, because differing
sources use differing categories. Third, 'The New Earnings Survey'
first divided clerical occupations into three types by level of
responsibility, but then recently changed to a classification by
industry. Thus the figures on national averages used here for a
time series are not strictly comparable. The Civil Servants I am
considering here are executive officers, clerical officers and
clerical assistants. The clerical assistant scale in the earliest
period is particularly low but this was in part because until 1950
it was an exclusively female grade.(14) Further, some of the
figures are for London only and are not national average figures
which have been consistently lower than London salaries. Finally,
I have not distinguished between men's and women's earnings in
this sector; first because of the difficulty in computing the
figures, and second because it is partly unnecessary since a

majority in the clerical officer and clerical assistant grades are
women, and in the executive officer grade are men. Furthermore,
since 1961 there has been equal pay for men and women in the Civil
Service.(15)

Executive officers (Table 4.5 and Fig.4.3)
In the mid-1930s the salaries of executive officers were below the
national average for clerks, although in the period immediately
preceding the Second World War changes in this scale kept pace with
the gradual increase in the national average. Throughout the 1950s
the levels of salaries of executive officers increased by 81 per
cent in the lowest grade and 61 per cent in the highest grade.
Nationally the percentage increase was 80 per cent. By the time
'The New Earnings Survey' was inaugurated the salary scale of
executive officers spanned the national average; however, the midpoint on the executive officer scale as well as the mean average
salaries of executive officers were below the national average.
(The mean salaries of executive officers would be below the midpoint because the greatest number of executive officers are concentrated at the lower end of the scale.) This position in relation
to the national average has been maintained into the 1970s. Empirically executive officers' salaries have declined in terms of pre-
war levels but have more or less held their own against national
averages for clerks in the most recent period. In terms of their
rate of increase they have not done as well as manual workers.
Indeed the bottom of the executive officers' scale has been lower
than the average for manual earnings since the mid-1950s. This
was not the case before the Second World War, and thus the absolute
pecuniary advantage enjoyed by executive officers has largely disappeared. In a general sense, based on relative changes there is
some evidence of income proletarianization among this group. This
is particularly interesting because this group have also been subject to the variety of other pressures associated with proletarianization. The group has been involved in the rationalization
process, and there is evidence of non-elite recruitment to it.(16)
Further, there is some evidence that this group have become more
militant in the last twenty-five years, which is precisely the
period in which income proletarianization could have been said to
have occurred.(17) Again generalizations are unwise but this group
of workers do present a classic case for the study of proletariani-
ation. This will be followed up later in the study.

Clerical officers and clerical assistants (Table 4.5 and Fig.4.4)
In the mid-1930s the range of Civil Service clerical salaries
spanned the national average for routine clerks. At that time
clerical earnings in the Civil Service were a little higher on
average than manual earnings although the low points on the scale
fell below this average. This is in part accounted for by the
fact that within the Civil Service at this time the lowest earnings
in these grades accrued to women, whereas the average for manual
workers with which the comparison was made was for men only. By
the mid-1950s the average earnings nationally of clerks and manual
workers were about the same, so on the whole all clerks do not
seem to have done as well as other groups of workers. At this time

TABLE 4.5 The salary scales of clerical officers, clerical assistants and executive officers compared with averages for other clerical occupations, 1931-78

Occupation / Year	National average for all clerks			Executive officer	Clerical officer	Clerical assistant
	With considerable responsibility	With some responsibility	Routine			
1931					320 (T) / 80 (B)	182 (T) / 71 (B)
1935	440		192			117 (B)
1936				379 (M)	350 (T) / 95 (B)	187 (T) / 117 (B)
1938					350 (T) / 105 (B)	
1945					428 (T) / 152 (B)	
1946						195 (T) / 125 (B)
1947					450 (T) / 230 (B)	265 (T) / 192 (B)
1950				700 (T)	500 (T) / 250 (B)	302 (T) / 208 (B)
1953				800 (T)	570 (T) / 295 (B)	437 (T) / 288 (B)
1955			523	870 (T) / 721 (M)	625 (T) / 331 (B)	505 (T) / 318 (B)

Year					
1956	549 (T) / 348 (B)	690 (T) / 380 (B)	1000 (T) / 745 (M) / 485 (B)		1480
1957	588 (T) / 421 (B)	760 (T) / 495 (B)	1050 (T) / 780 (M) / 510 (B)		1850
1960		788 (T) / 479 (B)	1154 (T) / 910 (M) / 598 (B)	682	
1961	612 (T) / 437 (B)	820 (T) / 498 (B)	1200 (T) / 946 (M) / 622 (B)		
1962	637 (T) / 433 (B)	852 (T) / 518 (B)	1236 (T) / 974 (M) / 641 (B)		
1965	656 (T) / 466 (B)	879 (T)	1273 (T) / 1003 (M) / 660 (B)		
1964	676 (T) / 481 (B)	905 (T) / 550 (B)	1408 (T) / 1118 (M) / 719 (B)		
1965	765 (T) / 517 (B)	968 (T) / 580 (B)	1457 (T) / 1157 (M) / 744 (B)		
1966	765 (T) / 536 (B)	1002 (TO) / 600 (B)	1457 (T) / 1157 (M) / 744 (B)		
1967	765 (T) / 567 (B)	1002 (T) / 631 (B)			

Occupation Year	National average for all clerks — With considerable responsibility	With some responsibility	Routine	Executive officer	Clerical officer	Clerical assistant
1968	1347	1071	905	1559 (T) 1238 (M) 796 (B)	1072 (T) 675 (B)	819 (T) 607 (B)
1969				1610 (T) 1295 (M) 830 (B)	1100 (T) 700 (B)	826 (T) 611 (B)
1970	1622	1248	1050	1835 (T) 1476 (M) 946 (B)	1253 (T) 797 (B)	942 (T) 697 (B)
1971	1768	1357	1160	2000 (T) 1590 (M) 1015 (B)	1358 (T) 892 (B)	1037 (T) 788 (B)
1972	1970	1529	1258	2150 (T) 1709 (M) 1101 (B)	1489 (T) 978 (B)	1123 (T) 874 (B)
1973	2168	1815	1596	2288 (T) 1763 (M) 1213 (B)	1601 (T) 1090 (B)	1235 (T) 985 (B)
1974	2590	2308	1882	2782 (T) 1926 (M) 1597 (B)	1882 (T) 1377 (B)	1456 (T) 1235 (B)
1975	3120	2758	2350	3492 (T) 2421 (M) 2043 (B)	2409 (T) 1747 (B)	1843 (T) 1524 (B)

1978	4387	4129	3510	4579 (T) 3659 (M) 3113 (B)	3280 (T) 2500 (B)	2608 (T) 2295 (B)

Sources: Appendices 1 and 3.

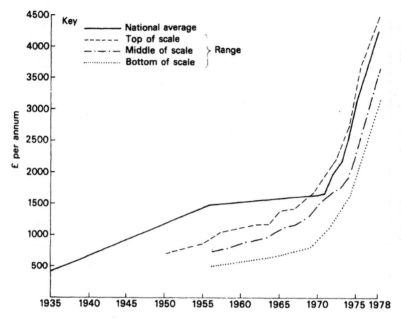

FIGURE 4.3 Graphical respresentation of changes in the salaries
of executive officers in relation to changes in the national
average for senior clerks

Sources: As in Table 4.5.

the earnings of clerical assistants had dropped to well below the
national average both for all clerks and all manual workers, while
the earnings of clerical officers straddled the average figures.
By the early 1960s clerical assistants had fallen further behind
while clerical officers maintained their position. This pattern
persists into the 1970s as both clerical assistants and clerical
officers maintain their fallen position relative to all other routine clerks. However, this period marks a decline in all clerical
salaries vis a vis manual workers. Not only have Civil Service
clerks lost out in relative terms over time and in relation to
other clerical workers, but they have also lost out in absolute
and relative terms to practically every other sector of the working
population (at least in terms of national averages). At this
level then there does indeed appear to be empirical evidence of
income proletarianization.

    Measured in money terms the low clerical grades in the Civil
Service have suffered considerable erosion of their differential
with practically all groups of workers since before the Second
World War. This is in line with trends in clerical work outside
the Civil Service. This particular group of workers has also borne
the brunt of many other changes associated with the concept of
proletarianization. They are the least socially exclusive of all
Civil Service groups, measured either in terms of father's occupation or in terms of educational background. In some cases they

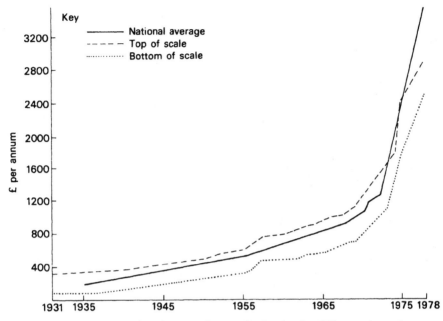

FIGURE 4.4 Changes in the earnings of clerical officers in relation to changes in the national average for routine clerks 1931-78

Source: As in Table 4.5.

have found themselves transferred from small work situations to
large clerical factories where the dual processes of rationalization and mechanization have impinged on their work task.(18) They
are also the most highly feminized group of Civil Servants.(19)

CONCLUSION

This chapter has examined the income levels of selected groups of
Civil Servants in Britain. Changes in their earnings levels have
been inspected over time in order to see if there is any evidence
of what has been called income proletarianization. On the basis
of these observations I concluded that although all Civil Servants
(except top-ranking scientists) are worse off than they were
before the Second World War in terms of purchasing power, only
laboratory technicians and clerks, and to a lesser extent executive
officers, had experienced acute income proletarianization. Among
top administrators in the service I observed that although their
position had declined in real money terms since before the Second
World War they still had absolute financial advantages over the
bulk of the population. Among top scientists there was an actual
increase in earnings over the rest of the population and this
belied any notion of proletarianization.
    Empirically the proposition that the salaries of white-collar
workers have fallen relative to manual workers, and that this was

therefore evidence of proletarianization, was found to be inconsistent and unsatisfactory. There is evidence of a narrowing
differential, but this must be tempered with other variables in
order for a clearcut indication of proletarianization to be
observed. The idea of income proletarianization can only be applied
selectively since there is no evidence that all non-manual workers
or all Civil Servants have experienced this. The changes that have
taken place in the wage structure since the 1930s have affected
different groups in different ways. On the basis of this I will
argue that income proletarianization has taken place for some Civil
Servants; yet as I argued in chapter 2, this is something of a
definitional trick since income proletarianization is not the same
thing as Marx's theory because the definition of class used here
differs from the Marxian usage.

Of the groups considered, those who had suffered most were also
the most militant. In subsequent chapters I will turn my attention
to whether this industrial militancy is based purely on economic
issues, or whether it is rooted in some form of class-conscious
behaviour. This finding is very significant because although
income alone does not define class, if the relative loss of income
generates class-conscious other-directed behaviour, then it is an
important element of the concept of proletarianization.

Chapter 5

THE MARKET SITUATION OF CIVIL SERVANTS II: SOCIAL ORIGINS

INTRODUCTION

In chapter 2 I showed that a number of writers had used as their main indicators of proletarianization factors associated with the social origins of white-collar workers. They argued that since the end of the nineteenth century the social character of the clerical workforce had altered in a number of very significant ways. Whereas the clerks of the nineteenth century were usually middle class or at the very least lower middle class in origin, and the vast majority of them were men, by the late twentieth century many white-collar workers originated from working-class backgrounds and a majority of them were women. I noted that some writers took either or both of these changes as evidence of proletarianization or as indicators of proletarianization. This chapter will examine the empirical evidence for these propositions in the British Civil Service utilizing the typology elaborated in chapter 2. Where possible I will examine trends over time to see if any long-term social process has been at work, although such analysis is hampered by the large gaps that exist in the evidence. The most complete survey of the Civil Service is that done in the mid-1960s at the behest of the Fulton Committee and I draw heavily on this material. (1) However before the mid-1960s the only material that was collected in any great quantity was on higher Civil Servants. Thus comparisons for routine clerks and scientists are difficult and on the whole less than satisfactory.

Throughout this chapter I will be making fairly frequent comparisons with the white-collar population as a whole. I do this in order first to compare the Civil Service with the white-collar world, and second to demonstrate how typical the Civil Service is of the rest of the white-collar workforce. Thus at one and the same time this chapter both tests the extent to which predicted changes have occurred in the social origins of Civil Servants as well as highlighting the extent to which the Civil Service is a good test-case for the propositions relating to proletarianization.

The white-collar sector of the working population has grown enormously in the twentieth century in Britain. (2) The growth has been both absolute and relative in terms of total numbers and as a

proportion of the workforce as a whole. This pattern has also
occurred in other advanced societies.(3) In Britain between 1911
and 1961 the number of white-collar workers increased 14 per cent
while the number of manual workers increased only 2 per cent.(4)
In the same period the white-collar labour force increased from
18.7 per cent to 35.9 per cent of the total labour force while the
manual share decreased from 74.6 per cent to 59.3 per cent.(5)
Although this is a general trend, there have been significant
differences in the various subgroups within the white-collar category; thus clerks have increased by 260 per cent, managers and
administrators have increased from 3.4 per cent to 5.4 per cent,
lower professionals and technicians have doubled, and higher professionals have shown a three-fold percentage increase.(6) (See
Table 5.1 and Fig.5.1). The most rapidly growing sector, although
still relatively small, is that of scientific and technical
employees. Thus for example draughtsmen have increased 376 per
cent, scientists and engineers 688 per cent, and laboratory technicians 1,920 per cent.(7) It is plain that different sectors of
the workforce have grown at different rates. In terms of my
typology category I has remained static or fallen slightly, category II has increased enormously, while category III has steadily
increased.

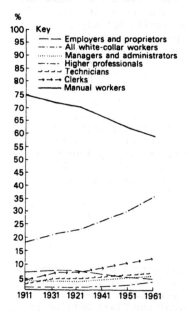

FIGURE 5.1 Graphical representation of major occupational groups
as a percentage of the total occupied population 1911-61

Source: Table 5.1.

TABLE 5.1 The occupied population of Great Britain by major occupational groups, 1911-61

Occupational groups	Number of persons in major occupational groups, 1911-61 (000s)					Major occupational groups as a percentage of total occupied population, 1911-61					Growth indices of major occupational groups (1911 = 100)				
	1911	1921	1931	1951	1961	1911	1921	1931	9151	1961	1911	1921	1931	1951	1961
1 Employers and proprietors	1,232	1,318	1,407	1,117	1,139	6.7	6.8	6.7	5.0	4.7	100	107	114	91	92
2 All white-collar workers	3,433	4,094	4,841	6,948	8,480	18.7	21.2	23.0	30.9	35.9	100	119	141	202	247
a Managers and administrators	631	704	770	1,245	1,268	3.4	3.6	3.7	5.5	5.4	100	112	122	197	201
b Higher professionals	184	196	240	435	718	1.0	1.0	1.1	1.9	3.0	100	107	130	236	390
c Lower professionals and technicians	560	679	728	1,059	1,418	3.1	3.5	3.5	4.7	6.0	100	121	130	189	253
d Foremen and inspectors	237	279	323	590	682	1.3	1.4	1.5	2.6	2.9	100	118	136	249	288
e Clerks	832	1,256	1,404	2,341	2,996	4.5	6.5	6.7	10.4	12.7	100	151	169	281	360
f Salesmen and shop assistants	989	980	1,376	1,278	1,398	5.4	5.1	6.5	5.7	5.9	100	99	139	129	141
3 All manual workers	13,685	13,920	14,776	14,450	14,020	74.6	72.0	70.3	64.2	59.3	100	102	108	106	102
4 Total occupied population	18,350	19,332	21,024	22,515	23,639	100.0	100.0	100.0	100.0	100.0	100	105	115	123	129

Source: G. S. Bain 'The Growth of White Collar Unionism', Clarendon Press, 1970, p.12.

THE SOCIAL ORIGINS OF CIVIL SERVANTS

The general argument in the sociological literature is that the
social origins of white-collar workers have changed since the nineteenth century in a very specific way in that they have become
more proletarian.(8)   This rather vague generalization is backed
up by a wide variety of fragmentary evidence. In order to examine
the social origins of Civil Servants I will concentrate on three
variables which I will take as indicative of social origin and
which will enable me to make some comments about the class position
of Civil Servants: father's occupation, place of birth, and education. These three factors are the variables which primarily affect
type of occupation. Also they are easily operationalized and faci-
litate comparisons between Civil Servants and other groups over
time. I use them primarily as indicators of social origins.

Father's occupation

There have been a number of studies of the social origins of Civil
Servants. The first of these was in the mid-1930s and so enables
us to compare changes over time in an albeit limited way. However,
a number of methodological problems exist with this material.
First, in using father's occupation as an indicator of social
class of origin we must refer to the Registrar General's census
of occupations. Unfortunately some of the census categories have
changed over time so the material is not strictly comparable, and
in addition the Registrar General's categories may not match sociological ones. Second, each study has had to address the problem
of the point in the father's life at which his occupation should
be classified, and each study has decided on a different point; so
again we have difficulties in making comparisons. Third, varying
research instruments were used in each study including subjective
impressions and highly structured questionnaires; this further
compounds our difficulties. Finally, and most seriously, all but
one of the studies concentrate on a limited section of the higher
Civil Service, so very little data actually exist on categories II,
III and IV. This seriously hampers a detailed comparison.

Top management and administration
Some general trends can be observed. The top administrators and
managers in the Civil Service tended to come from social classes I
and II in the Registrar General's census categories, and this has
been the case for many years.(9) Just after the Second World War,
social class I accounted for only 3.4 per cent of the adult male
working population of working age, but it provided for 29.3 per
cent of the fathers of top Civil Servants. Moreover, when social
classes I and II are computed together they accounted for 18.4 per
cent of the total census sample but provided 70 per cent of the
fathers of top administrators in the Civil Service.(10) In a very
small sample of administrators who joined the Civil Service in 1956
social classes I and II together accounted for 74.3 per cent of
entrants; social class II alone 54.3 per cent; class III 17.1 per
cent; class IV 2.3 per cent; and class V 6 per cent.(11)

TABLE 5.2 The social class origins of Civil Servants as measured by father's occupation, 1966-8 (%)

Father's occupation	Administrative class	Executive class	Clerical class	Top scientist	Intermediate scientists	Technicians
I Higher professional	21	6	3	15	7	5
II Intermediate and managerial professional	46	28	20	38	26	28
III (i) Skilled non-manual	10	16	11	13	16	12
III (ii) Skilled manual	13	32.5	37	27	40	39
IV Semi-skilled	4	13	} 22	} 7	8	10
V Unskilled	2	2				2
Other	4	2.5	8	1	3	4
Total	100	100	100	100	100	100
(N)	(571)	(1,021)	(366)	(403)	(446)	(352)

Source: A. Halsey and I. Crewe, 'Social Survey of the Civil Service', HMSO, London, 1969, pp.52, 125, 160, 314, 360, 385.

The typical member of category I in my typology comes from
social class II and since in both its upper and lower levels this
pattern is repeated there is good reason to suppose that this proportion has remained stable over a long period of time.(12) If
anything there has been a tendency in recent years for the top
Civil Service to become even more exclusive.(13) This contrasts
markedly with the pattern observed among the staff directly
recruited to the top scientific grades, where there has been a
tendency for staff to be appointed who originated from social
classes III, IV and V.(14)

Scientists
Among top scientists (category II) the typical member came from
social class II, with 15 per cent coming from social class I and a
large proportion having fathers who worked in manual occupations.
Thus the top scientists are a less socially exclusive group than
top administrators.(15) Intermediate grade scientists on average
come from social class III(i) and this group is no more middle
class in origin than the national population of similar status and
age although fewer are the children of semi-skilled and unskilled
workers.(16) Among the laboratory technicians and low grade scientists the most typical member was the son of a skilled manual
worker.(17)

Middle management and clerical grades
Within the middle management level of the service (category III)
there is a tendency for individuals to be recruited from wider
social backgrounds than in industry and commerce. However there
are subtle differences in the category itself. Women in middle
management tended to have superior antecedents to the men, and in
the lower grades of the executive class the social backgrounds of
both men and women were broader than in the higher grades. This
is possibly attributable to the greater frequency of individuals
with origins in social classes III, IV and V among the promotees
in the lower grades. A comparison of both promotees and direct
entrants in the different grades suggests a broadening of the
social recruitment all round to middle management.(18)
    Among clerical workers the pattern of women having higher social
origins than men repeats itself, although in this group the differences are less then elsewhere. The typical clerical worker in the
Civil Service is the son or daughter of a skilled manual worker.
Most recruitment is from social classes III(ii), IV and V and this
tendency has increased since 1945. Clerks in the Civil Service
are more 'proletarian' in origin than either category I or II and
more so than clerks in industry and commerce.(19)

Summary
Thus in terms of the social class of origin of Civil Servants there
are a number of differences between the various categories. Among
administrators there is a high concentration of individuals from
elite backgrounds. This is marked also to some extent among scientists but many more scientists come from more modest backgrounds.
Middle management and the clerical grades are less socially exclusive than the administrative grades and indeed than comparable

occupations in commerce and industry. Although no absolutely
reliable time series data exist we can discern fairly categoric
proof that the administrators have been an elite group for a long
period of time and the democratizing tendencies of modern society
have left them relatively untouched. In contrast the other categories all show limited signs that there has been a gradual 'proletarianization' measured by father's occupation over the last
fifty years. This tendency is perhaps most marked among the
clerical workers although scientists show similar signs.
     In the lower grades there has been an apparent tendency for the
recruitment of individuals from what might loosely be described as
working-class backgrounds. This is especially marked in the clerical grades and it is noteworthy that this group of Civil Servants
have consistently been in the vanguard of militant action in the
service. It seems reasonable to assume that some relationship
exists between the background of the person recruited and his
subsequent industrial behaviour.

Educational background

There is a large body of literature which has noted the profound
effects that changes in educational practices have had on rates of
social mobility.(20) It is also argued that the education acts of
the nineteenth and twentieth centuries and the associated changes
in the levels of literacy have significantly altered the life
chances of a large number of hitherto underprivileged groups in
society. This is thought to be particularly important in terms of
the recruitment to white-collar occupations and is therefore significant in any discussion of proletarianization. It is argued
that when literacy became universal it was henceforth theoretically
possible to recruit clerks from all sectors of society, not just
from a social elite who could read and write. This potential
supply of labour included some sons and daughters of manual
workers. Further, the increased demand for white-collar labour
meant that some recruitment of this kind was inevitable. Throughout the twentieth century this trend continued and gradually
increased in importance and hence it is argued that the influx of
the sons and daughters of manual workers had made the white-collar
workforce more proletarian.(21) In this section I will examine
the evidence for this in the Civil Service.

Category I: administrators and managers
Top administrators and managers in the British Civil Service are
mainly graduates with a median school-leaving age of eighteen
years.(22) This marks them off from the bulk of the population
who are neither graduates nor attend school for the maximum statu-
tory time. However, top managers and administrators are even more
of an elite than this indicates in that they have traditionally
been educated at public fee-paying schools and Oxbridge.(23)
Indeed in the mid-1960s only 42 per cent of this class had been
educated in the state sector, and the percentage who had been
educated in the private sector has fallen only slightly since
1950.(24) Among top administrators education strongly correlates

with social class of origin with more than two-thirds of those
whose fathers had been manual workers having attended local educational authority grammar schools.(25)   Sixty-four per cent of
administrators who were born in social class I went to public or
other fee-paying school as against 35 per cent of all administrators and less than 15 per cent of those with origins in social
classes III(ii), IV and V.(26)

The median school-leaving age of administrators was higher than
all other Civil Servants except top scientists.(27)   On the other
hand, promotees to the top administration had left school at an
earlier age than direct entrants, and early school-leavers contributed disproportionately to the non-graduate section of this
group.(28)

The vast majority of graduate administrators took their degrees
full-time at a university; about two-thirds took a degree from
Oxford and Cambridge, with the remainder coming in equal proportions from London, the Scottish and other English and Welsh universities.   This is quite striking especially in the context of the
shrinking proportion of Oxbridge graduates in the national graduate
population.   This type of Oxbridge domination has been reported in
many studies.(29)   In terms of the subjects studied at university
by the administrators there has been a prolonged dominance of the
classics and history graduate, some 71 per cent of these administrators having read arts and humanities, 28 per cent social
science, 11 per cent natural science, and 2 per cent applied
science.(30)

These findings on the senior Civil Servants show that it is an
educational elite within an educational elite.   The sort of education enjoyed before entry to the Civil Service by many administrators and managers is different from that received by the vast
majority of the population.   In this respect top administrators
in the service are not typical of the rest of the population.

Category II: government scientists
The scientific Civil Service is also an educational elite and on
the whole the scientists have higher qualifications than their
administrative colleagues, although these qualifications were
generally obtained in less prestigious educational institutions.
There is a marked tailing off of qualifications in the lower
grades.   Top scientists tended to be ex-grammar school with about
57 per cent having attended local educational authority grammar
schools, 15 per cent direct grant schools, and 20 per cent public
or other fee-paying schools.(31)   The great majority of top
scientists stayed at school after the age of 17 with those who
left earlier being the more likely to be promotees.(32)   Among
the intermediate scientific grades 51 per cent left school at 16
or 17, and 14 per cent left school at 15 or earlier.(33)   The average school-leaving age for technicians was 16.2 years although 45
per cent of them left school at 17 or later.(34)

One-third of top government scientists possess higher degrees.
(35)   Unlike administrators, top scientists tend to be graduates
from London, the Welsh and the provincial universities, with only
one-fifth coming from Oxbridge.   Even so, that one-fifth tend to
be concentrated in the higher grades.(36)   The standard of degree

obtained by top scientists tended to be very high with a large
proportion having first class honours degrees.(37) Among intermediate scientists 36 per cent possessed HNC, HSC or 'A' levels as
their highest qualification on entry.(38) Thirty-nine per cent
had only GCE 'O' levels and 23 per cent had a degree or diploma.
About one-fifth of these intermediate scientists had received some
form of higher education, and men in the upper grades were more
likely to have a degree than in the lower grades; the proportion
of women who were graduates was higher but the general standard of
degree was low with only one-third having higher than a third class
honours degree.(39) Of scientists and technicians in the very
lowest grades the predominant qualification at entry is GCE 'O'
level, although higher qualifications are not unknown. Twenty-two
per cent of men and 8 per cent of women were unqualified on
entry.(40)

Category III: middle management and clerical grades
Within the middle management and routine clerical grades in the
Civil Service a variety of qualifications are found. Clerks were
the least well-qualified desk grade in the Civil Service with
nearly half of them possessing no qualifications on entry and
only 14 per cent having obtained any certificate subsequent to
entry.(41) The typical executive officer went to a local education
authority grammar school although about one-third of middle managers attended fee-paying or direct-grant schools. In the lowest
grades in this category, where promotees from other classes are
concentrated, just under one-third went to secondary modern, technical or comprehensive schools.(42) For executive officers the
median school-leaving age was 16 or 17, but the lower in the grade
the lower the school-leaving age. Promotees in this group had a
lower school-leaving age than direct entrants, only 28 per cent of
them having stayed at school until 17.(43) Nearly half the male
clerks left school at 15 or earlier (49 per cent) and the average
school-leaving age was 15.6 years with women tending to have
slightly later school-leaving ages than their male colleagues.(44)
Among Civil Service clerks there is a correlation between the
school-leaving age and social class of origin with a later school-
leaving age being associated with a higher social class; there was
also a correlation between school-leaving age and educational
qualifications, with those who left later tending to have higher
qualifications.(45)
   This part of the workforce is not as educationally exclusive as
the administrative grades or the top echelons of the science group.
In the mid-1960s the majority of the executive officer class
entered the Civil Service as non-graduates (46) although in recent
years there has been a trend for increased graduate recruitment to
the ranks of middle management; for example in 1975 nearly one-
quarter of new entrants to this grade were graduates.(47) The
normal (median) educational qualifications of direct entrants to
this sector were GCE 'A' levels or HNC or HSC, but promotees from
the clerical grades often had 'O' levels only. In the lower ranks
of middle management nearly one-third had no qualifications at
all.(48) Clerks in the Civil Service are not on the whole very
well qualified relative to other Civil Servants, with about half

the men and 40 per cent of the women having no formal qualifications on entry.(49)

Summary
This examination of the educational backgrounds of types of Civil
Servants reveals a number of things. First, there are a wide
variety of qualifications held by Civil Servants. Second, top
administrators and top scientists are an educational elite which
in the case of the administrators is reinforced by social class
origin factors. There is little evidence that in the British Civil
Service the education acts of the twentieth century have opened up
the top grades to all comers. However there is no reason to doubt
that the effects of the education acts have been to open up the
ranks of middle management and clerkdom to persons with rudimentary
educational qualifications. The evidence shows that for some sons
and daughters of manual workers, entry to the Civil Service clerical grades was a form of upward social mobility. This has accordingly made the clerical grades more proletarian in origin, but it
is altogether another matter as to whether this could be regarded
as proletarianization in a Marxian sense.

The geographical origins of civil servants

In this section I will examine the geographical origins of Civil
Servants. This is to be regarded as important in the overall context of social origins because Britain is composed of geographical
regions which are socio-structurally different and enjoy differential access to factors affecting life chances. Similarly the
demographic make-up of different regions in the United Kingdom
show differing characteristics.
      There is a general tendency for Civil Servants to have been
born in or around London.(50) London and the South East account
for two-fifths of administrators and managers, with the other
regions being correspondingly under-represented. Among the higher
levels of middle management there was disproportionately heavy
recruitment from the Greater London area and the South East.(51)
The Northern region however provided the greatest proportion of
clerks and the actual proportion is close to or even slightly under-
represented in the regional distribution of the population.(52)
Senior scientists had a relatively high proportion of officers born
in the North or outside England, though in the lower grades this
proportion drops to about one-quarter.(53) Top scientists are on
the whole very close in their distribution by geographical origin
to the present population distribution. This is in contrast with
other Civil Servants and especially intermediate scientists, a
particularly high proportion of whom were born in London, the South
and the Midlands, a figure well in excess of the proportions of the
national population resident in these areas.(54) The subordinate
scientists in the Civil Service are completely nationally unrepre-
sentative in terms of geographical origins with the non-metropolitan
South and Midlands contributing most to this group (37 per cent).(55)
      An examination of the geographical origins of Civil Servants
thus reveals that wide differences are to be found from category to

category. No accurate time series data are available so it is
difficult to assess changes over time. But given the growth and
structure of the Civil Service a number of observations can be
made. First the classes which are the oldest appear to be the
most geographically exclusive with higher metropolitan concentrations than other classes. Further, those clerical occupations
which are dispersed nationally seem to recruit locally. Scientists
however do not fit into this pattern, being regionally biased
heavily towards the South and Midlands.

Conclusions

In this section I have examined the social backgrounds of a group
of British Civil Servants in order to determine whether there is
any empirical substance to the idea that white-collar workers, as
exemplified by the Civil Service, have become increasingly proletarian in origin. I have examined father's occupation, educational
background, and regional background, which were used as indicators
of social background. On all three variables marked differences
were found to exist between the various categories of my typology.
In category I we find a social and educational elite recruited from
and based mainly in and around London. There is no evidence that
this category has ever been, or is likely to be, dominated by
persons of lowly social origins. There are exceptions but these
are insufficient to back up any claim of social proletarianization.
On the other hand, among other categories there is evidence that
at all levels the Civil Service is less socially exclusive than it
once was and top scientists although recruited nationally and
based nationally form an educational elite within the Service. It
is in the lowest categories of clerical work and to a lesser extent
among subordinate scientists that evidence of large-scale recruitment of the children of manual workers, and particularly in the
case of clerks local recruitment, is to be found. Thus within
these groups some evidence of what might be termed social proletarianization may be said to have occurred. This statement must
however be interpreted along with the fact that this is not really
proletarianization as a process of change, but rather that proletarianization has occurred in those sectors of the Civil Service
which have expanded greatly in the twentieth century. Thus what
has occurred is not a process of proletarianization in the sense
that many of these jobs were once done by persons of middle-class
origins, and now a large proportion of persons doing them come
from working class backgrounds; but rather that a high proportion
of the workers had working-class backgrounds from the beginning.
The only sector where anything like a process may be said to have
taken place is among the clerks. It is true that in the mid-1960s
this section was more proletarian than it had been before the
Second World War. However, it is impossible to determine whether
this process is the result of Civil Servants of working-class
origins taking over jobs previously held by Civil Servants of
middle-class origins, or whether persons of working-class origin
have been recruited into the expanding sectors of the clerical workforce which has increased steadily in the twentieth century.(56)

The data which I have used is unsatisfactory since most previous
observers of the Civil Service have concentrated on the upper
grades, so my conclusions remain speculative rather than definitive, but trends are observable nevertheless. Quite a complex,
though incomplete, picture emerges. The overall view gives the
lie to notions of proletarianization in the market for all Civil
Servants. The exceptions are found at the base of the hierarchy,
and even in these instances we cannot be sure that this is a
process or a relatively new innovation as work loads have expanded.
Thus this conception of proletarianization finds only limited
support using the empirical data on the Civil Service.

FEMINIZATION

When considering feminization in the white-collar workforce as a
whole a number of things are immediately evident. First there is
the extent to which women are in a majority in this sector of the
working population, and second there is the extent to which women
as a percentage of this sector have increased since 1900 (see
Table 5.3). Thus by 1960-1 the population of women in the clerical
sector was two-thirds of the total in the United Kingdom and the
USA.(57) In 1966 clerical employment had become the most highly
feminized occupational group in Britain with women comprising 70
per cent of all clerical employees.(58) In other areas of non-
manual work the extent of feminization was nowhere near as marked.
Thus there are still very few women in the higher professions or
in managerial or supervisory grades, but they do form a majority
among lower professions (teachers and social workers) and miscel-
laneous non-manual groups like shop assistants.(59) Similarly
there are low concentrations of women among scientific, technical
and supervisory occupations.(60)

TABLE 5.3 The percentage of female workers in major occupational
groups in Great Britain, 1911-61

Occupational group	1911	1921	1931	1951	1961
1 Employers and proprietors	18.8	20.5	19.8	20.0	20.4
2 All white-collar workers	29.8	37.6	35.8	42.3	44.5
(a) Managers and administrators	19.8	17.0	13.0	15.2	15.5
(b) Higher professionals	6.0	5.1	7.5	8.3	9.7
(c) Lower technicians and technicians	62.9	59.4	58.8	53.5	50.8
(d) Foremen and inspectors	4.2	6.5	8.7	13.4	10.3
(e) Clerks	21.4	44.6	46.0	60.2	65.1
(f) Salesmen and shop assistants	35.2	43.6	37.2	51.6	54.9
3 All manual workers	30.5	27.9	38.8	26.1	26.0
4 Total occupied population	29.6	29.5	29.8	30.8	32.4

Source: G.S. Bain, 'The Growth of White Collar Unionism',
Clarendon Press, Oxford, 1970, p.14.

TABLE 5.4 The percentage of women in selected Civil Service
grades, 1975 and 1977

Grade, class	Percentage of women 1975	1977
Assistant secretary	4.8	5.0
Senior principal	3.0	3.1
Principal	7.7	8.3
Senior executive officer	8.2	8.5
Higher executive officer (A)	27.7	26.0
Higher executive officer	14.4	15.1
Administration trainee	31.3	30.2
Executive officer	31.7	33.7
Clerical officer	61.0	61.0
Clerical assistant	79.8	79.0
Higher scientific officer	7.5	8.3
Scientific officer	17.8	18.6
Assistant scientific officer	31.3	30.1

Source: Civil Service Department, 'Civil Service Statistics 1975',
HMSO, London, 1975, p.13. 'Civil Service Statistics 1977', HMSO,
London, 1977, pp.22-3.

TABLE 5.5 The percentage of women in the Civil Service, 1972-5

	Numbers 000s Men	Women	Total	% of women
1 January 1972	303.1	201.3	504.4	39.9
1 January 1973	300.8	203.3	504.1	40.3
1 January 1974	301.1	210.2	511.3	41.1
1 January 1975	300.1	218.9	519.0	42.2

Source: Civil Service Department, 'Civil Service Statistics 1975',
HMSO, London, 1975, p.12.

About 40 per cent of all Civil Servants are women,(61) although
the majority of women are employed in the lower grades, and in all
grades except the clerical women are in a minority.(62) The proportion of women Civil Servants is however increasing (see Tables
5.4 and 5.5). Comparisons are difficult because of changes in the
names of grades; however we can make a number of broad comparisons. In the mid-1960s approximately 8 per cent of top management
were women (63) and this had increased slightly by the mid-1970s.
(64) Among middle management there was an increase in the percentage of women from 20 per cent to 34 per cent 1966 to 1977,(65) and
among clerks there had been an increase in the percentage of women
employed in the same period (clerical officers 44 per cent to 61
per cent, and clerical assistants 63 per cent to 79 per cent).(66)
In the scientific grades the number of women has remained small
but in percentage terms this has been the sector where feminization

has been most rapid, particularly at the lowest levels; among top
scientists the percentage of women has increased from 2-3 per cent
in the mid-1960s to 8.3 per cent in the mid-1970s while the most
subordinate scientists have increased in percentage terms from
17 per cent to 30 per cent.(67)

The Civil Service is therefore highly feminized and becoming
more so. This is in line with changes in the rest of the working
population. Women are most important in the clerical grades while
men retain their advantage in the administrative, managerial and
scientific hierarchies, although in recent years there has been a
dramatic increase in the numbers of women in the lowest scientific
grades. We can argue with some certainty that the clerical sector
of the Civil Service is different in terms of sex composition than
it was in the nineteenth century. The extent to which this undeni-
able feminization will cause proletarianization is debatable.
Indeed some writers have argued that, if anything, feminization
will be an important element in tempering the radical elements in
the workforce.(68) Yet the case of the Civil Service belies this
since the grades in which women are found in the highest concentrations have been the most radical and militant, viz. clerks and
subordinate scientists. Hence although exact cause and effect is
indeterminate we can demonstrate that feminization has occurred
along with developments which are sometimes taken as indicators of
proletarianization. Women are concentrated in the regions away
from London,(69) and it is interesting that it is among these
grades in the regions that support for militant action has been
strongest.

Whether feminization is to be taken as an indicator of proletarianization is problematic, but since some writers have used it
in such a way then we can argue that, using this definition of
proletarianization, it has taken place in the Civil Service particularly in the lowest grades of scientists and among clerks. To
do so however raises all the problems of feminization and class
which I discussed in chapter 2.

CONCLUSION

In this chapter I have examined elements of the social origins of
British Civil Servants. I observed that some writers on proletarianization had claimed that if the white-collar workforce becomes
increasingly proletarian in origin then proletarianization has
taken place. Generally such writers have concentrated on two
indicators; social origins and sex composition of the workforce.
I examined social origins of Civil Servants with reference to their
father's occupation, their education, and their geographical
origin. These three indicators were tested against the four types
of workers; higher management, middle management, routine clerks,
and scientists. It was found that generally persons of working-
class origin (which generally correlated with educational experience and geographical origin) were not to be found in higher
Civil Service positions, only in the lowliest grades. I also
examined the sexual composition of the Civil Service workforce and
found that there was a large amount of evidence that feminization

of large (particularly subordinate) sectors of the Civil Service
was taking place. However, in spite of this a number of reservations must be expressed about this evidence of proletarianization.
Even if I had observed that the Civil Service was dominated by
women of working-class origin, I do not think that this would meet
a rigorous definition of proletarianization, particularly a Marxian
one. Marx viewed proletarianization as a downward shift of the
middle class toward the proletariat, whereas what we have in
essence been concerned with here, and found only limited evidence
of, is the intergenerational upward social mobility of the offspring of the working class as they have entered lowly Civil
Service jobs. This is scarcely overwhelming proof of proletarianization.

WORK SITUATION: THE EXTENT OF BUREAUCRATIZATION AND MECHANIZATION IN THE CIVIL SERVICE

INTRODUCTION

In chapter 2 we saw that a number of writers had linked together
the concepts of proletarianization, bureaucratization and mechanization.(1) Primarily these writers noted that changes in technology had brought about changes in the work situation which were
purported then to affect political attitudes and behaviour. I
argued that the different writers had concentrated on different
types of worker, e.g. clerks, scientists, professionals or managers,
and I also pointed to a number of deficiencies in the propositions.(2) In summary I concluded that there were two broadly
different emphases in the literature; one that concentrated on
increased bureaucratization and one that concentrated on levels of
technology. This chapter examines the evidence of these processes
in the Civil Service.

BUREAUCRATIZATION

Thematically we can reduce the writings of those authors who have
linked proletarianization to bureaucratization to two basic propositions which are allegedly the effects or results of the
processes mentioned above. First, for specialists, scientists and
professionals there is a loss of professional autonomy since
employment in bureaucratic organizations allegedly reduces these
workers to the level of all other employees. At the same time new
specialisms develop (particularly technocratic ones), and the
employees in these new specialisms become an extremely important
group, because although potentially they are very powerful in terms
of the esoteric knowledge at their fingertips, they are in a subservient position in the hierarchy. Both these developments are
taken either as evidence of proletarianization or as favourable to
the development of a militant industrial-political workforce. The
second proposition concerns individuals in the administrative/
clerical hierarchy and states that for those near the bottom of
the hierarchy, especially clerks, larger work units have increasingly become the norm. At the same time clerical work becomes yet

more routinized and subdivided, and the workers' sense of isolation
and dissatisfaction with work increases. This type of environment
is again thought to be conducive to the development of a militant
workforce and hence is taken as evidence of proletarianization. I
wish to examine the evidence for both these propositions within
the Civil Service. I will do this first by evaluating the extent
of bureaucratization and rationalization within the service, and
second by testing to find whether the effects of this are the same
as those predicted in the literature.

I wish at this point to define bureaucracy and bureaucratization. The concept of bureaucracy has had a long and chequered
history in the social sciences,(3) but many sociologists agree
that the most useful starting point for discussion is the work of
Weber.(4) I will define bureaucracy with reference to Weber's
ideal-type construction. Further, since I will be considering
bureaucratization in relation to proletarianization I will link
Weber's concept of bureaucracy with his writings on stratification.(5) In doing so I will make explicit the link which some
writers have assumed. The linking concepts are those of power and
domination - therefore it is pertinent to begin this discussion
with an analysis of power.

Weber noted that individuals could have power in a variety of
ways, but for the organization of human affairs a special instance
of power was important; this he termed authority.(6) The distinction between power and authority was developed in Weber's study of
organizations, and specifically the role of legitimate authority
in organizations.(7) Power is the probability that one actor in a
social relationship will be in a position to carry out his own
will despite resistance, regardless of the basis on which this
probability rests.(8) Authority on the other hand is the case
where directives issued by the one in control are voluntarily
obeyed: the subservient group obey because they consider the
source of authority as legitimate.(9) Thus the major criteria of
authority are voluntary compliance with legitimate commands and a
suspension of judgement in advance by those in subordinate
positions.(10)

Weber distinguishes three types of legitimate authority; char-
ismastic, traditional and legal-rational.(11) Although I am
concerned only with legal-rational authority it is worth noting
the two other types. The distinguishing feature of charismatic
authority is that the leader is thought to possess charisma, that
is either magical, supernatural or at least superhuman powers,
some quality which sets him apart from ordinary men and the
everyday.(12) The leader is supposed to be inspired by a divine
mission and deference is paid to him accordingly.(13) Charismatic authority tends however to be unstable and therefore sooner
or later all charismatic movements are confronted by the problem
of continuity, succession and routinization.(14) Traditional
authority has a number of contrasting characteristics.(15) First
the status quo is regarded as sacred, unchangeable and permanent.
(16) Those in authority are there because of traditional rules
and hereditary claims.(17) The administrative staff of the traditional leader are not officials but personal retainers (Diener)
and obedience is owed not to abstract rules but to the person who

holds the superior position.(18)   The subject groups are bound to
their chief by traditional ties of loyalty and other social rein-
forcements such as for example the Divine Right of Kings.(19)

The third type of authority with which Weber was concerned was
legal-rational authority.   Weber set out five related premises on
which legal authority depended.   First, that a legal code had to
be established which could demand obedience from members of an
administration.   Second, that this legal system of abstract rules
would be applied to particular cases and that within the bounds of
the legal system the administration would look after its own interests.   Third, that any person administering the legal code would
also be subject to it.   Fourth, that only as a member of the
organization would the member obey the law.   And finally that
obedience within the administration would be due not to individuals
but to the office they held.(20)   On the basis of this Weber
argued that legal-rational systems of administration had a number
of bureaucratic characteristics.   First, the organization would be
continuous and bounded by a system of rules.   This meant that all
problems facing the administration would be dealt with according
to these rules or according to precedent, and also that problems
would not be dealt with individually but as examples of particular
classes or categories of phenomena.   Second, bureaucratic admini-
strations would have a highly developed division of labour, and
thus each employee would have a specific sphere of competence.
This would lead in its turn to a subdivision of competence, and
provision would be made for the official to have the necessary
authority to carry out his functions.   Third, that the organization of offices and departments would follow the principle of
hierarchy.   In other words each office would be under the control
of a superior one and thus strict internal control would be
assured.   Fourth, that the principles which regulate the conduct
of an office would be fully rational rules or norms, and that
these rules would define the specialized training and qualifications for posts.   Fifth, that the administrative staffs would be
completely separated from the ownership of the means of production,
and thus sixth, the official positions would not be freehold and
could not be appropriated by the officer.   Finally all the administrative acts would be recorded in writing and thus the files
would be very important.(21)

On the basis of this Weber claimed that there were a number of
important implications for the bureaucrat or office holder.   First,
the official would be personally free and subject to authority
only in relation to his impersonal obligations.   Second, the
officials would be organized within the bureaucracy in a clearly
defined hierarchy of offices.   Third, each office within the
bureaucracy would have a clearly defined sphere of competence in
the legal sense.   Fourth, the office would be filled by a free
contractual relationship and thus in principle there would exist
free selection.   Next, the candidates for office would be selected
on the basis of technical qualifications such as examinations or
diplomas, and accordingly officials would be appointed not elected.
Also the official would be remunerated by a fixed money salary
usually with pension rights, the salary scale itself primarily
graded according to the rank in the hierarchy with allowances made

for responsibility and status. In addition, the officials's occupation would be treated as his main or primary occupation which
would constitute a career with a system of promotion according to
seniority and merit or both. Finally, the official would not own
his office and he would be subject to strict and systematic discipline in the conduct of his office.(22)

I will now specify Weber's concept of stratification in order
to link together bureaucratization and proletarianization. Weber
separated three elements in his discussion of stratification;
class, status and party. Again Weber's starting point is power
which he says may be defined socially or economically and these
two types of power need not overlap although sometimes the two
types do. Indeed economic power may condition social power or
prestige but this is not necessarily so.(23) Weber argues that
classes, status groups, and parties are phenomena of the distribution of power in the community.(24) For Weber, classes are
determined by the market situation in the sense that a group of
people share the same market situation by virtue of similar life
chances and opportunities for income in a market economy. This
determines class situation and a class is any group sharing a
similar class situation.(25) According to Weber, in the market
economy the most important element determining life chances and
opportunities for income is the possession of or non-possession of
property. But class situations are further differentiated by the
type of property an individual possesses and the type of service
he can offer in the market; thus for example Weber distinguished
between the entrepreneurial class and the rentier class.(26)
Because class situation is determined economically Weber suggests
that class interests will probably also be determined economically
but this is not always the case, although he does note that the
notion of class interests only makes sense in terms of some other
competing interest.(27)

The next facet which Weber distinguishes is status. Status
groups are those groups who are in receipt of a positive or nega-
tive estimation of honour by others.(28) Status and prestige may
overlap with class position, but this is not always the case since
possession of property does not automatically qualify an individual
for high status, and indeed others in possession of the same property may have higher status.(29) Status honour is normally
expressed in life-style which is sometimes socially reinforced
through intermarriage.(30) According to Weber the fullest expression of status groups are segregated ethnic groups or castes. The
major difference between status groups and classes for Weber is
that classes can be distinguished in terms of production while
status groups can be distinguished in terms of consumption.(31)

The third aspect which Weber details are parties who are concerned neither with production nor consumption but with the
acquisition of power and may be recruited either from status groups
or classes.(32)

In this work I have drawn attention to class position, consciousness of class position and political action. I have argued
that the three elements are important in the work of Marx. In his
discussion Weber makes explicit the link between the three concepts and introduces another concept, status. Further, Weber has

argued that either class interests *or* status interests may provide
the impetus for political action. This is all the more interesting
because one of the features that some writers have drawn attention
to is the loss of status and hence the spur to political action
which might come about because of bureaucratization and changes in
authority relations within an administrative organization. Further,
some authors have linked the loss of status and autonomy and frag-
mentation of work tasks to the bureaucratic tendencies of modern
organizations. In this section therefore I will explore two separate issues. First, whether the Civil Service is or has become a
bureaucratic organization, and I shall do this with reference to
Weber's ideal-type construction of bureaucracy, and second whether
these changes have altered status, authority or class relations in
the Civil Service. In a later chapter I will examine a third
issue, that is whether these changes have been an important impetus
to political or industrial action. Finally I will determine
whether this can be adequately understood, if it has taken place,
as proletarianization.

Weber does not discuss explicitly the concept of proletarianization, yet interestingly many authors have a neo-Weberian theory of
proletarianization embedded in their work.(33) It is worthwhile
expanding at this point what a Weberian theory of proletarianization would be. The most important element within the concept of
bureaucracy is the related notion of authority. The official is
said to possess the necessary authority to carry out his work.
This is laid down in the impersonal legal code. Since possession
of authority is both part of the class situation and the status
situation, a loss or relinquishment of authority would constitute
a change in class situation and status situation. Further,
should this provide for a change in political or trade union
behaviour then we could argue that it constitutes a change in
class relations and hence leads to proletarianization. The major
feature of this process is that the authority accruing to the
bureaucrat is in some way curtailed. If we wished to study proletarianization from an explicitly Weberian point of view then
the variables of authority, status and work relationships would be
the ones subjected to closest scrutiny. Many writers in fact have
done this. In this work I have followed closely the Marxian
formulation. I have introduced the Weberian elements at this
point because using the notions of authority and status we can
gain a better understanding of the relationship between bureaucratization and proletarianization.

Bureaucratization in the Civil Service

In fact an examination of the rational and bureaucratic tendencies
in the Civil Service is straightforward since there is a good deal
of historical material on the subject, and the steps which the
Civil Service took in applying rational bureaucratic principles
are clearly defined. The development of bureaucratic tendencies
in the British Civil Service was in part a spin-off from developments in the East India Company, and indeed the term Civil Servant
originated in India among the employees of that company.(34) Until

1800 when that company's activities had ceased to be purely commercial the only qualifications required for entry were those of a rudimentary commercial kind, but in 1809 a college for the training of Civil Servants who were to go to India was set up. The curriculum included oriental languages and literature, mathematics, natural history, classical and general literature, law, history and political economy. At this time appointment to the East India Company was by nomination, but in 1833 in the debate on the India Bill, T.B. Macaulay sought to establish a system of appointment by competition although it was not until 1853 when the last Charter Act abolished the practice of recruitment through nomination by directors that appointments were thrown open to competition. The demands for change in the Indian Civil Service led to similar demands in the home Civil Service, and in April 1853 the Treasury asked Stafford Northcote and G.M. Trevelyan to prepare a report on the home Civil Service. The result was the celebrated Northcote-Trevelyan Report.(35) This document is interesting because it is a manifesto of the rising bourgeoisie in mid-nineteenth century Britain. It extols the virtues of industry and merit as opposed to indolence and dilettantism, open competition rather than aristocratic patronage, and efficiency, thrift and economy rather than waste and extravagance. The main points of the Northcote-Trevelyan Report are significant because they represent the first thoroughgoing attempt to apply rational organizational principles, in a Weberian sense, to the organization of the Civil Service. The proposals were that the business of government should be carried out by an *efficient* body of workers, and business could not and should not be conducted in any other way. Therefore, the report argued, a permanent stable workforce was a prerequisite. They found that in the mid-nineteenth century the existing Civil Service had a number of structural weaknesses, which was a serious failing in their view since they believed that the profession of government service ought to attract the most able recruits instead of the unambitious, the lazy and the incapable whom the Civil Service attracted at that time. This they thought was a serious drag on efficiency and a blot on its public esteem. Second, the authors recognized that a number of specific difficulties affected the public service, for example within the existing promotion system both the hard-working as well as the lazy rose together and industry and merit went unrewarded. In addition patronage at all levels in the service meant that sometimes individuals of doubtful ability were being appointed while meritorious candidates were being passed over. Third, Northcote and Trevelyan believed that the service was over-fragmented into different departments, promotions were being blocked while a narrow-minded prejudiced outlook was fostered in different departments who were jealous of their autonomy. They therefore recommended the selection on merit of intellectual young men to the service whose promotion would depend on ability and hard work. To do this they proposed the introduction of a system of competitive examinations.

The report aroused a good deal of controversy with eminent Victorians springing to its defence or to attack it, but in 1855 an order in council was authorized which set up the Civil Service Commission as the central examining board.(36) The setting up of

the Civil Service commission did not however abolish patronage
immediately and really nothing more than a check on its blatant
abuse had been instigated.(37) A select committee on patronage
appointed in 1860 reported that patronage was found still to exist
in large areas in the Service. It was not for another ten years
that a proper system of competitive examination was established.(38)
Along with competitive examination came the division of the Civil
Service into two grades, higher and lower, with a separate class
of copyists or writers below them. Thus a distinction based on
the division of labour into special competences, viz. intellectual,
routine and copying was established.

The major structural alterations which relate to bureaucratization of the Civil Service have mostly come in the wake of Royal
Commissions, or committees of enquiry since that time.(39) In 1875
the Playfair Committee reported that it had discovered that
although open competition had been introduced comparatively few
people had actually been recruited in this way and that the distinction between intellectual and mechanical work was largely dis-
regarded. Playfair made a number of recommendations, but only
those affecting the lower divisions were executed. As a result
two lower divisions began to emerge as an all-service class,
meaning that for the first time all junior or lowly Civil Servants
were to be treated in the same way and not according to the
department in which they worked.(40) Equally important as a
bureaucratizing agent was the Ridley Commission (1887-8) which
introduced conformity of salaries, hours, sick leave and holidays
throughout the whole Civil Service. At the time of the Ridley
Commission the Civil Service consisted of five classes. These
were first, those recruited between the ages of 22 and 24 years by
the Class One examination, and others placed in the Upper Division
(or First Division as it was called from 1890); second, the Second
Division, recruited by examination of candidates between 17 and
20 years of age; third, a group called staff clerks; fourth, a
class to perform mechanical functions; and finally professional
officers recruited at a more mature age.(41)

Over the next few years the Civil Service greatly expanded and
an intermediate class developed which was recruited from a competition for young men between the ages of $18\frac{1}{2}$ and $19\frac{1}{2}$ of a higher
educational standard than the second division. Classes of boy
clerks, women and girl clerks had also developed.(42) The
MacDonnell Commission was appointed in 1912 and was dismayed to
find a lingering network of patronage in the service. The majority
report of the commission dealt with the administrative and clerical
field and recommended the setting-up of three classes: first a
junior clerical class recruited from boys at the age of 16; second
a senior clerical class of young men recruited from the age of 18;
and last an administrative class recruited in the main from university graduates; but the First World War prevented any action on
these proposals.(43) However after the war the consideration of
the organization of the classes was taken up again, this time by a
committee of the newly constituted Civil Service national Whitley
council known as the Reorganization Committee. This committee
maintained that clerical work in the Civil Service fell broadly
into two categories, that which was mechanical and routine, and

that which was concerned with the formulation of policy. To this
end they recommended that the Service be divided into four major
classes. First, the writing assistant class for very simple mechanical work; second, a clerical class for the better sorts of
clerical work; third, an executive class; and finally an administrative class for the better sort of policy work. Each class was
to be divided into grades recruited successively from the grade
below, while the major input to the classes was to come from the
output of different levels in the educational system according to
qualification and certification. The report was adopted and members
of the existing classes were assimilated into the new classes
although certain departmental classes, notably in the Ministry of
Labour, Inland Revenue and the Customs and Excise, were maintained.
(44)

In 1929 the Tomlin Commission was appointed and this endorsed
the grading structure laid down in the reorganization report, but
did suggest one minor modification which was adopted, namely to
extend the duties of the writing assistants because this group had
attracted recruits of a higher quality than had been foreseen.
The class was called the clerical assistant class and was to overlap with clerical officers at the lower grades, a modification
which was introduced in 1936.(45)

The bureaucratization of scientific work situations can also be
traced to the implementation of various government investigations.
(46) In 1931 two classes of scientists were established as a
result of the Carpenter Committee - scientific officers and
scientific assistants - and common pay scales and conditions of
service were introduced.(47) Another report in 1945 recommended
that the scientific staffs be reorganized into three classes
reflecting the output of British educational institutions, and
the scientific officer, experimental officer and scientific assistant classes were established.(48) At the same time a scheme of
centralized recruitment was introduced. In 1945 also, other
specialists were organized into classes along with standardized
rates of pay, conditions of service and centralized recruitment.(49)

Until 1970 the structure of the Civil Service was based on the
output of British educational institutions, with prospective Civil
Servants recruited at 'O' level, 'A' level, or degree level. There
was little movement between classes, and rigidly defined career
patterns existed which reflected the explicit division of labour
and tasks. However in 1966 in the wake of a new Labour administration whose avowed intention was to modernize Britain, and a particularly unflattering Estimates Committee report, a new major
investigation into the Civil Service was ordered.(50) This
investigation report is known as the Fulton Report.(51) The
authors of Fulton found a good many faults with the Civil Service,
particularly the rigid class structure and lack of movement
between the classes. It was argued that the distinction between
the higher and lower classes was neither valid nor appropriate in
the mid-twentieth century and the distinction between graduate and
non-graduate entry was deemed to be anachronistic, since to operate
efficiently it was thought that ability at all levels should be
drawn upon.(52) Indeed the rigidity of the class system was held
to be responsible for inefficiency and career blockage as well as

being a damper on innovation.(53) The report therefore recommended that the tripartite class system be abolished and a continuous hierarchy be introduced.(54)

The first major changes in structure came into effect on 1 January 1970 when the old administrative, executive and clerical classes were merged to form the administration group.(55) In the following year specialists of all kinds were merged into one group, and throughout the service the old class system was replaced by a streamlined hierarchy.

The modern British Civil Service is undeniably a legal-rational structure. The legal code on which its authority rests is defined by the statutes governing recruitment, promotion, pay, and the varieties of legislation which govern the work of the departments. The Civil Service does proceed according to these rules and regulations and Civil Servants are subject to the laws and principles which they administer. The organization of the Civil Service is continuous and is bounded by a system of rules. Within the Civil Service there is an extreme division of labour based on departmental and on specific competences of individual grades. The departments and grades clearly follow the principle of hierarchy. Recruitment to the Civil Service is on the basis of qualification, and the bureaucratic records exist in abundance. These principles were introduced over a hundred-year period and by tracing this development we can specify that the British Civil Service does closely resemble the Weberian ideal-type. Therefore the British Civil Service would appear to be a perfect testing ground for the theories of those writers who have argued that bureaucratization has a number of significant effects on the employees in that structure. In the next section I will specify those effects.

The effects of bureaucratization on the Civil Servant's working conditions

Having outlined the major developments in the bureaucratizing process in the Civil Service I am now in a position to test the various propositions which have been discussed. These were as follows: first, that professionals employed in bureaucratic structures lose autonomy; second, that a technocratic elite will come to hold important positions in that bureaucracy; and third, that the conditions of work for the majority of routine operatives will deteriorate and come to resemble factory conditions. Thus status, autonomy and work relationships will be examined. These propositions are supposed to be taken as evidence of proletarianization or create the conditions which are favourable to the generation of a proletarian class consciousness. Thus the overall process of bureaucratization is linked to proletarianization. I consider the propositions in turn as they relate to the Civil Service.

Scientists and specialists: loss of autonomy and the rise of the technocrat
In the first place there is little point in discussing the loss of professional autonomy of Civil Service specialists. As I have shown, bureaucratization has been occurring in the British Civil

Service since 1855.   By the First World War a well-established
bureaucracy was in existence.   Apart from some technical activities
in the Admiralty Dockyards direct governmental involvement in
science did not occur until 1915-16.(56)   Thus there is little
question of loss of professional autonomy for Civil Service
specialists.(57)

Civil Service specialists and technocrats do work in a bureaucratic system, but it is difficult to judge the extent to which
this leads to a process of proletarianization.   Pay, conditions of
service, terms of contract are all rigidly defined; but this is
common to all Civil Servants and most specialists working outside
the Civil Service.   The existence of bureaucratic forms of authority cannot in this case be taken as evidence of proletarianization.
The work situations of most specialist Civil Servants do not
resemble manual working conditions although the working conditions
of scientists and technicians in the Civil Service are extremely
varied.

It is however not merely the working conditions which are of
significance but also, in the case of the scientific elite and the
technocrats, the extent to which they can control their work situation.   Indeed within the Civil Service, scientists and other
specialists are effectively barred from the main lines of the
decision-making process in spite of the fact that such decisions
may impinge directly on their speciality.(58)   This stems from the
rigid separation of the administrative function and specialized
function which is a distinctive feature of Civil Service organization.   Also, there has been until recently in the British Civil
Service a decidedly anti-specialist mentality.   Thus one senior
administrator could blandly comment that although senior specialists would be consulted on any matter of importance which fell
within their province, this did not mean that their opinion would
carry any weight.(59)   This subservient position was firmly
institutionalized by the mid-1960s.   The number of specialists in
the Civil Service is about the same as the number of higher and
middle management, but very few specialists before the mid-1960s
held senior management posts and their chances of promotion and
their earning prospects were less than top management.(60)   Even
then the Treasury could find little wrong with this state of
affairs.(61)   In addition the actual execution of a specialist
function was often hampered by administrative interference; even
during the war it was possible for a scientist's account of a
technical matter to be rewritten by a non-specialist before sub-
mission to a minister, and sometimes ministries took decisions on
technical matters without discussing them with the specialist concerned at all.(62)   Indeed the arrogance of top management in
relation to specialists has often been commented upon,(63) and as
late as 1964 the Ministries of Labour, Transport and Aviation did
not employ a professional economist.(64)   It has even been suggested that top management in the Service deliberately conspired to
keep specialists out of the decision-making process.(65)

The limited evidence suggests several general points about the
Civil Service specialist.   Certainly their work situation is subject to rigid bureaucratic control.   Secondly, there appears to
have been a tendency for the scientist to be unable to become

involved in the decision-making process. Thus two basic conditions
exist which meet the criteria established by writers who have
linked bureaucratization and proletarianization. But this is not
prima facie evidence of a direct link between proletarianization
and bureaucratization. As I argued above, even highly bureaucratic
organization does not in its own right amount to proletarian
working conditions. Whether proletarianization has occurred in
relation to industrial behaviour will be considered below.

The emergence of the clerical factory situation
The second proposition derived from the literature relates specifically to clerical workers. It is argued that with increased
bureaucratization the nature of the work unit has changed
(although from what is not always specified) as it has become
larger, more impersonalized and routinized. I will examine this
proposition in relation to the Civil Service.

In spite of the ubiquitous bureaucratization in the Civil
Service the large clerical factory is still exceptional although
the number of such work situations is increasing. In this respect
the centralizing of the Vehicle and Driving Licensing Centres in a
computer-based complex at Swansea and the move of the National
Savings Bank to Glasgow are important developments. Yet the vast
majority of Civil Servants work in old buildings which were not
purpose-built and which are in some cases quite unsuitable for
office work.

In fact the environments in which Civil Servants work vary
greatly in style and quality. Government offices have to be provided for a variety of different purposes accommodating units of
staff which vary in number from two or three to several thousand.
The Civil Service had in the mid-1960s at its disposal some 40
million square feet of office space net in the United Kingdom.(66)
Approximately a quarter of this was in Central London, about 60
per cent occupied by regional, district and local office staff,
and the remainder by headquarters staff. A large amount of headquarters' accommodation in London was built before 1900, and the
standards of working conditions that are in force are the result
of a review of working conditions which took place after the Second
World War. Staff are given space to work in according to their
rank. Thus an assistant secretary or his equivalent is entitled
to 200-250 square feet per head, an executive officer 75-90 square
feet, and a clerical officer only 35-65.(67) Lighting standards
are determined according to the type of work which is undertaken
and heating standards are in line with the Offices, Shops and
Railway Act. On the whole the Civil Service has tended to make a
value out of austerity and this has caused some discontent. One
principal, for example, when asked what he disliked most about his
job replied: 'Mainly the squalor of the practical environment,
depressing offices and a lack of secretarial assistance....'(68)

It was common to find two principals sharing a room, or a principal sharing with three or even more subordinates.(69) Standards
vary widely. For example, at the Civil Service Clerical Association's conference in 1967 one delegate who worked in Somerset House
told conference:

Half our members work in a building which is classified as an

ancient monument. It is a very fine building in some respects
but hardly suitable for office accommodation. Some of us are
lucky and work in large rooms, beautifully decorated with
elegant friezes and paintings. Others are unfortunate to be
tucked away in dingy poky little rooms behind back staircases
in damp dirty vaults. Practically no improvements can be
carried out without sanction from the ancient monuments section
of the Ministry of Public Buildings and Works. They are
usually reluctant to authorise anything in case the character
of the building should suffer.(70)

Another clerical officer in a similar vein reported:
The office where I work has tiny rickety stairs. There are
cracks and the walls and floors slope into the centre so that
you have to put books in front of the cabinets to prevent them
opening. There are three pale grey walls, another in dirty
yellow and it is finished off with a pink door. The ceilings
are white with brown patches and the building has no fire
escapes.(71)

These conditions more closely resemble Dickensian clerkdom
rather than technological clerical factories. However, in contrast
to these squalid and bizarre situations, bureaucratization and expansion has brought about some large-scale factory-like developments. These are most commonly found in branches or departments
which deal with very large amounts of paper or documents which need
to be routinely processed. Before computerization the department
which dealt with National Insurance contributions and benefits was
an interesting example of this. The department was housed in long
low single-storey blocks of brick. The blocks were only distin-
guishable by numbers since they all looked exactly the same.
Records branch, for example, occupied a series of huge blocks
which were interconnected by main corridors:
a square tunnel of painted brick which runs straight down a
slight incline until it disappears into obscurity four hundred
yards away. Branching off it on either side are the spurs, the
large rooms in which the sections of clerical officers work.
These are well spaced with pleasant strips of grass [sic] separating them from each other; the large windows give plenty of
natural light.(72)

Records branch in this particular department was divided into
one hundred rooms of six men and women each performing exactly the
same task on one hundredth of the insured population of the United
Kingdom. In a typical room in these offices two sections were
situated, one down each side with executive officers at one end.
The two sections were divided by a long line of cabinets which
held the National Insurance contribution cards. The clerical
officers sat in pairs at desks which stretched down the rooms in
long parallel rows, 30 inches apart.(73)

Elsewhere Civil Service clerks do not work in purpose-built
environments. For example, the Department of Health and Social
Security in Coventry was housed in a building which was originally
built as a Hotchkiss machine gun factory during the First World War,
and afterwards was used for the building of Morris car engines. It
was bombed in the Second World War and after repairs the Civil
Servants moved in. Similarly, the Leeds South East area office of

the Department of Health and Social Security was accommodated in a
building erected in 1903. The building had subsequently functioned
as a Conservative club. Although originally condemned in 1958, in
1976 it housed forty Civil Servants, some of whom worked in offices
which were in a room with a roof 30 feet high while the partitions
separating offices were only 8 feet high.(74) It is significant
that many Civil Servants regard poor accommodation as the most
potent source of complaint after pay.(75) However, it is ironic
that the complaints are about poor, outdated conditions rather than
about clerical factories. The majority of clerical workers in the
Civil Service undoubtedly work within bureaucratic constraints
with regard to the way they do their task. However, within the
Civil Service there is only a relatively small number of Civil
Servants working in what could accurately be called factory conditions. Where factory-like conditions do exist, using a narrow
definition of proletarianization, there is limited evidence of it
in the Civil Service. In chapter 7 I explore the effects these
conditions have on industrial behaviour.

MECHANIZATION AND AUTOMATION IN THE CIVIL SERVICE

This section of the chapter will examine the extent of mechanization and automation in the Civil Service. These topics will be
examined because certain theorists have linked proletarianization
to the mechanization and automation of the clerical work situation.
For the writers in this tradition the links are based on the broad
proposition that along with changes in the division of labour,
transformations in the techniques and technologies of production
have altered the function and nature of white-collar work as it
has become de-skilled. This has speeded up the rationalization of
office work. Thus some clerical work is done entirely by auto-
matic systems, and clerks become nothing more than machine minders.
This supposedly completes their proletarianization or affects
their industrial behaviour in such a way that they exhibit 'proletarian' tendencies.(76) At the same time this automation requires
a new type of specialist to organize and service the technology.
The power of these specialists in the organization is allegedly
very great because of the importance of the technology to which
they have access. Yet the specialists are denied access to the
highest positions in the management hierarchy. This denial of
power leads supposedly to the generation of radical political
attitudes.(77)
      This section will analyse these two propositions by first exam-
ining in some detail the meaning of the terms 'automation' and
'mechanization'. This is necessary because the authors do not say
precisely what they mean by these terms even though there is a
long sociological tradition examining this phenomenon. Having
then defined automation more closely, I then consider the extent
to which it is occurring in the Civil Service and whether, if it
is occurring, it has affected Civil Servants in the way Braverman,
Denitch and Hopper believe it will.
      In fact the term mechanization can be reduced to four basic
types: first, the mechanization of conventional manual processes,

for example, the mechanical shovel or typewriter; second, the
mechanization of processes in which machines are linked together
for continuous production as found, for example, in an oil refinery;
third, it can mean the application of computers and the like to
paperwork, and fourth, the use of computers in the decision-making
process.(78) The first and third types of automation are at present the most important in the non-manual work situation. Social
scientists have long noted the impact which mechanization and automation have had on the working environment. The findings from the
industrial setting are numerous. Changes in the division of labour
which come about as the result of the introduction of automation
change the relations of production and allegedly the workers'
feelings about work.(79) The level and extent of technological
advance is related to work group formation and attitude to the
job,(80) and the nature of the functioning of an organization is
related to technology as is the very structure of the organization
itself.(81)

In the white-collar sector of the workforce the effects of automation are less well-known, although many writers have commented
on the 'revolution' that has taken place in office organization.(82)
It seems most likely that the introduction of office machinery
such as the typewriter and adding machine only occurred after the
office had been rationalized to a degree.(83) The introduction of
machinery led to centralization and an increased division of labour
although in its extreme form this process is only a recent development.(84) Mechanization proper was only slowly introduced into
office work and this late development was most probably because of
the intrinsic difficulties in doing so, in the sense that some
white-collar work does not lend itself easily to rationalization
and routinization.(85) More recently a new wave of machines have
been introduced into office organization. These are computers and
related sophisticated information retrieval systems. This development has sometimes had dramatic results.(86) It has, for example,
slowed down the growth rate in white-collar employment, and indeed
in the early 1960s in the USA the rate of growth of white-collar
employment in non-automated companies was approximately 15 per
cent per year, while white-collar employment in automated establishments grew at about 7 per cent.(87) But it is in the actual
task undertaken in the office where the most marked effects are
likely.(88) The long-term effect will be to create a new division
of labour in the office itself where one lowly group of workers
will be employed in routine tasks and will operate the machine
whose tasks are rationalized and subdivided, while above them a
new group of controllers with specialist knowledge will emerge.(89)
Finally, mere automation may itself be overtaken by cybernetic
systems technology, where the process can function because of the
operation of feedback systems with little need of human interference at all.

The basic thesis of the authors considered in chapter 2 was
that these changes were inevitable and they would have important
effects on the political-industrial behaviour of the workers
involved. I will now examine the extent of automation and mechanization in the Civil Service.

The Civil Service was not an early user of automated office

equipment. The Treasury used to evaluate the use of office equipment by the criteria that it should only be introduced wherever and whenever 'the resultant increase in efficiency (measured in terms of savings in money, staff, or improved services) [was] commensurate with the capital outlay involved.'(90) The main types of office machinery introduced in the ten-year period 1956-66 is shown in Table 6.1. These are examples of type 1 mechanization where machines carry out functions which had previously been done by clerks' hands and brains.

TABLE 6.1 The extent of mechanization in the Civil Service, 1956-66

	1956	1966	% increase
Typewriters	79,298	91,609	16
Duplicators and photocopiers	10,251	20,451	100
Adding, accounting and calculating	19,116	26,501	37
Addressing	2,880	3,481	20
Dictating	2,634	13,388	400
Miscellaneous	2,969	8,459	190

Source: HM Treasury, The Adequacy of the Provision of Office Machines in the Civil Service, in 'The Civil Service Vol. 4; Factual, Statistical and Explanatory Papers', HMSO, London, 1968, p.644.

In recent years, however, there has been automation of whole processes. Much Civil Service clerical work is inevitably of a routine nature and the processing of endless streams of documents and papers characterizes much of the execution of Civil Service business, especially in relation to the provision of health and welfare services. There are large inputs into the system in the form of the collection of taxes and other revenues, and at the output level, insurance benefits, unemployment payments and social security handouts. Much of this work is repetitive and requires merely the manipulation of fairly simple data and the application of standard rules and for the average clerical worker involved, very little decision-making of a fundamental kind is required. In most recent years it has been to this type of work that the Civil Service has introduced cybernetic technology. Thus today national insurance, taxation, drivers and vehicle licences, and some personnel functions are among those areas covered by computers.
Where this has occurred there has been a resultant change in the organization of work for the Civil Servants involved. Reallocation of the total task to other sites and other employees was the first result. This was followed by a reduced demand for middle quality clerical work, while demand for high level computer programmers and analysts and for machine operators increased.(91)
The first computer was installed in a government department in the early 1960s and by 1972 there were some 200 computers.(92) In the

period 1967-72 computer power in the Civil Service increased at an average rate of 50 per cent per annum, and a new specialist group of systems analysts emerged with some 2,000 of them by 1972.(93) Central government is now the largest user of computers, the biggest spender on computers, and the largest employer of computer operatives and programmers in the United Kingdom.(94) By 1973 there were 258 computer systems in the Civil Service worth about £100 million, which cost £60 million per annum to operate and employed about 3,700 Civil Servants to programme, 1,700 to operate, and 4,500 to prepare the data for the computers.(95) Twenty separate government departments are involved although there is some attempt at co-ordination by the Central Computer Agency. Interestingly, many outsiders, i.e. non-career Civil Servants, have been brought in and are employed by the computer agency and departments are encouraged to do the same.(96)
    The Civil Service has therefore in recent years mechanized and automated some of its work routine. As yet this affects only a small percentage of Civil Servants (1.4 per cent) but this percentage is increasing. Many of the predictions concerning the introduction of this type of automated process in relation to working conditions hold true for this small but growing sector of the Civil Service. Thus there is unquestionably evidence that mechanization and automation have taken place in the Civil Service and have brought about changes in the work situation of a relatively small number of Civil Servants. The working conditions of this group are considerably different from clerks in other sectors of the Civil Service. However, the link which some authors claim between proletarianization and automation remains problematic. For if we simply take the existence of automated working environments as evidence of proletarianization it may be said to have occurred in a few limited cases. But if proletarianization is to be related to industrial and political behaviour the mere existence of automation does not necessarily provide the causal link. These automated conditions are alleged to create an environment where political attitudes and behaviour are conditioned in a certain way. I will consider the evidence for this in chapter 7.

SUMMARY

This chapter has examined the extent to which bureaucratization and mechanization have taken place in the Civil Service, and has tentatively examined the links between bureaucratization and mechanization and the concept of proletarianization. The rationale underlying this discussion was the fact that a number of writers had linked these concepts in various ways. I began by demonstrating which writers had made the link between bureaucratization and proletarianization, but since they often used the former term in a vague way I specified the concept more rigorously with reference to Weber's ideal-type construct of bureaucracy. Then having specified the nature of bureaucratization I examined the historical growth of the Civil Service and looked at the extent of its bureaucratic tendencies. It was found to be a highly bureaucratic institution. I then examined different groups of Civil Servants

and found that to a limited extent the effects which other writers
had predicted for bureaucratization had actually occurred in the
Civil Service. I also noted that if proletarianization was
defined simply as bureaucratic working conditions then to some
limited extent we could observe proletarianization among Civil
Servants.

I then turned my attention to mechanization. I specified the
effects of automation/mechanization as defined in the literature
on working conditions. With these concepts in mind I examined the
extent of this process in the Civil Service. It was found that
although the Civil Service was the largest user of computers in
Britain it was a late user of these and other mechanical aids, and
cybernation only affected a small proportion of Civil Servants.
But for those Civil Servants there was a marked difference in their
organization of work when compared to traditional white-collar
workers. Once more if we simply define proletarianization as an
automated work situation then there is evidence of proletarianization of a small number of Civil Servants in this respect. But
since the writers considered usually linked these concepts with
industrial political behaviour no causal link was established in
this chapter.

On the basis of the evidence presented in this chapter, we note
that the British Civil Service is a highly bureaucratic organization. Also we note that to a limited extent mechanization and
automation have affected the working conditions of Civil Servants.
I argued in an earlier chapter however that proletarianization
could only be understood with reference to the three concepts of
class position, consciousness of class position, and industrial
and political action. In the following chapter I will explore the
relationship between mechanization and automation in relation to
class consciousness and industrial behaviour.

Chapter 7

THE INDUSTRIAL BEHAVIOUR
OF CIVIL SERVANTS

INTRODUCTION

Up to now this work has concentrated on the factors which various
authors have specified as the possible causes of changes in the
political attitudes and behaviour of white-collar workers. I have
argued that these possible causes could be limited to five key
variables which could be empirically measured; namely pay relativities, the extent of feminization, the extent of recruitment of
working-class individuals, the extent of bureaucratization, and
the extent of mechanization. It has been proposed that alterations
in these variables lead to changes in the industrial behaviour of
white-collar workers. In the preceding three chapters I have
tested these variables in the British Civil Service and have found
the evidence to be equivocal in relation to proletarianization.
Therefore this chapter which is devoted to the study of the industrial behaviour of Civil Servants is crucial. In this chapter I
concentrate on trade unionism in the British Civil Service historically and contemporarily, and I will link this to the five variables highlighted in chapter 2 and examined in chapters 4, 5 and 6.

THE DEVELOPMENT OF TRADE UNIONISM IN THE CIVIL SERVICE (1)

In the early part of the nineteenth century the Civil Service was
not highly bureaucratic. At that time it was a series of more or
less autonomous departments, and only after the instigation of the
Northcote-Trevelyan proposals and subsequent Royal Commissions did
the Civil Service begin to approximate to a bureaucracy proper.(2)
In the decentralized independent departments management was auth-
oritarian but 'tempered with a degree of paternal benevolence'.(3)
According to rigid Victorian social convention, social inferiors
were expected to know their places and most clerks in the Victorian
Civil Service probably did. For the clerks there was no bureaucratic means of articulating grievances or dissatisfactions, and
the attitude of senior Civil Servants was that if a clerk was dis-
satisfied he always had the option to resign. A limited and vague
form of grievance procedure did exist in that it was the practice

for clerks either individually or in groups to present grievances
to their immediate superiors. This practice was known as peti-
tioning.(4)   Toward the end of the nineteenth century some clerks
found themselves subject to increasingly bureaucratic forms of
control, and as the rate of bureaucratization increased so did the
number of petitions.(5)   Thus the first strivings of protective
action were spurred on by the gradual bureaucratization of the
Civil Service.   The first formal departmental associations and
combinations appeared in the revenue departments and by 1858 two
different associations were in existence.(6)   The links with the
phenomena of clerks protecting themselves and centralization and
rationalization were further marked by the fact that in 1871 when
writers became the first all-service class it was not long before
they joined forces with other low grade clerks and formed the
Association of Temporary Clerks and Writers.(7)   In the nineteenth
century the Post Office was the largest and most bureaucratic unit
in the Civil Service and unions and other forms of protective
associations prospered there.   The first moves by postal workers
to form protective associations seem to have been prompted by economic concerns.   In 1854 an economy drive was instituted to
increase the Post Office's profit and as a result some work was
down-graded without any corresponding alteration in payments to
the workers.   Thus a situation arose where a man was doing precisely the same work as a colleague but received only one-quarter
of the latter's wage.   Soon afterwards the first combinations
emerged to protest at this.(8)   Further development of combinations
and associations was affected by the legal status of trades unions
of all sorts, in that it was not until the passing of the Trade
Union Act in 1871 that properly consistuted combinations appeared,
and even then the Postmaster-General did not actually acknowledge
the postal staff's right to form or join an association.   This
right was granted in 1890; even at that time the Postmaster-General
effectively stifled expert organization by insisting that any
applications from the association had to be submitted by the Civil
Servants immediately concerned and not by some third party.
Accordingly the possibility of an association employing full-time
officials was curtailed.(9)
     In the rest of the Civil Service a five-class structure had
emerged by the last quarter of the nineteenth century,(10) but the
lowly clerks in this new structure were earning on average one-
fifth of what old-style Civil Service clerks had earned, and they
enjoyed considerably fewer fringe benefits.   Complaints about this
on an individual petition basis were ineffective and more broad-
based protest began to appear.   Thus common service grades which
had emerged from the bureaucratic reforms began to submit petitions
on a service-wide basis.   In this case a mixture of bureaucratization and pressure on salaries seems to have been the major impetus
to the growth of protest which was channelled through organized
associations.
     The first *national* Civil Service union was the Postal and Tele-
graph Clerks Association which was founded in 1881.   This was
followed in 1887 by the United Kingdom Postal Clerks Association,
by the Fawcett Association in 1890, and the Postman's Federation in
1891, until by 1902 there were nine postal organizations.(11)

Other associations had appeared in different departments (for
example, the Admiralty in 1884) and by the end of the century there
were twenty-eight departmental and national associations in the
Civil Service.(12) The attitude of management in the service was
not favourable to trade unionism, and since at this time many Civil
Servants worked in small-scale closely controlled situations the
pressures against unionization were quite formidable. The response
of the Board of Inland Revenue to a pay claim in 1890 is typical:
    The Board will be glad if you will inform those clerks who
    signed the petition that if they are dissatisfied with the
    weekly wages which the surveyor of taxes is authorised to pay,
    it is open to all of them to give one week's notice and seek
    employment elsewhere.(13)
The period of the early twentieth century was one of further
expansion of unionism in the Civil Service particularly among subordinate grades, especially the clerks. The mainsprings to this
continued expansion appear to have been economic and bureaucratic
while at the same time the diehard resistance of management to
trade unionism was declining. The assistant clerks were one such
group to take advantage of this. They first met as a group in
Exeter Hall in the Strand on 2 March 1903 and agreed to form an
association.(14) The organization was at first loose and informal
without any annual subscriptions, although collections were to be
made because funds would be needed. By 1904 this association had
554 members.(15) The formation of this association was in direct
response to the single interest group of clerks established in the
1890s after the Ridley Commission.(16) Yet the formation of an
association did not lead automatically to recognition, and it was
not until 1906 that the first Civil Service union was granted full
legal recognition. This occurred in part because the new Liberal
government was more favourable to trades unions than the erstwhile
Tory administration.(17) In February 1906 Mr Stanley Buxton, the
Postmaster-General, announced that he was prepared 'frankly to
recognize any duly constituted association or federation of postal
servants and was willing to receive representations from the members or representatives of the association through the secretary
of the association whether or not he was a serving officer'.(18)
The postal unions therefore held the most favourable position of
any union in the Civil Service. Other groups in the Civil Service
began to make headway at about this time. These were the departmental groups which included the tax inspectors, the Customs and
Excise officers, and specialists in the Admiralty.(19) At this
time the Civil Service was not fully bureaucratized and hence these
departmental associations enjoyed an advantage over service-wide
associations in so far as the latter were effectively barred from
dealing directly with the Treasury and instead had to make applications to individual departmental heads. Typical of the problems
faced by service-wide associations were those of the Boy Clerks
Association. Boy clerks were taken on by the Civil Service at the
age of 16, and two years later three out of every four were dis-
missed and replaced by newly recruited 16-year olds (the odd one
in four was promoted). This fostered a good deal of resentment
which manifested itself in the formation of the Boy Clerks Association. When the MacDonnell commission was appointed in 1911 a group

of militants at the large savings bank (noted even then for its
rationalization and routinization) organized themselves to make
representations to the commission. When a meeting was called at
the Savings Bank some three hundred boy clerks enlisted and an
organizing committee was formed for the purpose of recruiting boy
clerks in the *fifty other* government departments where boy clerks
worked. Within a short while the organization had a membership of
3,000.(20) By the outbreak of the First World War Civil Servants
were joining trades unions or other protective associations in
increasing numbers. The major impetus to this growth was the
steadily growing bureaucratization of the Service because this had
led to the concentration of Civil Servants in larger work groups,
and the application of rational management principles led not only
to a similarity of work experience for many Civil Servants, but
also to a similarity of experience of grievance. The major source
of grievance was low pay. At the same time conditions in society
at large were becoming increasingly favourable to the growth of
trades unions in so far as legal recognition had been granted
gradually in the last quarter of the nineteenth century. The
claims of the boy clerks and the assistant clerks were far from
militant, merely an expression of an attempt to control their work
environment to a limited extent. They sought to be responsible
and to be accepted as such. This mirrors the development in the
manual craft unions of an earlier period who sought respectability.(21) The hankering after respectability is significant because
the period immediately before the First World War was one of the
most stormy in the history of industrial relations in Britain.
There were few overt links between the Civil Service unions and
other unions or the Labour party; what links did exist were where
an individual Civil Service trade unionist was also a member of
the Independent Labour party.

Perhaps the most significant event in relation to Civil Service
trade unionism was the First World War itself, which disrupted the
Civil Service to a great extent. Not only were many more functions given to the Civil Service because of the exigencies of war,
but also much actual or potential manpower was removed to the
fighting forces. Two main effects on the trades unions can be
noted; first there was an enormous speeding-up of the growth of
unions hastened by the greater and more widespread experience of
grievance, and second the war offered better opportunities for
obtaining demands because the government very often had to act out
of expediency.(22) The specific grievances related to pay and conditions and were therefore fundamentally economic. The pressures
of war-time work meant that overtime was increased, some work was
downgraded, and many promotions were blocked. On top of this the
cost of living rose steeply. Civil Servants observed that outside
the Civil Service workers' wages were increasing while theirs
remained static. The postal workers were the first to campaign
for an increase and their claim went to arbitration which awarded
a war bonus to some Civil Servants while others like the boy clerks
were denied not only the increase but also the right to arbitration.
Discontent festered and other associations demanded full recognition. It was finally agreed about one year later than the associations outside the Post Office would go to arbitration. By this

time the postal workers were organizing for another increase.
This arbitration settlement resulted in the extension of the first
postal settlement to the rest of the Service.(23)
    A still more decisive issue arose, again one which was primarily
economic. In 1916 an attempt was made to alter the terms which
governed the hours of the clerical, executive and administrative
grades. Hitherto hours had been fixed at seven per day with
additional hours counting as overtime. By 1916 many Civil Servants
were working up to twelve hours each day.(24) It became known that
the Treasury wished to extend the length of the working day to
eight hours and that this was to apply beyond the duration of the
war, thus permanently lengthening the working day without any
financial recompense. This created much resentment among the
desk classes. The Assistant Clerks Association was very active on
this issue and petitions were organized to each head of department
and MPs were lobbied.(25) The Treasury action offended many Civil
Servants and it appears to have been instrumental in spurring many
non-members to join trades unions.(26)
    However as these economic issues were making many Civil Servants
either join or seriously think about joining unions or other protective associations a significant development occurred which was
to be singularly important in making trade unionism respectable in
the Civil Service as well as leading to the fully-fledged development of trades unions in the Service. The wartime government was
extremely alarmed by the state of industrial unrest in industry
which was seriously threatening war production. A committee was
appointed under the chairmanship of J.H. Whitley 'to make and consider suggestions for securing a permanent improvement in relations
between employers and workmen'.(27) The interim report of the
committee dealt with 'the problems of establishing permanently
improved relations between employer and employed in the main industries of the country in which organizations fully representative
of both sides were in existence'. This report describes in outline the machinery for consultation between management and unions
at a national, local and works level. In October 1917 a second
report dealt with those industries in which employer and employee
co-operation was not well developed. Importantly for the Civil
Service it contained a reference to employees in central and local
government and recommended: 'that such authorities and their work
people should take into consideration the proposals made in this
and in our first report with a view to determining how far such
proposals can suitably be adopted in their case.'(28)
    The Civil Service staff associations, especially those in the
Post Office, seized enthusiastically on this proposal as an opportunity for legitimate and established bargaining rights. In 1918
the War Cabinet decided in principle to adopt the application of
the Whitley Report, with 'necessary adaptations' to government
establishments where conditions were similar to those in outside
industry. Another committee was set up with the task of drafting
a suitable Whitley system for government employees. The committee
drew attention to two factors which caused difficulty. First, that
the state as an employer was unlike a private employer since the
state was also the government of the country and therefore had a
dual role; and second, the problem of ministerial responsibility,

which is to say that in the terms of the conventions of the un-
written British Constitution a minister is held responsible for all
that occurs in his department, and to set up a committee of Civil
Servants to decide on staff matters would impinge on the minister's
executive power. So this committee recommended that Whitley
councils in the Civil Service should not have executive power but
simply be consultative; and that the scope of the councils should
be limited to the conditions of service. This effectively ruled
out of court matters relating to organization, method and management.

The government put these proposals to a representative conference of Civil Service unions in April 1919 where the Chancellor of
the Exchequer, Austen Chamberlain, proposed the adoption of the
recommendations. The staff associations however rejected the proposals on the grounds that they refused to accept a constitution
which they had not helped create. The associations demanded co-
operation on equal terms with their employers. The Chancellor
agreed to this and the unions congratulated themselves on what
appeared to be a famous victory. In some respects, however, it was
a hollow victory for the unions and it seems likely that the Chancellor realized this, since even an accepted Whitley system would
only have as much power as the government or its representatives
would allow it. In the early years of operation it effectively had
no power. A provisional joint committee was appointed to work out
a modified constitution for Whitley councils in the Civil Service
and work began in April 1919. A constitution which allowed for
equal representation on both sides was produced. The constitution
established that the chair would always be taken by representatives
of management, that the councils would not vote but reach decision
by agreement, and decisions were to be reported to the Cabinet in
order to overcome the problem of ministerial responsibility.

By the end of 1919 the basic formal structures which were to
influence the course of industrial relations in the Civil Service
were established. The unions had achieved organization, recognition, negotiation and arbitration rights, and large numbers of
individual Civil Servants were now members. There appear to have
been two major reasons why trade unionism in the Civil Service had
reached this stage. The first was economic in so far as Civil
Servants banded together for economic protection. The issues
related not only to pay but also to hours and conditions of service.
At the same time the bureaucratic rationalization of the Civil
Service was important because it created unified conditions and
therefore unified experiences of grievances. At a secondary level
certain social-demographic factors may have been important. In
the Civil Service in the earliest days of trade unionism the less
socially exclusive grades were the first to organize and unionize,
particularly in the Post Office. The factors of feminization and
mechanization do not seem to have been particularly important in
the early moves to trade unionism. Outside developments in
society's attitude to trades unions was also significant because
they created the conditions favourable to unionization. The late
nineteenth century up to the First World War saw the tremendous
growth of all forms of trades unions in Britain. This was moreover
the period where legal recognition was given to them (despite some

legal setbacks). This gradual alteration in the legal status of
trades unions gave both encouragement and protection to Civil
Service unions although it was not until 1906 that the Civil
Servants' employers acknowledged this. Civil Service trade unionism was never particularly militant nor syndicalist at this time
which marks it off from a good deal of manual unionism of the
same period. Thus we can argue that Civil Service unions remained
reasonably independent of mainstream developments in industrial
unionism yet basked in the glow of the legal recognition afforded
to it.
   The legal-formal structure of the Whitley system created the
situation whereby trades unions in the Civil Service could take an
active part in the internal affairs of their organization. I now
examine the extent to which the trades unions were able to utilize
this formal structure and what were the causal elements underlying
this.

THE TRADES UNIONS TAKE AN ACTIVE ROLE IN THE INTERNAL AFFAIRS OF
THE CIVIL SERVICE

The formal structure established in 1919 is still more or less
intact. There have been a number of modifications. In this section I will describe the formal structure and then examine the
extent to which it has helped or hindered the unions' attempt to
be involved in the affairs of their organization. There are two
distinct elements in the formal structure, the Whitley structure
and the unions. I deal with each in turn.

The formal system

The trades unions and staff associations
I concentrate on three unions in particular because they represent
the key grades of Civil Servants with which I am concerned in this
book: the Civil and Public Services Association, CPSA (formerly
the Civil Service Clerical Association) representing the clerical
grades; the Society of Civil and Public Servants, SCPS (formerly
the Society of Civil Servants) representing middle management; and
the Institution of Professional Civil Servants, IPCS, representing
scientists and specialists. By concentrating on these three
unions I can provide a good test for the ideas outlined in chapter
2.
Membership Generally speaking the staff associations and unions
are organized on a horizontal basis representing one class or grade.
The main exception is IPCS which is organized vertically representing nearly all scientists of all grades in the Civil Service.
Some staff associations are service wide, i.e. they are found in
many different departments; thus both the executive officer in
the Department of Health and Social Security and the executive
officer in the Ministry of Defence belong to SCPS. Some associations are however found in only one department and these are known
as departmental associations, e.g. the Inland Revenue Staff Federation. All Civil Servants are potentially members of an association.

Some writers have taken the proportion of actual members in relation to potential members as an indicator of the level of activity
of a union.(29) In the Civil Service the figure on membership as
a proportion of potential members is very high but the actual
figures are difficult to calculate because the staff associations'
figures on membership include individuals who work in quasi-Civil
Service bodies like the Airports Authority, the Atomic Energy
Authority and even the public corporations like the Post Office.
One study found that 4/5 of top management, 2/3 of middle management and approximately 1/2 of scientists were members of their
associations.(30) This high percentage is in no small part due to
the'fact that the Civil Service encourages new recruits to join the
associations:

> A Civil Servant is free to be a member of an association or
> trade union which will admit him under its rules of membership.
> Civil Servants are, moreover, encouraged ... to belong to
> associations, for the existence of fully representative assoc-
> iations not only promotes good staff relations but is essential
> to effective negotiations on conditions of service.(31)

Recognition The staff associations vary greatly in size. National
recognition is granted by the Civil Service Department to associations representing national service grades, but departmental
recognition is granted by the department concerned relating to
staff in that department. In order to be recognized an association
must show that it represents the staff it says it does, although no
precise percentages are laid down as to what would constitute
reason for national recognition.(32)

Union structure (i) CPSA The Civil Service unions are themselves
typically bureaucratic and hierarchical. In 1979 the CPSA had
218,000 members in over 100 departments and quasi-Civil Service
offices all over the United Kingdom. There were over 900 branches,
varying in size from less than a dozen to more than seven thous-
and.(33) The union itself has no easily definable organization.
This is the result of the piece-meal development of the union
through amalgamation and the vagaries of Civil Service reorganization. Broadly the structure consists of branches, areas, a
national executive and the national conference.(34)

Union structure (ii) IPCS The IPCS was formed in 1919 in the wake
of the setting up of the national Whitley council with the stated
aims of advancing efficiency in the Civil Service, increasing
promotion for scientists, helping to improve and maintain the
status of the scientific Civil Service, protecting the rights of
the Civil Servant and representing scientists and professional
Civil Servants in the Whitley council.(35) Membership of the
Institution has increased markedly since then (see Table 7.1).(36)

Until very recently IPCS was not registered as a trade union,
but it was nevertheless concerned with negotiating the terms and
conditions of professional Civil Servants as well as attempting to
cater for their professional needs.(37) The IPCS now represents
nineteen general service categories or classes and nearly four
hundred departmental classes.(38) Every member of the Institution
is a member of a branch and there are 117 branches varying in size
from under fifty to over five thousand. Generally the branches
are organized on a departmental basis; thus in some departments

TABLE 7.1   Membership of IPCS, 1919-78

1919	1,000
1933	8,000
1939	15,000
1942	21,000
1945	30,000
1965	57,000
1973	96,000
1978	99,051

there is only one branch covering all the Institutions' members
while in others there are several branches, each catering for a
particular sector of the membership - for example those in a particular management area of the department or those in one profession.   Branches are broken into sections or sub-sections and the
section or sub-section is the local organization which is the
individual point of contact.(39)   The governing body of the
Institution is technically the annual delegate conference which is
made up of delegates from all branches.(40)   The branches and the
national executive committee put down motions for discussion, conference takes decisions on them, and those motions which are
passed become Institution policy.(41)
Union structure (iii) SCPS   This organization represents middle
management in the Civil Service.   It is also organized into
branches and sections of which there were 384 branches and 18
sections in 1970,(42) and by 1978 membership was over 106,000.(43)
Formally the Society consists of an executive council of twenty-six
which is elected by the annual conference of branch delegates.   The
annual conference has approximately two hundred delegates who come
direct from the branches.   Branches vary according to the nature
of the departments.   In large departments the structure is one of
a section which covers a number of branches with each section
having its own conference and executive based on the branches.
Branches are not work-place based, although their average size is
five hundred members.   There is one branch meeting annually at
which business is transacted and at which motions for conference
are put up.   The rest of the time business is done by branch committees.
     In principle and formal structure there is a highly elaborate
apparatus within the Civil Service trades unions.   The unions are
large with a high proportion of their potential membership.   They
are bureaucratically organized so that in theory ordinary members
have a direct line to policy making.   On top of the individual
union bureaucracy another level of bureaucracy exists, namely the
Whitley councils.   I now turn to a consideration of these.

Whitley councils in the Civil Service (44)
General   Whitley councils operate at three different levels;
nationally, departmentally and locally.   Each however has common
principles of procedure.   On each Whitley body there is a division
between the official side which represents management and the staff

side which through the unions and associations represents the ordinary Civil Servant. The chairman of a Whitley body or one of its
sub-committees is always a member of the official side and the
vice-chairman is always a member of the staff side. If a chairman
is absent, the vice-chairman does not take over but the official
side appoints another chairman. The size of the committee is a
matter for agreement, but the composition of each side is a matter
for itself to decide. Although strictly speaking decisions are not
reached by voting and each side speaks formally the business is
conducted more or less informally between the individuals representing either side.(45) The minutes are normally drafted in the
first instance by the official side secretary and then agreed to
by both sides. At national level it is convention that the minutes
will record what was intended rather than what actually was said.
Nationally The national Whitley council is supposed to be concerned with all matters affecting the conditions of service of non-
industrial Civil Servants at all levels. The *stated* functions of
the national council include the provision of the best means for
utilizing the ideas and experience of staff, greater staff participation in decisions affecting them and determining the conditions
of service. The official side always contained Treasury officers
and more recently members of the Civil Service Department, heads
of departments and other top Civil Servants.(46) The members of
the staff side are appointed by the staff associations acting
individually or collectively and is made up of full-time trade
union officials, many of whom are former Civil Servants.(47) Representation on the staff side is not logically calculated and
indeed the allocation of the seats has only a crude relationship
to figures on membership and the diversity of represented interests. The membership has changed over time (see Table 7.2). The
larger associations forego some of their strict entitlement according to membership in order to accommodate the smaller unions and
associations and make the staff side as representative as possible.
(48) In spite of the facility in the constitution of the national
Whitley council that states that decisions must be reported to the
Cabinet, this rarely happens in practice unless they impinge on
matters of national importance, for example pay policy.(49)
Agreement is apparently reached so often that to report it to the
Cabinet would be impractical. The ultimate legitimation for the
official side lies with the minister, and for the staff side with
the staff associations. Much of the consultation that goes on is
supposedly very friendly and the whole national Whitley council
actually rarely meets as a collective body. Most business is transacted by sub-committees on the staff side, the most important of
which are known as committees A and B. The former is the more
important and meets fortnightly with an agenda coming from a
variety of sources, for example the staff side or an individual
union.(50) Committee B meets monthly and deals with issues of
equal importance but less urgency. The policy is agreed among the
members of committees A and B before they meet the official side
for negotiation. The full staff side meets monthly to review the
work of committees A and B and its other sub-committees, and to
consider resolutions passed by the unions and staff associations.(51)
When agreement is not reached between the official side and the

TABLE 7.2   The national staff side: changes in composition, 1963-79

1963		1974		1979	
Society of Civil Servants	2	Society of Civil Servants	3	Society of Civil and Public Servants	4
IPCS	2	IPCS	4	IPCS	4
First Division Association	1	First Division Association	1	First Division Association	0.5
Civil Service Alliance	6	CPSA	7	CPSA	7
Civil Service union	1	Civil Service union	2	Civil Service union	2
Association of HM Inspectors of Taxes	1	Association of HM Inspectors of Taxes	1	Association of HM Inspectors of Taxes	0.5
Association of Officers of the Ministry of Labour	1	Prison Officers Association	1	Prison Officers Association	1
Customs and Excise	1	Inland Revenue Staff Federation	2	Inland Revenue Staff Federation	2
Federation of Civil Service Technical and Professional Staff	1	Association of Government Supervisors and Radio Officers	1	Association of Government Supervisors and Radio Officers	1
Union of Post Office Workers	6				
Post Office Engineering Union	2				
Association of Post Office Controlling Officers	1				
Smaller Post Office bodies	1				
	26		24		22

Sources: The Civil Service national Whitley council; R.L. Hayward, 'Whitley Councils in the United Kingdom Civil Service: A Study in Staff Relations', 1963, p.5; 'Civil Service Opinion', vol.52, 1974, p.157.

N.B. Post Office groups no longer took part in the proceedings of the Whitley council after 1969 when the Post Office became a public corporation. In 1979 the First Division Association and the Association of HM Inspectors of Taxes shared one seat.

staff side, the staff side has the right to present its claim to
the Civil Service arbitration tribunal the decision of which is
binding on both parties.(52)

Departmental Whitley councils There are numerous departmental
Whitley councils (reflecting the number of government departments),
varying in size according to the nature of the department. Usually,
though not invariably, the head of department will chair the
official side and other members of the official side will be heads
of divisions. The staff side will be composed of representatives
of associations that are recognized by the department and can
include both service-wide associations or departmental associations.
The departmental council is only concerned with domestic matters
other than the implementation of national agreements at local
level. In practice the departmental Whitley councils do their
work in sub-committees which meet regularly and formally although
as with the national council some informality exists.(53)

Local Whitley councils The third level of the Whitley system is
the local level, generally located in the actual place of employment, the local offices and branches. There are a very large number
of these and they are concerned wholly in dealing with local questions, although like the departmental councils they are important
in implementing national agreements. The chairman of the local
committee is the local manager and the rest of the official side
is made up of section heads while the staff side is made up of
serving Civil Servants. The committees meet regularly and tend to
be more formal than those at the national level mainly because in
these situations consultation is between supervisor and supervisee.
The local councils are fully autonomous and have no necessary
organic link with the national council, and neither is the national
council a final court of appeal from the local or departmental committee.(54)

   This highly elaborate structure would seemingly provide both
unions and ordinary Civil Servants through their unions with the
opportunity to take an active and decisive role in the internal
affairs of their organization. Indeed much Civil Service and
Whitley council literature gives this impression.(55) However an
examination of the system in practice fails to justify such optim-
ism.

The Whitley system at work
When in 1919 the Treasury finally accepted Civil Service unionism
and the Whitley structure was erected there were no immediate consequences in the sense of a change in the pattern of industrial
relations in the service overnight. Power still rested firmly in
the hands of management and this absolute power was not relinquished
in any meaningful way until the Second World War. The balance of
power between individual Civil Servants and their superiors, and
between individual departments and the Treasury, remained largely
undisturbed. If anything, because the Whitley system embodied
these distinctions in the staff and official sides, the status quo
was strengthened. In addition, the provision for agreements to be
reported to the Cabinet and then to become operative was a fiction
because agreements under this system were never made and then
reported to ministers, but rather the decisions were first

authorized by the minister and were then reached. Even so, immediately after the establishment of the Whitley machinery the unions held on to their limited gain and exerted a small degree of influence in staff matters, but usually in uncontentious and uncontroversial matters. Following the débâcle of the General Strike the staff side was both split and demoralized and in this state faced the problems of the Depression.(56)

An example of the ineffectiveness of Whitleyism in this period was the action on Civil Service salaries. During the 1920s Civil Service salaries were on a sliding scale where a cost of living bonus was adjusted every half year according to the average retail price index of the preceding six months. Thus as potatoes, bread and meat fell in price so did Civil Service salaries. Most of the staff associations were determined to 'stop the drop', either by stabilization or consolidation i.e. going for a regular wage in the belief that prices would remain low or continue to fall, or gambling on prices beginning to rise again while wages stayed where they were. The Treasury first proposed a plan that the bonus would be stabilized within a wider range of movement, but this was rejected. When the government announced a plan for a Royal Commission whose terms of reference were to include pay the staff side became even more divided among itself, and management could dictate matters. The 1929 election put a Labour government in office which in September of that year suspended the sliding bonus. But early in 1931 the government reversed its decision. Later when this government split over proposed cuts in public expenditure and a coalition government came to power the Civil Service bonus was reduced to its lowest level ever. The continuing split in the staff side, between consolidation and stabilization which seemed likely for a time to cause the final break up of the Whitley machinery, was only resolved when the government proposed consolidation which came into effect in 1934.(57)

From the trades unions' point of view the first twenty years from the setting up of the Whitley council were not successful. The unions did not establish any kind of real advantage over the Treasury, and the influence the unions were able to exert on major matters remained limited and often ineffectual. There were a number of reasons for this. First the architects of Whitley did not necessarily have a clear idea of what it was they actually wanted to create and probably had very little idea of how it would work in practice. There was no exemplar for them. Second it was an established fact that the two parties were not equal. The power of the Treasury was supreme while the unions were divided among themselves. In addition the unions and their leadership were relatively inexperienced, with some only establishing themselves after Whitley had come into existence (notably IPCS). But the unions' internecine feuding and jealousy as well as the personality clashes of their leaders seems to have seriously hampered any kind of prolonged unified approach to the Treasury by the staff side, and this held back the capacity for individual unions to become effectively involved in the internal affairs of their own organization.(58)

The available evidence suggests that in the early days of Whitleyism anything but negotiation and consultation went on.

Indeed anything approaching a general discussion at the national
council meetings was exceptional. Each side presented a single
case and in a large body of fifty people discussion was virtually
impossible. One participant in these early discussions recalled:
    Each side viewed the other with some distrust ... some meetings
    of the council were chilly gatherings of about fifty men and
    women brought from overworked desks, to sit, most of them mute
    and idle, while the more or less formal business was transacted;
    others were red hot rows.(59)
From its earliest days the work of the council on specific subjects
was delegated to committees and the council tended to act as a
rubber stamp for their reports. Those debates which occurred were
rather phoney and any real negotiation rarely took place.(60)
This ritualism and formalism continued until 1939 when most
observers agree that the official side changed its attitude to the
staff side.(61) In all probability this change was actually a
matter of administrative convenience as far as management was concerned. The formal atmosphere was certainly not particularly conducive to harmonious relations, and it was not a particularly
efficient system of consultation. Faced with the need for more
effective control over its employees during the war the official
side entered into negotiation with the staff side and joint emergency committees were formed which were given the power to reach
decisions as fast as the circumstances demanded. In these committees business became less formal and this tradition endured up
to the mid-1950s at least.(62)
    During the war and after, the Whitley system carried on its
business and on a number of minor matters undoubtedly provided
Civil Servants with a number of benefits. But individual unions
within the Whitley system have tended to become increasingly dis-
satisfied with the way Whitley operates and this is indicative
that Whitley and all the rest of the elaborate machinery actually
does not give unions access to the control of the internal affairs
of their organization.(63) In 1973 for example the CPSA passed
the following resolution at its annual conference: 'That this conference instructs the National Executive Council to review the
Whitley procedure with the view to obtaining an alternative negotiating system.'(64) The conference registered dissatisfaction
over the divisibility of the staff side. The speakers to the
motion felt that Whitley seriously curtailed the independence of
individual unions and that militant action was not possible
because the unions in the staff side have had to submerge their
differences in the interests of making Whitley work.(65) This
amounted to a forced consensus among the staff side and in part
accounted for the lack of any unified direct action for the period
since the setting up of the Whitley system and the early 1970s.
Indeed the system of consultation and negotiation embodied in
Whitley and expressed in its highly elaborate structure has functioned as a delaying mechanism (see below in relation to the
scientists' pay claim). This is not to argue that Whitley was
conceived of to do this, but rather to point out that the self-
proliferation of committees acted as an obstacle to the clear
pursuit of goals by the staff side. From the unions' point of view
the divisibility of the national staff side means that no strong

leadership emerges as the unions have attempted to maintain their
own spheres of influence. The factional jealousy and demarcation
disputes have often been more vigorously pursued than any attack
on the official side. There has consequently been a tendency for
the staff side to agree on the lowest common denominator policy
and unions wishing to pursue more militant goals have found this a
serious constraint.

Within the structure of Whitleyism itself there tends to be a
lack of democratic control, with the full-time staff working on
Whitley doing most of the negotiation and being only indirectly
answerable in practice to the annual conference. This has produced
a reaction among some rank and file members of Civil Service trades
unions. In CPSA, for example, a militant rank and file unofficial
group has operated with its own publication called 'Redder Tape'.
There is some evidence of and suspicion among membership of
oligarchic leadership developing in unions and still the suspicion
remains that it is a very simple matter for the Civil Service
Department to dictate policies to the staff side. Indeed even in
the 1970s the balance of power remained firmly in the hands of
the management, and the staff side were unable to pursue issues
either at the speed they wanted or to the conclusion they wanted.
From the management's point of view Whitleyism provided an added
form of control over their staffs through the oligarchic trade
union. Whitleyism is undoubtedly part of the 'establishment' and
hence it is hardly surprising that management encourages new
recruits to join their respective associations.

This review of the formal structure of the system of industrial
relations in the Civil Service and brief examination of its workings reveals a number of things pertinent to the discussion of this
chapter. First, there is no question that trades unions in the
Civil Service have established the right to participate in the
decision-making process in regard to the internal affairs of the
Civil Service. But second, there are numerous constraints which
prevent the trades unions being anything like equal partners in the
organization. The main issues with which trades unions have been
concerned have been economic, but a highly bureaucratic super-
structure has confounded their efforts. However, the trades unions
have not been completely impotent and ineffective, and they have
managed at various times to struggle free of the bureaucratic
straight-jacket of Whitleyism. It is to this that I turn in the
following section.

INDUSTRIAL ACTION IN THE CIVIL SERVICE

In this section I will trace the history of recent disputes in the
Civil Service and the way Civil Service trades unions have resorted
to traditional forms of trade union militancy and try to determine
to what extent if any these militant actions can be explained with
reference to the thesis of proletarianization or the key factors
of money, feminization, bureaucratization, automation or social
demographic composition which are purported to be associated with
proletarianization.

The pay pause: the threat of a work to rule, 1961-2

In 1957 two well-respected students of public administration wrote:
there has never been any official strike of Civil Servants
organized by one of the recognized staff associations. It is
difficult to imagine circumstances in which it would be good
tactics to attempt to further a claim in this way.(66)
This statement seems quite well representative of official side
(and probably some senior staff side) thinking in the post-World
War Two era. The first serious challenge to the ethic of harmony
and understanding occurred in 1961. At that time the Conservative
government was attempting to control incomes and prices, and the
Chancellor of the Exchequer, Selwyn Lloyd, initiated a pay pause
in the Civil Service. In this instance the government did not
consult the staff side on the Whitley council and thus contravened
the 'spirit' of consultation which Whitley supposedly epitomized.(67) The unions responded by calling the national staff
side together to show united opposition to the pause,(68) and it
was decided to lobby MPs and call local protest meetings.(69)
Civil Service union leaders expressed disquiet because although
the Chancellor's pause was supposed to apply to all wages it was
only those sectors like the Civil Service who could not, or in
their case would not, strike or even threaten to strike that the
pause was in any way effective. This was demonstrated when in
turn haulage workers and later electrical workers threatened to
strike and were then awarded a pay rise.(70) At this point some
of the trades unions decided to back up their campaign with a form
of direct action, and thus a ban on overtime and a work-to-rule by
Civil Service clerks were proposed, and called for January 1962.(71)
At the same time the staff side put in a central pay claim for 5½
per cent on the basis of a 5.5 points movement in the outside wages
index.(72) On 1 January 1962 the Union of Post Office Workers
began a work-to-rule, and the Civil Service Clerical Association
planned to begin theirs on 17 January. But on 16 January the chief
secretary of the Treasury informed the staff side that he hoped the
pay pause would end on 31 March and that the salary awards for the
previous year would then become operable.(73) The CSCA promptly
called off its campaign. Following further negotiations the
official side offered a 2 per cent increase which the clerks rejected and the claim then went to arbitration; this awarded 4 per
cent from 1 April 1962.(74)
    In this instance the union of the clerks had not actually
resorted to direct action but had merely threatened it. But nevertheless this in itself marks a turning point because the government
only made any kind of promise at the eleventh hour and were not
presumably prepared to call the clerks' bluff. The primary factor
in this dispute was money, this was the casus belli. Yet several
other factors were also significant. First, the group of workers
who proposed to use direct action were the most highly feminized
in the Service.(75) Although in no way could this be regarded as
a causal factor in the dispute (unless the Treasury thought that
such a group as clerks should only receive low pay and were a
non-priority group who could be squeezed in a pay pause because the
majority of them were women), it is significant in the context of

the broader issue of white-collar militancy. As I have already
noted, sociologists have traditionally argued that a high level of
feminization blunts militant behaviour.(76)   This and subsequent
action by Civil Service clerks certainly calls the sociological
assertion into question.   Second, the clerks who were threatening
to use direct action were the most socially proletarian of all
Civil Servants (77) in that the clerical grades contain the highest
number of individuals (both absolutely and relatively) whose
origins are in the working class.   Again we cannot identify any
causal relationship but as with feminization it may have been an
important conditioning factor which gave the Union's executive
committee the confidence to threaten the Treasury with direct
action knowing they had grass roots support.

    Following the threat of direct industrial action a motion was
put at the next annual conference of the CSCA to adopt a fully-
fledged strike policy: this was however lost.(78)   In the following year a similar motion was also defeated.(79)   But by 1968 the
mood of the membership was more militant as the prices and incomes
policy of the Labour government began to squeeze the public sector,
and at conference that year there were numerous demands for the
adoption of a strike policy.(80)   A motion was adopted which
stated that in certain instances CSCA would back up its claims
with a withdrawal of labour, and a motion calling for the adoption of a strike policy was overwhelmingly carried.(81)   The arguments that the protagonists used in favour of a strike policy were
pragmatic and instrumental and indicate strong economic concerns.
Thus it was argued that a trade union with a strike policy was in
a much more powerful bargaining position, and that specifically in
the case of public employees, the increase in government interference in negotiating procedures with pay pauses, freezes, prices and
incomes policies was an interference in free collective bargaining
and accordingly highly unsatisfactory for a union that could not
fight back.(82)   Thus a document was drawn up which set out the
CSCA's policy.   This was circulated to all branches and at the
1969 conference the document was adopted as policy.   At the same
time the CSCA registered its disapproval of the government's prices
and incomes policy and the government's proposed reform of industrial relations.(83)

    In the same year the Society of Civil Servants began to discuss
the question of industrial militancy and at their 1969 conference
they agreed not to nullify any action taken by the Civil and
Public Services Association if the latter ever used selective
strike action.(84)   In the following year their annual conference
endorsed by a narrow majority a resolution to use militant action
including strike action and the setting up of a fighting fund.(85)
Not all of the membership of the Society of Civil Servants were
behind this move and the Society received a number of abusive
letters and there were a small number of resignations.(86)   However
both unions were ready to launch a campaign of industrial action
and back up their claims that way by 1970.   The spark came eventually in the Post Office.

The Post Office dispute: strike action by Civil Servants becomes a reality, 1970

On 1 October 1969 the Post Office became a public corporation and was thus technically no longer part of the Civil Service, nor were its employees Civil Servants. However the Civil Service unions which had represented workers in the general classes in the Civil Service and Post Office, like the CSCA and SCS, continued to represent their members in the new public corporation. In October 1968 the Posts and Telecommunications group of the CSCA had prepared a claim for Post Office clerks and a formal claim was lodged with the Post Office on 11 September 1969.(87) The Posts and Telecommunications group threatened industrial action late in 1969 to try and force the new Post Office Corporation to name 1 January 1970 as the operative date for any settlement that might be agreed.(88) In the absence of any offer from the Post Office a one-day stoppage was organized for 19 January 1970. A Civil Service union thus took the step of organizing a strike, albeit in a body which had just been hived off from the Civil Service. The strike was well supported by Post Office clerks.(89) The one-day stoppage was followed by a series of guerrilla strikes in the third week in February with five telephone managers offices and London telecommunications region branches taking part and with about three hundred union members involved. On 4 February the first offer from management was received and rejected by the union, and then in the last week of February six new branches took the place of the original five and 573 members of CSCA went on strike. A second offer of management was received and again rejected. On 12 February half day strikes commenced and walk-outs were organized where higher grade staff had been assigned to clerical duties.(90)
    At this point the Post Office instructed local management to take a stronger line and to withdraw privileges and facilities. Some strike breaking was organized and management withdrew all pay offers. When twenty-four CSCA members were sent home by management, 10,500 CSCA members in twenty different branches walked out in protest. In the fourth week of industrial action there were one-week strikes in three computer centres which involved 620 CSCA members in Derby, London and Leeds, as well as telephone managers offices in Bradford, Coventry, Edinburgh and Leeds being on strike. When on 25 February 2,000 CSCA members in Manchester staged a mass walk-out and demonstration the general secretary of the TUC was called in to mediate.(91)
    This industrial action by clerks in the Post Office marks a turning point in the history of unionism in the Civil Service. It is significant for several reasons; first, that the first ever strike by Civil Servants should occur in the Post Office is not pure chance. The Post Office has always been the leading sector in relation to industrial militancy in the Service. Indeed the earliest associations were found in the Post Office. This early development and leading role may in part be due to the fact that the manual grades that exist in the Post Office have usually behaved more like manual workers than clerical workers. This in its turn may have encouraged the clerks in the Post Office to

follow suit. Second, because technically the Post Office was no
longer part of the Civil Service perhaps Post Office clerks felt
that they could break with the tradition of passive unionism found
in the Civil Service. However, whatever the factors were which
created conditions favourable for the clerks to take strike action,
the fact remains that they went ahead and did it. The prima facie
reason appears to have been economic, but a number of other significant facts emerge from an observation of the strike. The major
motive was economic; however support was strongest for the strike
in the postal clerical grades which were both highly feminized and
highly bureaucratized. Of equal significance is the fact that
computer workers were involved and thus automation and mechanization seem to have also played a significant part. Further, it is
noteworthy that the guerrilla action took place in areas of traditional working-class militancy so we may assume (because of local
recruitment) that social proletarianization may have also been
significant.
     Thus in the case of clerks in the Post Office and their first
ever strike we are presented with a case where proletarianization
was apparently important, especially where it created the conditions favourable to militant action. First there was a perceived
fall in income of clerks relative to other workers. This group
were working in large-scale bureaucratically organized automated
work situations, in areas of traditional working-class militancy,
and had been largely recruited from working-class families. It is
impossible to locate cause and effect but here indeed the factors
isolated in chapter 2 appear to be significant. Of equal significance as far as future trends in industrial behaviour in the Civil
Service were concerned was the fact that a white-collar Civil
Service union had passed the motivational edge of militant industrial behaviour and it was now probably only a matter of time
before it would flex its industrial muscle in the Civil Service
proper. This it did three years later.

The desk workers' strike: Civil Servants adopt strike action to
further their claims, 1973

Under the established procedure, by 1 January 1973 most non-
industrial Civil Servants were due for a pay research settlement.
In fact their pay had not been revised by the pay research procedure since 1 January 1970 for some and 1 January 1971 for the majority and the movement in outside pay, particularly during 1972,
pointed to the likelihood of substantial 'catching up' increases.(92)
However these increases were not to be paid until the Conservative
government's pay freeze was over. The CPSA arranged a series of
mass meetings to protest against this.(93) In addition the less
militant union of the middle managers (SCS) organized a series of
local protest meetings and launched a campaign to educate the
public about Civil Service grievances.(94) On 8 January Civil
Service union leaders met the Prime Minister and since the unions
felt that nothing very positive emerged from this and other meetings, on 10 January CPSA and SCS members (clerks and middle management) staged walkouts, and rallies and protest meetings were

organized over the country.(95)   The government remained adamant
and three unions, CPSA, SCS, and the Customs and Excise group
decided on direct action with a national one-day strike on 27
February 1973.   Members of these unions who were not strictly
speaking Civil Servants, for example those working in the Post
Office and British Airports Authority, were called out as well.(96)
The programme of direct action consisted of an overtime ban, withdrawal of co-operation, and a strike.(97)   In this instance, then,
Civil Service union leaders were urging their members to adopt
traditional trade union tactics to back up a claim.   The extent to
which the membership actually followed the union's instructions is
more difficult to assess.   The union estimated that 75 per cent of
the membership took part in the strike,(98) but estimates by the
management were much lower and indeed Civil Servants at the Department of Education and Science voted by a two to one majority not
to strike.(99)   In Whitehall only about half the clerical and managerial staff joined the strike.   In the Customs and Excise it was
estimated by management that about 57 per cent of the department's
staff of 23,000 joined the strike.   What is apparent is that there
were large regional variations in support of the strike and that
support was strongest in the industrial regions away from London.
In Barnsley for example the strike was almost totally effective as
the town's three hundred Civil Servants closed down both of the
town's DHSS offices.   A group of about sixty people picketed the
Department of Employment although the Employment Exchange was kept
open by a skeleton staff.   In Bradford all DHSS offices were
closed.(100)   Following the one-day strike the industrial action
continued with selective strikes over the country.   On 8 March 1973
selective action began at the Customs and Excise at Southend and
on the VAT computer.   On 12 March 1973 selective action commenced
in Customs and Excise, the Department of Agriculture, National
Savings, Departments of Employment, Environment, Health and Social
Security, the Ministry of Defence and the Stationery Office.(101)
A sporadic campaign of protests lasted into April.   Settlement was
finally reached in November 1973 when the anomalies settlement
averted the worst effects of the government's phase two pay restraint and ended any further industrial action in the Service.(102)
   This direct action is extremely significant, because for the
first time Civil Servants had been on an official strike.   The
immediate impetus was money and particularly the relative decline
in clerical and middle management salaries as the government held
down wages and salaries in the public sector.   But also a number of
background factors are significant.   The then government had been
constantly in a state of open conflict with the trade union movement throughout its period in office, and a number of strikes by
key groups such as miners and power workers as well as the government's attempt to enforce legally a code of industrial relations
had made the period 1970-3 one of the most stormy in recent British
industrial relations history.   A pervasive sense of militancy perme-
ated the trades unions and similarly must have influenced the Civil
Service.
   Against this background of disorder measured in terms of a number of spectacular strikes by groups of manual workers, a number
of specific factors were at work in the Civil Service.   This becomes

clear when we examine those Civil Servants who actually supported
the direct action. First, support seems to have been strongest in
the lowest grades, in the largest most bureaucratic departments,
among workers dealing with machines, and in areas away from the
metropolitan South of England. The clerks among whom support was
strongest were the lowest paid group of Civil Servants who perceived that they were about to bear the brunt of a Conservative
government's penal income policy. Thus as predicted by various
theorists some form of proletarianization seems to have occurred
in these grades in the Civil Service at that time, in the sense
that a group of white-collar workers were resorting to traditional
manual workers' forms of protest to back up their claims.

The scientists' dispute: professionalism reaffirmed

In the early 1970s a systematic attempt was made by management to
apply the principles of scientific management to governmental
research. This took the form of the establishment of the so-called
customer-contractor principle. The idea underlying customer-
contractor is very simple. It is based on the premise that
research must be channelled in a specific direction in order that
certain well-defined needs be met. The customer, in this case the
government, sets down what it wants in the way of scientific or
other specialized commodities, and this is supplied by the contractor, namely Civil Service scientists or other specialists. The
idea was promulgated by Lord Rothschild when he was head of the
government's 'Think Tank'. The main argument in favour of customer-
contractor was that highly expensive applied research ought to have
defined practical application, and that scientific development
ought not be left to a form of scientific Russian roulette.(103)
This apparent infringement of scientists' professional autonomy
caused outrage among some scientists.(104)
    With this background of apparent removal of scientists' autonomy
a pay dispute arose in the Civil Service science grades. Early in
1970 the national staff side of the Whitley council submitted a
central pay claim which aimed at putting the Civil Service on a
par with outside movements in pay.(105) The agreement which was
reached went back beyond the 1969 pay settlement and took account
of movement in wages and salaries from 1968.(106) The IPCS was
highly critical of this settlement because it did not take account
of scientists' special grievances on pay, and at their 1970 conference they debated the possibility of using militant action to
further their aims.(107) In the following year the issue of pay
was again to the forefront and negotiations between the national
staff side and management broke down over the central pay claim.
Management offered 8 per cent while the staff side pointed out
that wage rates had increased 13.2 per cent at least in the preceding twelve months.(108) The staff side argued that the offer
was unacceptable and management thereupon offered 9 per cent which
was accepted by the staff side. IPCS however did so only grudg-
ingly because some of their members even with a 9½ per cent
increase were still a long way behind outside comparisons.(109)
Accordingly in May 1971 IPCS decided on unilateral action and began

negotiations with the Civil Service Department (CSD) on pay for
scientists, basing their claim for special treatment on the fact
that some scientists had not had the pay research procedure for
ten years.(110) However the CSD and the IPCS could not agree on
the interpretation of the pay research report. Scientists began
therefore to organize a protest campaign beginning with a mass
meeting in London in August 1971.(111) Negotiations broke down
when the government refused to improve an offer which gave approximately half of government scientists no increase. IPCS argued
that refusal to offer 'fair' salaries to scientists was a deliberate
attack on all scientists in Britain and not just those in the Civil
Service, since the Civil Service employed a majority of all scientists in Britain; thus by keeping this sector's salaries low, so
all others would be artificially depressed.(112) The claim went
to arbitration which awarded 5 per cent to those grades who got
nothing in the previous offer.(113) IPCS said that this offer was
unsatisfactory because it failed to take account of the main issue
which was now described by IPCS as the failure to base the award on
internal relativities in the Civil Service (i.e. it did not compare
scientists with administrators but rather compared government
scientists with non-government scientists - the latter were low
paid anyway). A joint committee was set up to examine the differences in principle but no agreement was reached as to the criteria
which ought to be used in determining the pay of government scientists.(114) IPCS then proposed the setting up of an independent
tribunal to consider the evidence, but the government remained
intransigent,(115) and IPCS therefore declared that they would not
accept any refusal to appoint an independent committee and that
'if negotiations fail we will have no hesitation in launching a
major campaign'.(116) At the same time 'catching up' increases
due to Civil Servants which had already been agreed were not forthcoming because of the government's freeze. So the Civil Servants
demanded that at the end of the freeze the increases should be
paid in full and that if these increases were not forthcoming
militant action would be the result. The timing of this was significant as far as scientists were concerned because this was the
very month when clerks had struck for more pay. The question of
scientists' pay was then referred to the Pay Board and although
the terms of reference were agreed the report was slow to arrive.
The IPCS put into the Pay Board for an interim increase and the
national executive committee gave official support to demonstra-
tions by members in support of the interim claim.(117) The membership seems to have wholeheartedly supported the protest although
the national executive committee of the union left the decision as
to the sort of action to be taken by the scientists to the scientists. At scientific establishments all over the United Kingdom
half-day strikes or mass walk-outs were organized. These with-
drawals were generally preceded by mass meetings at which resolutions were adopted calling upon local management to recognize the
problems of scientists. At the same time some groups adopted a
policy of non-co-operation including refusals to work on Saturdays
and overtime bans. IPCS decided that this helped their case and
when the Pay Board promised to speed up its report the policy of
non-co-operation was suspended on 8 February. However the report

still did not appear and as the Pay Board continued to deliberate,
although it looked to the union like prevarication, there was a
half-day strike by scientists.(118)   In April the Pay Board's
report was published and negotiations began again, but not until a
year later, in April 1975, did negotiations for the whole of the
Civil Service arrange an increase of 26 per cent for *all* Civil
Servants including scientists.

In the case of the scientists the main issue was pay, and particularly the relationship of their pay to scientists outside the
Service and managers within the Service.   It is significant that
the scientists should have adopted a policy of 'going it alone'
when the other unions were acting in a united way.   This is perhaps
indicative of the scientists' self-image as professionals rather
than trade unionists.   This attitude is especially marked because
it was not pay alone which was the significant issue.   Throughout
the period under discussion the Rothschild customer-contractor
proposals were being implemented.   Scientists perceived this to be
an erosion of their professional liberty and probably responded
accordingly.   A good case can actually be made that nothing in
fact changed after Rothschild, because customer-contractor had
always been in operation in government science anyway.   The
Rothschild proposals were merely a bureaucratic recognition of the
status quo.   This perceived attack on the professionalism of the
scientists may be the reason they then acted unilaterally in
relation to their outstanding pay claim, although eventually they
too resorted to strike action.   The structure of IPCS is also
significant here because it represents all grades of scientists
from laboratory technicians to the technocratic elite.

A number of authors have posited that in modern industrial
society, scientists will be the most highly militant group of the
white-collar workforce.(119)   Such militancy is brought about
allegedly by virtue of the 'contradictions' inherent in their work
situation.(120)   Yet the case of the British government scientists
belies this - indeed the scientists appear to be the least militant group in the Service excepting only the top administrators.
This is indicated by IPCS clinging to its autonomy, seeking professional rather than trade union goals, specifically in its
reluctance to join with other Civil Servants and strike for more
pay.

The 1979 dispute

The next major industrial action in the Civil Service took place
in 1979.   This dispute involved a lengthy strike by a number of
Civil Servants, and involved grades of Civil Servants who had not
previously taken strike action.   The 1979 dispute was therefore
markedly more militant than any previous dispute and provides an
interesting test of the concept of proletarianization.   The strike
action had its roots in the pay settlement of 1974 when after a
year of almost continuous negotiations the procedure of fair comparison of Civil Service salaries with outside occupations was
updated to take account of inflation.   The important changes introduced in the procedure were the provision for annual pay research

settlements and an inflation adjustment to outside pay rates in
line with the Retail Price Index. After these new arrangements were
introduced there was only one settlement and set of negotiations
under the new procedure and that was in 1975. Four months after
the 1975 settlement the agreement was suspended by the government
and even though CPSA organized a week of protest against the suspension the government announced that the pay research procedure
would not be reintroduced until 1979.(121)

In 1977 the CPSA voiced doubts about the government's willingness to reintroduce pay research at all and if it did whether it
would allow pay research to function properly.(122) Both CPSA and
SCPS protested at the government's policy of suspension of pay
research but since in 1977 and 1978 the government's pay policy
seemed to be holding, both unions saved their main attack for 1979
when the pay research procedure was due to be reinstated. In
October 1978 the Civil Service unions began to draw up contingency
plans for industrial action, because they estimated that the
government would not honour its agreement and reintroduce pay
research.(123) In November the Whitley council staff side approved
of a £1 million fighting fund to support possible selective strike
action and CPSA and SCPS drew up joint plans for selective disrup-
tive strikes.(124) This was resolved after the Prime Minister had
insisted that the 5 per cent pay guideline of his government's pay
policy would apply in the public sector in spite of anything
recommended by the pay research unit in excess of 5 per cent.(125)
In the last week of November and the first week of December the
SCPS consulted its members on the proposed strike action and a
large majority of members favoured the plans.(126)

On 11 December 1978 the Minister of State for the Civil Service
department, Mr Charles Morris, refused in a House of Commons
debate to give an undertaking that the government would implement
the full pay increases recommended by pay research.(127) At this
SCPS and CPSA strengthened their determination to fight for the
full implementation of pay research and not just 5 per cent.(128)
In preparation SCPS drew up plans for an additional strike levy of
£1 per week per member to pay for what now seemed inevitable
industrial action.(129) At the end of January CPSA announced that
its members had voted in favour of action over pay and that plans
were in hand for a joint one-day stoppage in February, followed by
further selective strike action. The selective strike targets were
chosen to cause as much inconvenience to the government and as
little harm to the public as possible.(130) The unions were
further angered when circulars appeared in government offices
threatening with disciplinary action any Civil Servant who manned
a picket line. The unions advised their members that such threats
were illegal.(131) Both CPSA and SCPS were by now making it quite
clear that their intention was to confront the government although
the unions regarded it primarily as the government's fault that
such a situation had arisen.(132)

On 6 February a meeting took place in London between Lord Peart
the Lord Privy Seal, and the Civil Service unions making up the
Whitley council staff side. SCPS and CPSA pushed for a 30 per
cent settlement based on the pay research findings, but the government regarded this as excessive.(133) At another meeting on 16

February the government offered to implement the pay research
settlement in stages but because the exact nature of these stages
was not specified, SCPS and CPSA decided that the offer was too
vague and therefore resolved to go ahead with their one-day strike
on 23 February followed by selective strike action.(134)

On the day before the strike the Prime Minister attacked the
Civil Service unions in a speech in the House of Commons. He
claimed that the Civil Service unions were breaking their agreement by striking while negotiations were still taking place.(135)
The unions replied that it was not they who were in breach of
agreement but the government, because the impending strike was not
solely about the pay claim but rather about whether existing agreements which defined the principle of fair comparison would be
honoured by the government.(136)   Indeed the unions later claimed
that the Prime Minister's remarks provoked some still uncommitted
Civil Servants to join the strike.(137)

On 23 February the unions claimed 90 per cent support for their
strike although the official side estimated only 50 per cent
support. The strike was followed by supportive and selective
action. The supportive action was that all union members would
refuse to work overtime, to use their private cars for official
business, to do the work of other grades and to travel on official
business in their own time. The selective action consisted of
selective strikes which began on 26 February in a number of different locations. The ones chosen were: the Department of Trade
offices in Companies House and Export House in London and Cardiff;
the Ministry of Defence at Chorley, Liverpool, Glascoed and
Bishopton; the Department of National Savings at Lytham; the
Ministry of Agriculture at Guildford; the Court of Sessions in
Edinburgh; the Sheriffs' Courts in Scotland; the Scottish office
in Edinburgh; the Customs and Excise in Southend; the Department
of the Environment at Hastings; the Foreign Office in London; the
Government Communications Headquarters in Cheltenham; the Royal
Mint; the Land Registry in Plymouth; the Inland Revenue Stampers;
and the Paymaster-General's Office in Crawley.(138)

These sites are interesting because a number of them are computer installations; for example at Lytham, Guildford, Southend,
Liverpool, Hastings and the Scottish office. In these locations
relatively few officials could be withdrawn and this would cause
maximum disruption. It is also notable that most of the locations
chosen were in areas with no history of trade union militancy;
for example Guildford, Hastings and Cheltenham.

After the selective actions began the unions announced that
they had enough resources to strike for at least three months.(139)
In certain areas the effects of the selective action were dramatic.
On 13 March the government had to introduce emergency legislation
to overcome the backlog of court cases in Scotland where the
judicial system was in chaos with the postponement of fifteen
High Court cases and 5000 summary cases.(140) The unions got no
further assurances from the government or the Civil Service department and when the Lord Privy Seal refused to meet the unions to
discuss the situation the unions decided to escalate their action.
Members were called out on selective strike at the Ministry of
Defence in Carlisle and Stafford, at the Department of Industry

Computer in Cardiff, at the Exports Credits Guarantee department
in Manchester and Cardiff, at the Department of Education in
Darlington, and in the Scottish office the strike was extended.
This action was backed up by lightning strikes by Customs men in
Newhaven, Dover, Holyhead and London.(141)
     The situation was exacerbated by threats of suspension. Since
the beginning of the dispute the official side had been making
threats of suspension without pay to Civil Servants. Indeed on 23
February the Civil Service Department wrote to SCPS to tell them
that the departments had the discretion to refuse to pay staff who
were not on strike but were refusing to carry out all the duties
normally expected of them.(142) This was aimed at the supportive
action being taken by the unions. The Scottish office was particularly persistent in its threats of suspension. Management in
the Scottish office eventually issued the following statement:
     Staff will not be required to undertake duties which are beyond
     their competence or inappropriate to the terms on which they
     were recruited or to the grades in which they are now serving....
     it has been made clear to all staff that refusal to undertake
     duties simply on the grounds that the work concerned is normally
     processed by computer or machine will be treated as a serious
     breach of their terms of service ... staff who refuse to under-
     take work required of them will be sent home without pay and
     not allowed to return until they are prepared to perform these
     duties required of them.... It can be confirmed that thirty-
     nine warning notices to staff on an individual basis have been
     sent out today.(143)
The unions instructed their members threatened with suspension to
report normally for work, while all other members in Scotland were
instructed not to report for work. The thirty-nine threatened with
suspension reported normally but were sent home for refusing to do
the work of other striking Civil Servants. Thirty thousand members in Scotland struck in sympathy. In the United Kingdom as a
whole about 200,000 Civil Servants came out on sympathy strike for
one day.(144) The Scottish office continued its policy and issued
another fourteen suspension notices to Scottish office staff. The
unions now saw the dispute as being concerned with two issues;
first, the need for government assurances on the full reinstate-
ment of the pay research procedure and second, what the unions
regarded as a lock-out of their members in the Scottish office.
     On 26 March the government made another offer to the unions of
a 7 per cent increase with effect from 1 April 1979, with the
balance due from the pay research findings payable on 1 April 1980.
This offer was put to the national staff side who rejected it.(145)
Four Civil Service unions then agreed to support a proposal for an
all-out strike on 2 April: these were CPSA, SCPS, IPCS and the
Inland Revenue Staff Federation. Even the First Division Association in an unprecedented move urged top management in the Civil
Service to support the strike.(146) In response to this the
government came up with a new pay offer of 9 per cent immediately
and further increases of up to 20 per cent or more by the same
time next year. CPSA and SCPS rejected this new offer, but nego-
tiators for the other Civil Service unions recommended the new
offer to their members and then tried to stop their members taking

part in the strike of 2 April.(147) Meanwhile CPSA and SCPS
planned to escalate their action to the County Courts and Crown
Courts in England, the Department of the Environment at Newcastle,
various driving test centres, further computer centres in the
Ministry of Defence, the National Savings Bank in Glasgow, air
traffic control assistants, customs officials and immigration
officials.(148)

On Monday 2 April the unions put on a major show of strength
with a one-day strike involving Civil Servants in practically all
government departments. The support varied across the regions but
the unions calculated on average about 90 per cent support throughout the country with support as high as 99 per cent in some places.
There were many meetings of striking Civil Servants and the
government's offer was rejected.(149) The Civil Service Department
estimated that almost 250,000 Civil Servants took part, but union
sources put the figure at about 300,000.(150) There were angry
exchanges among the national staff side as only two unions (SCPS
and CPSA) had gone ahead with the strike, but the resolve of all
the unions on the national staff side was hardened when on 3
April the government restated that it had made its final offer.(151)
One by one all the unions on the national staff side rejected the
offer and each union resolved to press for more than 9 per cent.(152)

Finally on Wednesday 11 April the unions and the official side
agreed an offer which gave 9 per cent immediately (plus £1 for the
lower grades), 5 per cent in August 1979 and a further increase on
1 January 1980. The unions rationalized the acceptance of this
offer by arguing that since the government was now totally immersed
in a general election campaign it was extremely unlikely that any
better offer would be forthcoming, even though the question of pay
research for future years was unresolved. The unions' executives
therefore recommended the settlement to their members.(153)

Some members were reluctant to accept their unions' recommendations. Opposition to the settlement was particularly marked in
Scotland where Civil Servants believed that they had borne the
brunt of the industrial action. A campaign was mounted in Scotland to reject the offer. The situation was eased somewhat when
the Scottish office revoked the suspensions.(154) SCPS consulted
all its branches in the United Kingdom about the proposed offer in
the week 23-8 April, holding 98 meetings. SCPS voted 25,755 for
acceptance and 7,522 against while CPSA voted 103,506 for and
29,543 against. After agreement was reached between the unions and
the Civil Service department that victimization of strikers would
not take place normal working resumed in the Civil Service on 2
May 1979.(155)

This dispute provides a very interesting case study for the
theories of proletarianization because the grades in the forefront
of the dispute (clerical and middle management) are those who have
been subject to many of the changes which this study has highlighted as being associated with proletarianization. These grades
have been subject to relative loss of income, demographic changes
in terms of social class of origin and education and have been the
grades most affected by computerization and mechanization. Since
the 1979 dispute was more militant than anything before in the
Civil Service, it would seem plausible to suggest proletarianization as a cause.

However a closer examination of the dispute reveals that to explain it with reference to proletarianization would be naive. The underlying cause of the strike was not a straightforward pay claim; instead the actions of the unions were aimed at protecting existing procedures for determining Civil Service salaries. The unions launched a highly sophisticated campaign to protect these procedures which was designed to cause the government much inconvenience and embarrassment. The memberships of CPSA and SPCS were highly organized at national level. The plans for the action were laid many months in advance of the dispute. What seems likely is that government and management harassment of some non-striking members, particularly in the Scottish office, did serve to galvanize the unions' rank and file, and indeed by the end of the dispute the rank and file in Scotland were thoroughly disenchanted with the national leadership. Thus in the early stages of the dispute it was not rank and file militancy which was important, but national leadership policies aimed at protecting middle-class living standards. The computer centres were chosen for this action, not because computer staff are more militant as predicted by the proletarianization literature, but because the computers are easily stopped by the withdrawal of a very few Civil Servants. It would be implausible to explain this strike therefore as a class-conscious political action.

The major impetus to the dispute was government insistence on maintaining a 5 per cent pay limit in the face of the established pay research procedure which had recommended more than 5 per cent. The government's reluctance to break its own 5 per cent pay guideline precipitated the dispute, not nascent class militancy of Civil Servants working in clerical factory situations. Later in the dispute militancy was kindled by other government action, but militancy was not itself the cause of the dispute.

Summary

It is significant that all three unions considered here have turned to forms of direct action in contrast to their policies of earlier years and in contrast to the ethic of harmony allegedly epitomized by Whitley. I have traced the various significant reasons for this. In the case of the clerks the main causal factor underlying this change of policy has been a real and perceived decline in salaries, although other factors seem to have created conditions favourable for militancy, namely large-scale feminization, geographical dispersion, rationalization and bureaucratization, automation and the recruitment of the sons and daughters of manual workers. The result for the clerical workers' union has been to pursue a form of instrumental-pragmatic unionism whose main goals were financial. Most importantly central government policy in relation to public service wages and salaries has led the clerks to use strike action. Also, since Civil Service industrial relations do not operate in a vacuum we may assume that outside developments may have affected the Civil Service unions. An examination of the industrial behaviour of the middle managers shows similar tendencies. The case of the scientists is very different to the clerks.

The scientists have been relatively slow to move to any form of
recognizable trade unionism and seem to have been reluctant to
forego their professional respectability. This is in spite of the
fact that to varying degrees the scientists have been subject to
many of the similar tendencies that have impinged on clerks, i.e.
decreasing real income, bureaucratization, mechanization, non-elite
recruitment, and feminization. The case of the scientists does
seem critical because, in the British Civil Service at least, the
scientists do not exhibit the militancy that writers such as
Touraine would expect.(156)

THE RELATIONSHIP BETWEEN CIVIL SERVICE UNIONS, THE TUC AND THE
LABOUR PARTY

In this section I will examine the extent to which the unions have
become involved in party political affairs. In fact many of the
developments in this field occurred concurrently with events
already discussed, but I treat the issues separately for analytic
convenience and because the political developments were quite
often independent of the instrumental developments.
     Throughout the First World War the Assistant Clerks Association
(later the CSCA) pursued a vigorous policy for recognition and
resolved at their annual general meeting in 1915 to affiliate both
to the TUC and the Labour party. A majority of members were in
favour of this step and in 1917 the ACA registered as a trade
union and in the following year affiliated to the Labour party.(157)
in 1920 the association decided to inaugurate a levy which could
be used as contributions to strike funds of any workers whom the
association decided to support and that same year the ACA granted
money from its political fund to support the 'Daily Herald'.(158)
     It seems likely that the ACA and later the CSCA would have con-
tinued their association with the political and industrial wings
of the Labour movement, and likewise a number of the smaller low
grade unions. However, this link was broken following the General
Strike in 1926 and marks a most significant development in the
relationships between Civil Service unions and outside party political organizations.(159)
     A number of Civil Service unions had affiliated to the TUC by
1926 and consequently held seats on the general council of that
body, and it was the general council of the TUC which in 1926
decided to support the miners against the coal owners. A court
of enquiry had already examined the coal industry and its problems
and this reported in 1925 in favour of the miners; the government
decided on a coal subsidy. But in the following year during negotiations between the government and the miners, printers in the
'Daily Mail' quite independently refused to print an issue unless
a certain provocative leading article was removed. There were a
majority of ministers within the Conservative Cabinet who thought
it intolerable for the government to have to negotiate under the
threat of a general strike, and it seems likely that they had been
seeking a casus belli. The 'Daily Mail' incident provided it.
Baldwin, the Prime Minister, broke off negotiations with the miners
and it was only a short time before a strike began in the mines

and certain other industries. Civil Service unionists, although
they had no particular axe to grind with the government or the
coal owners at that time, because they sat on the general council
of the TUC were party to the decision to call a strike. No Civil
Service union actually went on strike but the penal legislation
which followed the strike effectively stifled the development of
links between Civil Service unionism and the Labour movement. The
government's punitive action stemmed in part from a directive
issued by the national staff side which seemed to the Tory ministers to be deliberately antagonistic. The national staff side
instructed members of the staff side:
> That advice be given to all civil servants not to volunteer to
> perform during the crisis any work other than their own normal
> duties and to report to the headquarters of their organization
> (through the local branches) any attempt to cause them to per-
> form any work outside the normal duties of their class or
> grade. Pending a further communication, however, all civil
> servants should obey the orders of the competent authorities
> making protests in the proper form if such orders conflict with
> the principles stated above.(160)

Whether this was just sabre-rattling by the staff side is difficult
to tell. However clause V of the Trades Disputes Act 1927 was a
deliberate attack on Civil Service unions. It stated:
> Amongst the regulations as to the conditions of service in His
> Majesty's Civil Establishments there shall be included regula-
> tion prohibiting established civil servants from being members,
> delegates or representatives of any organization of which the
> primary object is to influence or affect the remuneration and
> conditions of employment of its members, unless the organiza-
> tion is an organization of which the membership is confined to
> persons employed by or under the Crown and is an organization
> which complies with such provisions as may be contained in the
> regulations for securing that it is in all respects indepen-
> dent and not affiliated to any such organization as aforesaid,
> the membership of which is not confined to persons employed by
> or under the Crown, or any federation comprising such organiza-
> tions, that its objects do not include political objects and
> that it is not associated directly or indirectly with any
> political party or organization.(161)

The penalty for disobedience was to be dismissal from the Service.
The staff associations promptly withdrew from the TUC. The
national staff side was in disarray because the Association of
the First Division (representing higher management) and two other
higher grade organizations split from the staff side. The leader
of the staff side, George Middleton, was replaced by William
Llewellyn. In the new reconstituted staff side IPCS held the
balance of votes between the Post Office and clerks. The divisions
thus established, it is not surprising that the staff side produced such a lacklustre performance over the next thirteen years.
The government were able to act with impunity in regard to the
Civil Service unions because the unions were now deeply divided
among themselves. The punitive legislation of Baldwin's government remained in force until 1946 when the Labour government
repealed the Trades Disputes Act, and therefore since 1946 it has

once more been possible for Civil Service unions to affiliate to the TUC.

For the CSCA there has been a determined effort to distinguish since that time between affiliation to the TUC and affiliation to the Labour party. In 1949 it decided not to reaffiliate to the Labour party but did reaffiliate to the TUC.(162) This it did on its own terms with a clearly defined non-party political role. Thus the CSCA and subsequently the CPSA does not take part in or vote on narrowly defined party political issues. The executive have consistently taken the line to the membership that it is a 'complete fallacy' (sic) to see any connection between the TUC and the Labour party and instead extols the instrumental and pragmatic virtues of a strong trade union movement.(163) Only dissident rank and file members who support the Tory party have publicly equated membership of the TUC with socialism and have proposed disaffiliation on those grounds.(164)

In contrast to the clerical union's long association with the TUC the unions of middle management and of the scientists have long shunned involvement with the TUC. In 1947 the SCS held a referendum on affiliation to the TUC but two thirds of the votes were cast against affiliation.(165) Conference decided in 1951 and again in 1952 not to reconsider the question of TUC affilia- tion.(166) In 1959 a conference motion instructing the executive council to seek affiliation to the TUC was defeated.(167) The same issue was revived in 1962 when the pay pause was introduced. In that year fourteen SCS branches tabled conference motions on the question of TUC affiliation and the executive council prepared a paper on TUC affiliation for discussion at the 1963 conference in which the executive emphasized the powerlessness of unions like SCS outside the broader power base of the TUC, especially when faced with a government determined to hold back the pay of the public sector. At the same time they played down any political or ideological consequences of affiliation. Conference decided on a postal ballot of all members and the result was 14,969 in favour of affiliation and 19,677 against affiliation in an 83 per cent poll of the membership.(168) The issue was pressed further by the executive and at the 1965 conference the following resolu- tion was adopted by a large majority:

That this conference notes the decision of NALGO to affiliate to the TUC and instructs the executive council to review the question of society affiliation in the light of this decision and the need to formulate a national incomes policy.(169)

The motion was introduced by the executive council on the grounds that the Labour government's decision to introduce a compulsory prices and incomes policy made it imperative that SCS became in- volved as a constituent member of the TUC; further, the executive council argued that with increased expansion of state planning in the NEDCS, SCS could *not* afford not to be affiliated. Once more the non-party political nature of the TUC was stressed.(170) This time the use of the referendum was rejected in favour of a vote at the annual conference at which delegates would be mandated by their branches. Once more the decision was against affiliation.

Finally in 1973 the SCS did affiliate to the TUC by a card vote at conference, the margin being 3,347 to 2,315 in favour, and thus

in June that year SCS joined the TUC.(171) The year of affiliation
is significant because this was the year when SCS had been involved
in militant industrial action in pursuit of a wage claim. Even so,
in the debate which preceded the conference vote the executive went
to great pains to emphasize the non-political nature of affiliation.(172)

When the executive committee of IPCS attempted to persuade its
membership of the benefits of affiliation to the TUC a similar
line was taken in emphasizing the non-party political nature of
the TUC although rank and file membership have been traditionally
sceptical about this claim.(173) The main impetus which has led
to repeated attempts by the union's leadership to take the membership into the TUC has been financial. In 1963 concern over the
government's policy on pay, following the pay pause, led the
executive committee to submit a report to the membership on the
nature of affiliation,(174) but a referendum which followed
decided against affiliation.(175) At the 1966 conference the
issue was raised again but got no further, as was the case in
1967. But in the following year the national executive committee
once more recommended affiliation and a referendum was held.
This time in a very small poll (34 per cent) the membership rejected the idea 71 per cent to 27 per cent.(176) In 1975 a referendum produced a 2 to 1 result against affiliation in a 43 per cent
poll but finally in 1976 the executive got their way. At the
annual conference motion 217 was adopted and IPCS agreed to seek
affiliation to the TUC. On a card vote the motion was carried
by 54,434 votes to 38,246.(177)

All three unions on which I have concentrated in this chapter
are now therefore affiliated to the TUC, but all three remain outside the Labour party. It is highly significant that in the discussions leading up to eventual affiliation the non-ideological
nature of affiliation was discussed and the instrumental value of
such membership stressed. The arguments in support of affiliation have been primarily economic. The union leaderships have
appealed to the clerical workers' sense of powerlessness outside
the big battalions of the TUC. This claim and the membership's
eventual acceptance of it highlight the extent to which financial
considerations weigh heavily with the membership. It is also significant in the case of SCS and IPCS that the decision was finally
taken by the membership after periods of militancy by Civil
Servants which had included for the first time strike action to
back up a pay claim. In this case the three unions were behaving
in a typically instrumental way. So even though the unions have
become involved in party political affairs the impetus to do so
was not political but economic. This is further highlighted by
the fact that because their employer is the state itself any action
over pay by Civil Servants becomes immediately political because
it is essentially challenging the state. The Civil Service unions
have then become involved in political issues but for apparently
economic motives.

Thus in spite of the frequent claims by the Civil Service
unions that they are apolitical there has been a tendency for
unions to become more closely involved in party politics in recent
years. Before the 1964 general election, for example, the SCS

adopted a neutral position and published the party platform of
each of the three major political parties.(178)   But after the
1970 general election the SCS expressed disquiet at the consequences for Civil Servants after the Tories' return to power.(179)
Other indicators of this increasing politicization are to be found
in a number of other events.   The clerical union have vigorously
opposed all government attempts to impose control over incomes.
This in part stems from the fact that because they are in the
public sector Civil Service salaries are more vulnerable than
salaries in the private sector.   Furthermore, when a government
interferes with Civil Service salaries in its role as the controller of the economy of the state, it infringes its role as an
employer who recognizes the right of its employees to free collective bargaining through the Whitley machinery.   This conflict
between the roles of the government has pushed the Civil Service
unions along a path to politicization.   This has manifested itself
in the CPSA's support for the miners' strike in 1972, and virulent
opposition by CPSA and SCS to the Heath government's Industrial
Relations Act which put further restriction on trades unions.(180)
The CPSA conference condemned the Industrial Relations Bill, and
when the bill became law CPSA did not register under the terms of
the act and thus followed the TUC's policy.(181)   Even the less
radical IPCS were alarmed by the proposals in the act although
initially they did register.   A year later however they deregis-
tered.   The SCS never registered under the terms of the act.(182)
     Although the Civil Service trades unions could in no sense be
considered to have adopted a fully-fledged political programme,
undoubtedly their position on pay has pushed them into an anti-
government position on a number of occasions and hence to a de
facto political position.   The main considerations for the unions
were economic, but without the other factors highlighted above,
namely changed recruitment, rationalization and to a lesser extent
automation, it remains problematic as to how far the union leaderships could have taken their memberships.

PROLETARIANIZATION COMPLETE?

Within the three groups of workers considered in this chapter there
is little evidence that, even among the most politically sophisticated and sensitive rank and file or leadership, the unions have
acted in an overtly class-conscious way.   There have been a couple
of examples of isolated individuals or small factions who have
discussed class conflict in an explicit Marxist way, and for a
time immediately after the Second World War the CSCA was communist-
controlled.(183)   But these were essentially minority movements
within the overall structure and certainly in terms of policies
and actions the unions bear little or no relationship to what
Touraine has called the 'vanguard of the proletariat'.(184)
Indeed most of the evidence presented in this chapter points to
the contrary: for example, the constant references by CPSA, SCS and
IPCS to their apolitical status, and their reluctance to involve
themselves in the political wing of the Labour movement.

CONCLUSION

The evidence presented in this chapter suggests that three groups
of workers - clerks, middle managers, and scientists - have responded in different ways to the five factors of decreasing relative
pay, increased feminization, recruitment from the offspring of
manual workers, bureaucratization and mechanization. The clerks
have increasingly tended to resemble an ordinary manual trade union
with a strike policy, the use of militant action, and involvement
over a long period of time in the TUC. The scientists on the other
hand have attempted to retain some autonomy within the overall
structure of industrial relations practice in the Civil Service
and have consequently exhibited tendencies more appropriate to a
professional association than a trade union. This was particularly
noticeable in their 'go it alone' attitude in the 1970s. The
middle managers represent something of a halfway house although in
recent years their association has moved toward a more conventional trade union position and indeed for some time there have
been discussions between CPSA and SCS on the possibility of a
merger. If this were to occur they would become one of the largest
white-collar unions in the world.
     It would be fallacious to consider these changes that I have
documented from the earliest combinations to the militant strikes
of the 1970s as indicators of a broadly based proletarian consciousness among Civil Servants. Instead the unions have responded to a number of specific grievances, particularly pay and
governmental interference in the determination of their pay. That
the prime issue is cash is hardly surprising in the light of our
knowledge of manual trades unions. First, pay is the legitimate
ground on which management and staff can argue and it is possible
that pay grievances are merely a reflection of a wider discontent
generated by bureaucratization and mechanization and fuelled by a
changing demographic structure.(185) Further, the fact that successive governments have attempted various policies of income
restraint has meant that the understandings and assumptions of the
Whitley system have been undermined. This elaborate negotiating
body has been overridden on a number of occasions, and because of
the constraints upon the government to stop public expenditure
rising to a politically suicidal level the Whitley system has
failed to deliver the goods. The unions constituting the staff
side have become increasingly disenchanted with Whitley and have
turned to traditional unionism.
     This is not to be read as evidence of proletarianization
because any kind of class consciousness seems to be distinctly
absent from Civil Service unionism. Again this should not be a
surprise given our knowledge of manual unionism, where evidence of
class consciousness in a Marxian sense is certainly exceptional.(186)
     In this chapter I have correlated the variables of pay relativi-
ties, feminization, social proletarianization, bureaucratization
and mechanization to the history of the political and industrial
behaviour of Civil Servants. I have argued that it is possible to
observe among Civil Service trades unions a movement since the
nineteenth century, from no trade unionism to a highly developed
conventional form of trade unionism, where trades unions take an

active interest in the internal affairs of the Civil Service, are prepared to use industrial action, including strikes, to back up their claims, and to a lesser extent are becoming involved in party political affairs.   I have found little or no evidence that this group of white-collar workers have a class-conscious view.   I have argued that the single most important factor in bringing about these changes has been pay, and therefore the income proletarianization outlined in chapter 4 seems to have been vital in this respect. It is ironic that writers on income proletarianization have had the least sophisticated theory of cause and effect in relation to political and industrial behaviour.   But pay alone would not have been sufficient.   Certain other factors have created conditions favourable to the development of instrumental unionism, viz. demographic change, bureaucratization and mechanization.   The exact cause-effect relationship remains problematic and among other things I tackle this in the conclusion.

Part Three

CONCLUSIONS

Chapter 8

SUMMARY OF KEY PROBLEMS AND MAIN FINDINGS

In this book I have discussed the concept of proletarianization with reference to the industrial behaviour of a group of white-collar workers in Britain. The study of proletarianization was prompted initially by the fact that there appeared to be occurring in Europe and the USA a nebulous process of politicization and radicalization of certain groups of white-collar workers which had been particularly marked in the late 1960s. Limited evidence suggested that a similar movement was occurring in the United Kingdom. The critical concept cited as an explanation for this was the so-called proletarianization of sectors of the middle class, and accordingly I undertook a study to examine this.(1)
    I began by reviewing the theoretical and empirical writings which had concentrated on the middle strata of western society. I found that in this literature there was a basic failure to distinguish between three distinct ideas, viz. class position (however measured), political action (usually measured by trade union activity), and class consciousness. I maintained the importance of making such a distinction for the purposes of analytic clarity. (2) The embryo of this confusion is to be found within the work of Marx, which much of the literature takes as its major point of reference. For Marx the concept of class is taken to be crucial in understanding social change, because class conflict provides the motive force of social development.\ Despite certain inconsistencies and ambiguities in Marx's treatment of these ideas, he predicted the emergence in capitalist society of a fundamentally dichotomous class structure. In this process, the polarization of society into two opposing classes is seen as the essential feature. The fact of polarization has far-reaching consequences for the middle levels of society, for if polarization were to occur then members of the middle classes would either sink into the proletariat or join the bourgeoisie. Hence the concern of writers on the middle strata with this aspect of Marx's work. Marx believed that the downward shift for the mass of clerical workers would be hastened by processes of work rationalization and the introduction of universal education, and he termed the process of downward movement proletarianization. However, Marx's ideas on class do not end at that point, for he also introduced the ideas of political action

and class consciousness at various points in his discussion. The
ideas on class consciousness may be summarized as follows: when
members of social groupings called classes became aware of and
therefore developed a consciousness of their class position in
relation to other classes, this would fuel and hasten the class
struggle and eventual polarization of the classes. Marx thought
that one of the primary vehicles of class consciousness would be
trades unions.(3)

Out of Marx's work there grew a literary tradition on the class
consciousness of white-collar workers. This has been a recurrent
theme in sociology in the twentieth century. The basic problem was
that some members of the middle strata of society were earning,
living and working in situations like those of manual workers yet
they consistently shunned involvement with the political and industrial action of manual workers; instead they preferred to identify
with management and the bourgeoisie in general. The charge of
false consciousness was thus levelled against them by their political opponents. Some of the early work, particularly in Germany,
harnesses this academic issue to the fact that it was precisely
this stratum of workers who were drifting into the fascist camp.
False consciousness was taken as the central problem in much of
the work in this field in the interwar years, but even though much
effort was expended in the discussion of this, sociological understanding was not advanced a great deal.(4)

Since the Second World War a new series of issues has come to
the attention of sociologists in relation to the study of white-
collar workers concerning the new technologies which have been
introduced into their work situations. With alterations in the
relations of production there appeared to be a good chance that
proletarianization was about to or had already taken place in the
office. Thus the question before the Second World War was essentially why had proletarianization *not* taken place, whereas in more
recent years attention was focused on when and how proletarianization would occur. The events in France in 1968 seemed to justify
such a theoretical position.(5)

Against this background I was able to outline a convenient area
of study. In reviewing the extant literature on proletarianization
I discovered that in the main writers had concentrated on work
situation and market situation, or a mixture of the two. I also
observed that the various writers had chosen to study various types
of white-collar worker, the most significant of which were clerks,
managers and professionals, and technologists and scientists.
There were two main problems confronting these positions: first a
logical failure to define class in accordance with the original
Marxian definition, and second an empirical failure to match the
indicators of proletarianization to the concept being discussed.
To simplify matters I traced through the various aspects of market
situation and work situation, and this work therefore took these
two variables as its central concern.(6)

In examining the market situation a number of different
approaches were observed in the literature. First, a concentration
on income. It was argued that the levels of income of white-collar
workers had fallen relative to those of manual workers and that
this had had two possible effects: either it reduced white-collar

workers to the level of manual workers financially, and/or in doing
so it created conditions which would or should produce a proletarian class consciousness.

I argued that there were a number of problems with this contention. There were computational difficulties relating to with
whom and when meaningful income comparisons could be made. Moreover, it was not exactly clear which group of white-collar workers
had been affected in this way. In addition, the extent to which
the overall decline in the differential was merely a function of
this computation rather than a real decline further compounded the
difficulties.

My first task therefore in the empirical part of my study was
to examine this income differential. A number of methodological
problems were evident, such as the fact that no satisfactory set
of comparative data existed for Britain, and accordingly I constructed my own comparative index. Also there were specific computational problems in relation to Civil Servants, but nevertheless a
number of trends could be observed. The main master trends were
that indeed there had been a decline nationally in the manual/
non-manual differential and this was reflected in Civil Service
salaries, but a number of other trends within this significantly
altered the force of the argument. Higher management both in the
Civil Service and in Britain as a whole still enjoyed considerable
pecuniary advantages over the rest of the working population.
This group were relatively less well off than they had been in the
pre-war era but on the whole a clear advantage existed, and
although the differential had narrowed it was still quite wide.
Technologists' and scientists' salaries revealed two distinct
trends. Top scientists had done relatively well in terms of the
rate of their salary increases, but middle ranking and subordinate scientists had not done as well. Indeed the majority of Civil
Service scientists were found to be worse off than the average for
all non-manual workers and were only just keeping ahead of manual
workers. In the ranks of middle management in the Civil Service
yet another picture emerged, where salaries have declined in purchasing power in terms of pre-war levels but have more or less
held their own against national averages for this type of occupation, although the differential between middle management and
manual workers continues to narrow. Finally, among Civil Service
clerks a very definite decline in salaries vis-a-vis manual workers
has occurred and Civil Service clerks have done even less well
than clerks in other occupations.(7)

Given these findings in the Civil Service one can argue that at
a general level income proletarianization has taken place in the
lowest grades in the hierarchy. Thus by taking simply the level
of income as an indicator of class position we have a situation
where some members of the middle strata have been proletarianized,
although this hinges on somewhat suspect definitions both of class
and proletarianization based on income.

At the level of political action and class consciousness yet
more significant findings emerged from this study. Throughout the
history of the modern Civil Service (from 1853) money has been the
most constant source of disagreement between management and the
Civil Servants, and moreover it was low remuneration and its related

issues which prompted the formation of the first protective associations in the Civil Service. Later, when Civil Service unions had
been recognized and had been granted a legitimate role in the
internal affairs of the Civil Service, pay was the most constant
source of dispute. Indeed it is hardly surprising that those
groups whose pay has declined most in relative terms, i.e. the
clerks, were unionized very early on and in the most recent period
were the first Civil Servants to back up their pay claim with
strike action. The scientists have not however been as active in
the field of militant unionism, even though in the lowest grades
they have done little better than clerks. Their response has
generally been of a more 'professional' as opposed to a trade union
kind. This may well be the result of the fact that top scientists
have done very well and may have discouraged militant action among
scientists. In terms of political action the issues are not very
clear. In the earliest period of trade unionism in the Civil
Service the clerical union (ACA) was associated with both the TUC
and the Labour party for what appear to have been primarily ideological reasons, but this is certainly not the case today. None
of the groups studied in this work currently have any formal links
with the Labour party although the unions of the clerks, middle
management and scientists all belong to the TUC. However this
involvement with the TUC seems to have been primarily instrumental
as can be seen by the nature of the campaigns conducted by the
union leaderships to take their memberships into the TUC. These
prolonged campaigns by the scientists and middle managers emphasized both the economic benefits which would accrue to members once
inside the TUC and the apolitical role of the TUC itself. Indeed
these campaigns were only successful after the members of IPCS and
the SCS had been subject to prolonged squeezes on their pay
packets. It seems unlikely therefore that attachment to the TUC
was related to any wider political point. This economism and the
careful attempts of clerks, managers and scientists to remain outside party political issues indicates an apparent lack of any
highly developed form of class consciousness inspired by economic
concerns. However, at the same time these unions have come into
direct confrontation with the government over pay and hence have
been forced into a de facto political position almost against their
will. This has been caused not by ideological concerns but by
economic matters.(8)
    Thus at three levels of class, class consciousness, and politi-
cal action the falling pay differential has had varying effects
which can only partially be termed proletarianization. For top
management the pay differential appears to have had few effects
industrially or politically. For clerks and middle management a
very definite fall in salaries vis-à-vis other groups of workers
has resulted in a more militant form of industrial action but no
highly developed ideological or class-conscious position. For
some scientists, although there has been a decline in their salary
position there has been only limited and muted industrial action
and no indication of class-conscious behaviour. Probably it is
therefore only theoretically or logically possible to talk about
proletarianization here in relation to clerks and middle managers.
This is in itself problematic because in doing so one is using a

definition of class based on income alone and is therefore devia-
ting significantly from Marx's exposition. Marx states that class
is not necessarily determined by level of income so we cannot
therefore, using this evidence, legitimately argue that the class
position of white-collar workers has changed. We can say that for
some white-collar workers erstwhile financial advantages have
disappeared and in that sense, and that sense alone, can we talk
about proletarianization. However, despite the fact that in
abstract theoretical or logical terms one can make a case for proletarianization, I would argue that this is not sociologically
legitimate.

I noted that another strand of argument in relation to market
position and income was evident in the literature. One writer,
Carchedi, conceptualizes proletarianization as the changing source
of the income of white-collar workers. He argues that in the
modern rational system of office management the white-collar
worker not only helps the capitalist expropriate surplus value
from other workers, but because of new techniques and changes in
the relations of production the white-collar worker produces
surplus value himself which is also expropriated. Proletarianization is thus said to occur where the clerical worker is more the
exploited than the exploiter. Although I noted this position
with interest I argued that it was highly dubious to erect a
theory of proletarianization on a classical theory of political
economy. More importantly, given the data available to me in
terms of level of income (and not source of income) it was
impossible to test such a proposition.(9)

The second feature of market situation to come under scrutiny
was the social origins of the workforce. I noted that it was
sometimes argued that the nature of the white-collar workforce had
changed considerably since the nineteenth century in two specific
ways: first, in that a great number of individuals whose fathers
had been manual workers were recruited into white-collar occupations and second, that the white-collar workforce had become
highly feminized. These factors it was noted, either in isolation
or together, were taken as proletarianization in terms of class
position or as proletarianization because such a reconstituted
white-collar workforce would be more likely to behave militantly
and develop a proletarian class consciousness. The mainsprings of
such developments, as indeed Marx had argued, were changes in the
relations of production and the expansion of universal education.
I therefore undertook an examination of these features in Britain
in general and the Civil Service in particular.(10) I found that
the total number of white-collar workers in Britain had increased
dramatically in the twentieth century although differences between
types of workers were observed; that is, higher management were
static, scientists had rapidly increased, while clerks and middle
management had steadily increased. The growth patterns were
repeated in the Civil Service.

I next looked at the concept of social origins as used in the
literature on proletarianization and found it to be vague and
ambiguous. For purposes of this study I separated it into three
key variables; father's occupation, educational background, and
geographical origin. These variables were, I argued, critical in

determining life chances and therefore crucial to a test of proletarianization. Unfortunately the extant data on these variables
was unsatisfactory although it was possible to observe a number of
trends. Thus I found that top management in the Civil Service
were a socio-geographic-educational elite, whose social origins
belied any notion of proletarianization. In contrast, scientists
were certainly an educational elite but their social class and
geographical origins were more modest; however, the widespread
recruitment of individuals from unskilled manual backgrounds was
exceptional in this sector. Finally, among clerks and to a lesser
extent middle managers there was a definite tendency for the
recruitment of individuals from manual worker backgrounds and this
appeared to have increased steadily throughout the twentieth
century. Among clerks I found the lowest educational qualifications in the service, while there was a tendency for middle management to have increasingly good educational qualifications. In
terms of social origins defined by father's occupation, educational
background and geographical origins, only the clerks showed any
definite tendency for social proletarianization. However it
remained problematic as to whether this could be accounted for by
a gradual change in the Civil Service employment practices or
whether it was a result of the increasing size and functions of
the Civil Service in the twentieth century. Some interesting
findings emerged in relation to industrial behaviour; measured in
terms of militant actions it appears that those grades containing
the highest proportion of individuals with manual worker backgrounds have been the most militant (the clerks) but no causal link
between social backgrounds and militancy could be established;
instead social origins appeared to act as a conditioning factor.(11)
    There was overwhelming proof that the Civil Service had and was
becoming feminized in line with trends in the rest of the white-
collar world. This was occurring most extensively in the lower
grades (particularly the clerical grades) and only to a limited
extent in the higher grades. I argued that if we take feminization as an indicator of proletarianization then indeed proletarianization is the case in the Civil Service (especially where it over-
laps with working-class recruitment). However the most significant
finding was in relation to militant behaviour because it was in the
most highly feminized grades that there was most militancy. This
contradicts most of the sociological conventional wisdom on the
subject. However it was impossible to establish a causal link
between feminization and militancy or to disentangle this effect
from the social origin-recruitment effect. The most likely explanation was however that feminization was a conditioning factor
toward militancy.
    Most significantly, the evidence I found was not of a downward
shift of members of the middle strata of society to the proletariat
but rather evidence of limited short-range inter-generational
upward social mobility. This is the opposite to what Marx had supposed would occur, and writers who have studied inter-generational
upward mobility in support of a theory of proletarianization have
redefined the concept of proletarianization.
    The next major element with which I was concerned was the work
situation.(12) Some of the literature which had examined this was

found to be the most interesting and adventurous and yet, in the
final analysis, the least satisfactory. I separated two distinct
strands in the discussion of work situation in the literature. The
first was concerned with organization of work and in particular the
introduction of rational bureaucratic principles. The second was
concerned with the manner of executing the tasks and in particular
the application of technological devices to operations. I showed
that a number of writers had posited that either or both of these
variables were extremely significant in the determination of class
position and class consciousness and were hence inextricably linked
with proletarianization. In fact the various authors limited
themselves to three key groups of white-collar workers. First,
scientists and technologists were alleged to find themselves in
work situations where, because of mechanization and automation
(especially the introduction of computers) and other forms of
sophisticated technology, and given the significance of this
technology in modern industrial society they were a very important
and powerful group of workers. But because of the tendency for
modern organizations to be ubiquitously bureaucratic this group's
potential power is denied and they are divorced from control of
their work situation. This phenomenon is taken to be proletarianization since these highly qualified scientists and technologists
are no more than ordinary employees when their autonomy is curtailed. This may in its turn generate radical political action
and in particular, examples of French technicians striking, ostensibly in support of radical student demands, is held to be evidence in support of this position. I argued that this position had
a number of severe weaknesses of a theoretical kind (redefinition
of concepts, teleology, explanatory adequacy) and of an empirical
kind (lack of comparative examples, ethnocentrism).

   At the other end of the white-collar spectrum the dual influence
of bureaucratization and mechanization are said to have had equally
far-reaching effects for clerical workers. It is stated that
clerical work has become increasingly rationalized and routinised,
and at the same time the clerks find themselves working in larger
and increasingly impersonal 'factory-like' situations. This
supposedly makes the clerical worker completely proletarian
especially where he or she is reduced to the level of a machine
minder.

   In order to test these dual notions I began by specifying what
was meant by the concepts of rationalization and bureaucratization.
I did so with reference to Weber's ideal type construction of
bureaucracy, and then examined the history of rationalization in
the Civil Service. I found that the Civil Service had passed
through a series of clearly defined stages as bureaucratic principles had been applied to the organization, until by the 1970s
the British Civil Service, in formal terms at least, closely
resembled the Weberian formulation. This application of rational
principles has had, I discovered, a number of effects on the work
situations of Civil Servants. I found that indeed scientists had
had their autonomy curtailed to a great extent by bureaucratic
exigencies, but I doubted whether, as far as government scientists
were concerned, the case had really ever been otherwise. The same,
I argued, was inter alia true of all Civil Service specialists and

professionals. Similarly higher management were subject to bureaucratic constraints. With reference to Civil Service clerks I noted that even though the Civil Service was very large and very bureaucratic, large-scale clerical factories were still exceptional and if anything clerks complained not so much of large impersonal bureaucracies but of dingy, damp and cramped old-fashioned working conditions. However bureaucratization did result in the routinization of tasks and had created a situation of unified working conditions and also unified experience of grievance.

The study then examined automation and mechanization, by first delimiting the concept (because of an original failure to do this in the literature). Armed with this specification I examined Civil Servants' work situations and found that extensive mechanization and automation is exceptional in the Civil Service and that even though the Civil Service is the largest consumer of computers in Britain the number of Civil Servants directly affected by this is very small. However, where computers have been introduced, the effects on the work situation were profound as routine clerical work diminished and a demand was created for machine operators and high level systems analysts.

The dual features of bureaucratization and mechanization were then considered in relation to industrial and political behaviour. (13) It was evident from an historical study of the growth of trade unionism in the Civil Service that the pressures to rationalize and bureaucratize the Civil Service were singularly important in establishing conditions which both made possible and also provided an impetus for trade union organization. Also in the more recent past bureaucratization which had been so important in establishing unionization also served to mute incisive involvement as the trades unions became enmeshed in the highly elaborate machinery of the Whitley council system. But concomitantly, as Civil Servants fought for more pay and resorted to militant industrial action, it was the more large-scale clerical units and those which were most highly automated and mechanized which provided some of the most active support for the strikes. In contrast the specialists and scientists of whom certain neo-Marxist authors expected so much - indeed who were supposed to be the vanguard of the proletariat - were the least militant group, and instead the scientists preferred to maintain professional goals and respectability. In this instance neither bureaucratization nor mechanization appears to have been in any way instrumental for either the clerks or the specialists in effecting changes in class consciousness or ideology, and the idea of proletarianization here remains problematic.

In the last section of my study on trade unionism in the Civil Service I attempted to link explicitly the variables of pay, social origins and feminization, bureaucratization and mechanization to the history of trade union development in the Civil Service.(14) I found that Civil Service unionism had passed from a period of repression, through recognition and legitimation to the use of strike action and limited involvement in organizations like the TUC. No union I examined manifested indicators of class-conscious behaviour. The major propulsive influence on the development of Civil Service unionism was pay or similar economic factors although the variables of social origins, feminization, bureaucratization and

mechanization have been, at various times and in different configurations, important conditioning (and sometimes limiting) factors.
However I also noted that Civil Service unionism did not develop in
a vacuum, and wider developments in unionism (both manual and non-
manual) appear to have set the parameters in which Civil Service
unionism could operate. This cluster of variables works quite
adequately for clerical workers in the Civil Service and to a lesser
extent for middle management as an explanation of industrial behaviour; but scientists provide a limiting case, because although they
have been subject to many of the same key variables (except feminization) they have not proved to be anywhere near as militant as the
clerks. From this we could conclude either that feminization is in
fact a more significant variable that sociologists usually assume
or that some other factor is at work, unique to scientists, which
acts as a brake on the development of a trades union consciousness.
Ostensibly we might conclude that this key variable is the professional self-image of scientists, but there is some evidence that
Civil Service scientists do not regard themselves as professionals
at all.(15) The limiting factor may be the structure of the union
which is organized vertically rather than horizontally, or it
might be the fact that scientists work in situations removed from
desk workers and so little cross-fertilization occurs. Whatever the
factor is, and I have no evidence to allow me to explain adequately
this deviation, it certainly occurs. And most significantly it
seems to give the lie to the technocratic theories of proletarianization, at least among government scientists and technicians in
Britain.(16)

Chapter 9

THEORETICAL ISSUES
AND CONSIDERATIONS

Beginning in the work of Marx and subsequently in the sociological
literature a number of problems concerning the conceptualization
of the middle strata of society have arisen. Attention has been
focused in particular on white-collar workers. There are two main
strands to this, one which concentrates on high level workers and
one which concerns itself with subordinate workers. The issue is
complicated because ostensibly from the same evidence about pay,
feminization, recruitment, bureaucratization and mechanization the
writers predict different things; first, that top level workers
will assume an increasingly important role in the class struggle
and indeed become the 'vanguard of the proletariat', and that subordinate white-collar workers will become just like ordinary manual
workers in respect of their industrial-political behaviour. Both
processes are referred to as proletarianization. Consequently I
have conducted a study to determine, if possible, which is the
correct hypothesis. My study reveals that both hypotheses are
more or less inaccurate, so at this point some kind of alternative
framework is required to understand the behaviour of white-collar
workers.

THE EXPLANATORY POWER AND GENERALIZABILITY OF THE CONCEPT OF
PROLETARIANIZATION

My main finding is that the proletarianization hypothesis is erro-
neous in the context of the British Civil Service. But by delimiting the main variables involved in proletarianization some
alternative explanations of industrial behaviour, if not changes
in the class structure, have emerged.(1) This is particularly true
in relation to the two features of pay and bureaucracy. Tentatively I wish to argue for a modified form of the cash nexus thesis
as a possible explanation of the industrial behaviour of this
particular group of white-collar workers.(2)
  My contention is that as bureaucratization has increased in the
Civil Service so too have bureaucratic dysfunctions. The result is
that even though the British Civil Service is a highly elaborate
and formal bureaucratic structure certain unintended consequences

have occurred as a result of this. Thus increased formalism, uni-
fication of grades, and centralization of pay negotiations have
reduced the individual Civil Servant's control over his work situation and created a situation where job satisfaction has decreased.
At the same time a unified experience of grievance has been created.
This has led in its turn to the formation of protective associations whose task of organization was made that much easier by the
Civil Service's administrative universalism. The trades unions
which operated in such a system were paid off with financial recompense for the worst effects of the administrative universalism.
This system worked well from management's point of view because it
facilitated an additional means of control over staff through what
amounted to incorporated house unions. The system was formalized
within the Whitley structure. This system was to a greater or
lesser extent in harmony especially since legislation debarred
Civil Servants from overt political action. Yet the system now
shows signs of breaking down. I maintain that this is *not* attributable to proletarianization but rather to other factors which an
examination of the Civil Service reveals.
     Increasingly the Whitley system and its elaborate formal
machinery has come to be associated with management per se and de
facto incorporation was recognized by unions and rank and file
members alike. Secondly, government interference with the negotiating machinery through the operation of successive incomes policies
has, by virtue of the state's dual role as employer and government,
removed the safety valve which allowed Civil Servants to be
bought off with relatively secure pay settlements. The trades
unions' denial of political involvement, and later their voluntary
cessation from party political affairs, meant that they had become
increasingly instrumental and pragmatic. Government interference
in pay negotiations denied the legitimacy and rationale of this
role and Civil Service unions had to seek an alternative style and
policy. The result appears to have been that there has been no
outlet for grievances other than through the use of direct action,
since the legitimate ground for conflict has been interfered with.
     At the same time the principles for determining Civil Service
pay, viz. the principle of fair comparison with outside similar or
comparable occupations, has been too slow to work decisively. As
a result the use of pay as a safety valve for grievances has disappeared and this has contributed to open and direct conflict as
the parties to the disputes tried to establish their new positions
in relation to each other. The result has been that even a traditionally non-militant group such as middle management have attempted
to protect themselves within a more openly aggressive and militant
instrumental policy within the ranks of the TUC. Considered from
this point of view there seems no question of any form of class
consciousness being the causal factor.
     At a higher level of abstraction we might argue that with
increased bureaucratization within the Civil Service the bureaucracy itself has become much more formal and rigid. The assumptions
between management and labour which operated in the period after
the establishment of Whitley have been eroded. The only legitimate
area of conflict has therefore become pay. However increased
bureaucratization and formalism within the mechanism for determining

pay (e.g. pay research, fair comparison and Whitley itself) cannot
and do not operate successfully, in that a form of goal displacement
occurs and their main function becomes procrastination, formalism
and so on rather than the determination of pay. Thus pay can no
longer act as the surrogate issue where various other grievances
could be aired. The most likely consequence of the concomitant
strains in the system are direct action by the unions to circumvent
the various bureaucratic obstacles. Indeed as Civil Service unions
now seem to operate as instrumental unions there is a good deal of
evidence for this.

I wish to argue that in many industrial settings conflict over
pay is recognized as a legitimate bargaining area between management and unions.(3) This is particularly so in societies such as
Britain where trades unions and management have had a long period
in which to work out the nature of their relationships.(4) This is
not to argue that the unions are purely economistic in orientation
or instrumental and pragmatic in practice, since this raises the
question of class consciousness. But rather that in advanced
capitalist societies the cash nexus is recognized as the legitimate
sphere of disagreement and negotiation.(5) Thus it is possible
for other grievances to be aired through the medium of institutionalized conflict over money. Since most trades unions, including those in the Civil Service, do not exert much direct influence
over the conditions under which the work task is organized, it is
necessary for the unions to use cash as a surrogate issue with
which to argue with management. The system of negotiated cash
conflict only moves into a situation of tension when management is
unable or unwilling to provide the cash resources to buy off the
workers. At times non-cash benefits may be negotiated such as
longer holidays or improved health and safety, and these may provide an additional safety valve. But as we have seen in the Civil
Service when both real cash and indirect cash resources dry up
then both unions and management have to reassess their respective
positions. At this point new forms of the expression of disagreement may emerge, such as Civil Servants resorting for the first
time to strike action.

It would be facile to account for the militancy in terms of
proletarianization, whatever indicators we choose to use of that
concept. I maintain this because repeatedly in this work I have
found the evidence relating to proletarianization and its indicators to be equivocal. I argue instead that industrial behaviour is
more readily understood with reference to the nature of the relationship between management and the unions. In an advanced society
like Britain, management and unions have got an agreed area of
disagreement: cash, or cash substitutes like holidays. When this
agreement breaks down either because of internal changes in the
organization or because of external pressures on management or
unions, new positions will have to be adopted by either side. The
extent to which the unions' response will be militant will depend
on several important variables - which are the type of occupation
of membership, the social background of the membership, the type of
working conditions, and other factors such as the degree of feminization and the structure of the union. My speculative hypothesis
is a more subtle explanation than either proletarianization or pure
economism.

I mounted this study with the explicit intention of testing the thesis of proletarianization, and found that however I defined and operationalized the concept I was unable to explain satisfactorily the industrial behaviour of Civil Servants in Britain in the last twenty-five years. Instead I profer a modified speculative version of the cash nexus thesis as a more plausible explanation. This raises the question of the extent to which my findings on Civil Servants can be generalized to other similar types of worker. Throughout my study I have made constant references to the similarity of the Civil Service to the rest of the white-collar workforce. Indeed, in many of the dimensions I examined the Civil Service was typical and similar. The salaries of Civil Servants are in line with trends outside the Civil Service, the growth rates of the various types of white-collar employment are similar, and the rate of feminization is comparable. The Civil Service and its employees are different from the bulk of the white-collar population in two respects; first its higher management is a more elite group than conventionally found in the white-collar world, and the Civil Service is more highly unionized than normally found in the white-collar situation. However, these differences are not important enough to prevent comparison since many of the other processes discussed in this book are at work in outside occupations. Thus I would not attribute recent changes in the industrial behaviour of white-collar workers outside the Civil Service to proletarianization. Indeed the growth of the numbers of persons joining such unions as ASTMS or APEX is rather a reflection of the fact that hitherto this section of the workforce was largely unorganized and that it is also the fastest growing sector of the workforce.(6)

Throughout this work I have argued that proletarianization is not a useful explanatory device because both the concept and the use of the concept are inadequate. My emphasis on the separation of the dimensions of class position, industrial behaviour and class consciousness signals that we must necessarily call into question the various writings on proletarianization which have either used market or work situations as the major indicator of proletarianization (but rarely used both together) and in doing so have conflated the dimensions of class position, political behaviour and consciousness of class. Thus as Goldthorpe and Lockwood argued in the context of manual workers and thesis of embourgeoisement,(7) for embourgeoisement to occur convergence on the three dimensions of the economic, normative and relational aspects of class had to take place. When considering proletarianization which is conceptually the opposite to embourgeoisement then a similar convergence ought to be considered. This was not so observed in my study of Civil Servants.

Several inferences can be drawn from the fact that no convergence appeared in this study. First, writers following Marx have not stressed the importance of this convergence and by taking only limited dimensions, which in their way appear to support the thesis of proletarianization, have claimed to find evidence of proletarianization. Second, since Civil Servants are quite typical of all white-collar workers we can argue that there is no evidence of proletarianization in the middle levels of British society as a whole, nor probably in other advanced societies. Third, to explain

changes in the political-industrial behaviour of white-collar
workers by reference to proletarianization is fallacious - instead
other explanations must be sought.

Indeed it would have been somewhat surprising if I had observed
that the main changes in industrial behaviour of Civil Servants
was caused by changing class consciousness given current sociological knowledge of manual workers' trades unions. Among manual
workers' unions revolutionary class consciousness is very rare. It
has been observed in certain extreme settings, but these appear to
be exceptional.(8) The issue is settled in regard to industrial
workers and it is therefore surprising to find it resurrected in
relation to non-manual workers. We might interpret this as the
fact that neo-Marxist writers have been increasingly turning to
ever more unlikely sources for confirmation of their theories.
Thus when French technicians began to behave, for a short while, in
ways which were atypical of white-collar workers and in a way which
could be taken as prototypical of a revolutionary vanguard, then
there was a switch in emphasis by some Marxist writers. The main
conclusion I draw from this is that writers such as Touraine hope-
lessly misinterpreted the actions of that particular technocratic
elite. In relation to lower level clerical workers the 'factory-
system' seemed to herald the ending of the clerks' hopeless self-
delusions to make them realize their 'true' class position. Thus
modern technology would heal one of the lingering sores in Marx's
system. Yet my evidence shows that nothing of the kind has
occurred to clerical workers. Thus concentration on the problem
of false consciousness has led writers to ignore critical issues.

WHITE-COLLAR WORKERS IN BRITAIN AND THE POST-INDUSTRIAL SOCIETY

At the beginning of this book I raised the issue as to whether the
events observed in France and the USA which prompted my concentration on proletarianization were similar to what was occurring in
Britain. I also considered whether the apparent changes in modern
society were part of a strong tendency to radicalization or merely
limited evidence of politicization. In some respects what I
observed in the British Civil Service was undeniably similar to the
sort of developments that had occurred in France and Italy in the
late 1960s as selective white-collar groups became militant and
radical. But in two important respects the British and French
cases are dissimilar. First, in France the action was far more
militant and dramatic, involving street fighting and 'sit-ins' and
on the surface at least proffered a highly sophisticated neo-Marxian
challenge to society with thoroughgoing demands for the restruc-
turing of that society. Second in Britain, in the main, it was
the lower echelons of the white-collar world who were most militant,
while in France it was the technocrats. A number of writers argued
that the French case was attributable to proletarianization. But
I have argued in this study that proletarianization is a suspect
notion when used as a scientific explanation. By generalizing from
the findings in this study I would argue that the French case
cannot be explained with reference to proletarianization either.
We must therefore seek reasons as to why this is not so. This is

a fairly straightforward matter which can be understood with reference to the different developmental paths of France and Great Britain, and the different structures which have evolved for resolving industrial disputes in those two countries. Britain was the first nation to industrialize (9) and labour and capital have had a much longer period to establish the 'rules of the game'.(10) The rates of economic growth have been different between France and Britain, and the behaviour of labour and capital in relation to one another have been different.(11) In Britain there has been a much stronger tendency to rationalize the bargaining procedure and both sides agree that the cash nexus is the fundamental question over which they will argue.(12) To a very great extent the trades unions in Britain have dropped any rhetoric of revolution or even socialism and apparently stick closely to the principles of instrumental economism.(13) In France on the other hand, which was much slower to industrialize and even up to the Second World War was still primarily a rural economy, management and labour have retained anachronistic practices while the unions have poured forth a revolutionary and socialistic rhetoric.(14) The system of industrial relations so constructed has had few safety valves and hence in France there have been periodic eruptions of unrest like general strikes.(15) In addition further distinctions must be made between Britain and France; the latter is highly centralized and bureaucratized (a tradition going back to Napoleon). This centralized control has meant that there has always been a division in French society between Paris and the rest. This dualism has led to recurrent conflicts in French society, and a fairly good case can be made that the eruptions of 1968 were nothing more than one of those periodic crises.(16) Finally, French unions are less well organized than either their British or American counterparts, and are infused with a definite Marxist tradition.(17) French unions have therefore been strong on ideology and weak on definite economic action, whereas in Britain they are the reverse. This in part explains the differences between the British and the French cases, and because of the specific factors at work in France we can call into question explanations of 1968 based on proletarianization.

My findings lead me to conclude that there is very little evidence of a widespread radicalization or politicization taking place in advanced society; instead we may infer limited evidence of politicization. There is little evidence of any thoroughgoing transformation of the middle levels of society. France is exceptional, but the conflicts there are best explained by the unique social configurations in that country, not by class polarization. Instead we may interpret the British case definitely, and other Western societies probably, as being an attempt by the middle levels of society to protect themselves, and this self-interest may be interpreted as a form of politicization. This small-scale politicization has led in some cases to the adoption of pragmatic trade union practices by certain groups of workers. This does not appear to herald the awakening of the 'true' class consciousness of these groups, though this is not to deny the possibility of this happening later on,(18) because if governments repeatedly fail to grant the cash on which the bargain is made this may indeed generate a more radical form of political consciousness.

IMPLICATIONS FOR THE STUDY OF THE MIDDLE LEVELS OF SOCIETY

I believe that a number of things can be induced from my study
which are crucial to this problem area in sociology. The first concerns the Marxian tradition in the study of white-collar workers
and the concept of proletarianization. Although class is an important concept in the work of Marx it remains a problematic concept.
Marx did not adequately define class, so we are left to define it.
Even more problematic is his idea of class consciousness and the
concomitant ideas elaborated by others of embourgeoisement and
proletarianization. However, I would like to argue that this
gap in the literature stems not from a failing by Marx so much as
the fact that in essence class and its associated ideas were actually peripheral to his central concern which was to understand the
workings of the then modern capitalist economy. This was his key
problem, especially toward the end of his life. However industrial
sociology has from its inception remained locked into the Marxian
problem of class and class consciousness and viewed the economy as
the peripheral concept. Thus I argue that by placing class as the
central concept this branch of sociology has tended to pose fundamentally the wrong types of question in relation to social structure, and although this has thrown up much useful material the
problems I have highlighted remain. On a different level an
additional confusion has been the infusion of Weberian concepts
(such as status) to the literature and a kind of debate between
Marxian and Weberian approaches has emerged. I argue that it
would have been much more fruitful had the writers on industrial
sociology unified theory and empiry rather than doing one or the
other. Generally however we are presented with sterile empirical
discussions or elaborate theory building. This has caused specific
operational problems with concepts like proletarianization and
embourgeoisement which transcend the empirical-theoretical divide.
    My own study has in a limited way, by working within an explicit
Marxian tradition, demonstrated the unsatisfactory nature of the
paradigm (19) and has pointed to the utility of unifying theory
and empiry. My explanations remain tentative because in some instances I do not have enough data, and also I did not set out to
construct a model of white-collar industrial behaviour but rather
to test the idea of proletarianization. The latter I have done and
found it wanting. I have therefore suggested reasons why this is
so and have suggested alternative means of studying it. Whether my
conclusion is justified can only be proven by replicatory studies
of other groups of white-collar workers.
    This study therefore calls into question one of the mainstream
paradigms of sociology, viz. Marxism. There are three possible
interpretations of my findings. First that the whole paradigm
ought to be rejected. I would not go as far as this because, on
the basis of the findings of this study alone, I do not think there
are sufficient grounds to challenge the total Marxian scheme. [1]
Moreover this would perhaps be rather rash since Marx's sociology
has indeed provided many useful insights into the study of society.
Second one might interpret my findings as demonstrating that there
are numerous problems with certain neo-Marxian theoretical developments. I would support this position since my own study has shown

some of the difficulties in applying post-Marxian Marxism to a study of modern society. Finally, my findings might be interpreted as showing that there is no utility in taking pieces of the Marxist paradigm and using them as explanatory devices. This selectivity does gross injustice to Marx's original thesis as well as providing little or no explanatory power.

APPENDICES

APPENDIX 1 Salaries of clerical, executive and administrative Civil

Grade

Per week

Year	Clerical assistant		Clerical officer		Executive officer			Assistant principal and later administration trainee[3]	
	B	T	B^1	T^2	B^2	M	T	B	M
1931	1. 7.11[†‡]	3.10.0[†‡]	80[‡]	320[‡]					
1935	2. 5. 0[†‡]								
1936	2. 5. 0[†‡]	3.12.0[†‡]	95[‡]	350[‡]			379[d]		509[d]
1937									
1938			105[‡]	350[‡]					
1939				350[a]			525[a]		
1945			152[‡]	428[‡]					
1946	2. 8. 0[†‡]	3.15.0[†‡]							
1947	3.14. 0[†‡]	5. 2.0[†‡]	230[‡]	450[‡]					
1950	4. 0. 0[†‡]	5.16.0[†‡]	250[‡]	500[‡]			700[a]		
1951	4.14. 0[‡]	7. 5.0[‡]							
1952	5. 3. 6[‡]	7.11.6[‡]	274.12.0[‡]	549.16.0[‡]					
1953	5. 9. 0[‡]	8. 8.0[‡]	295[‡]	570[‡]			800[b]		
1954	5.15. 9[‡]	8.16.6[‡]	312.10.0[‡]	595[‡]					
1955	6. 2. 1[‡]	9.14.6[‡]	330.10.0[‡]	625[‡]		721[d]	870[a]		743[d]
1956	6.14. 0[‡]	10.11.0[‡]	380[‡]	690[‡]	485[‡]	745[‡]	1000[‡]	605	815
1957	8. 2. 0[‡]	11. 6.0[‡]	465[‡]	760[‡]	510[‡]	780[‡]	1050[‡]	635	855
1958	7.16. 0		450	739	510	785	1055	635	860
1959									
1960			479	788			936[d]		
1961	8. 8. 0	11.15.6	498	820	598	910	1154	738	1004
1962	8.14. 6	12. 5.0	518	852	622	946	1200	768	1044
1963	8.19. 6	12.12.6		879	641	974	1236	791	1075
1964	9. 5. 0	13. 0.0	550	905	660	1003	1273	815	1107
1965	9.19. 0	14.14.6	580	968	719	1118	1408	895	1247
1966	10. 6. 0	14.14.6	600	1002	744	1157	1457	926	1291

Servants, 1931-78

Occupation

Higher executive officer		Senior executive officer[4]		Principal			Senior chief E O post-Fulton senior principal mid-upper grade	Assistant secretary		
B	M	B	T	B	M	T		B	M	T
						1017^d				
	650^a		860^a			1100^a				1500^a
	865^a		1075^a			1375^a				2000^a
	995^b		1230^b			1570^b				2200^b
	1090^a		1325^a			1595^a		2000	2300	2600
1055	1225	1285	1530	1375	1650	1950	2000	2100	2400	2700
1110	1285	1350	1605	1450	1730	2050	2200	2200	2400	2700
1120	1290	1355	1610	1460	1740	2070	2240			
								2350	2650	2950
						2181^d				3115^d
1222	1430	1508	1872	1716	2106	2418	2564			
1271	1487	1568	1947	1837	2244	2569	2715			
1309	1532			1894	2311	2646	2743	2800	3150	3500
		1845	2250	1951	2330	2725	2929	3300	3800	4300
1521	1811	1910	2329	2174	2629	3002	3500	3500	4000	4500
1574	1874	1977	2411	2250	2721	3107	3500			

								Grade
Year	Clerical assistant		Clerical officer		Executive officer			Assistant principal and later administration trainee[3]
	Per week							
	B	T	B[1]	T[2]	B[1]	M	T	B M
1967	10.18. 0	14.14.6	631	1002	744	1157	1457	
1968	11.13. 6	15.15.0	675	1072	796	1238	1559	991 1381
1969	11.15. 0	15.18.0	700	1100	830	1295	1610	1020 1430
1970	13. 8. 0	18. 2.6	797	1253	946	1476	1835	1162 1630
1971	15.15	19.95	892	1385	1015	1590	2000	1260 1740
1972	16.80	21.60	978	1489	1101	1709	2150	1355 1871
1973	18.95	23.75	1090	1601	1213	1763	2288	1467 1998
1974	23.75	28.00	1377	1883	1597	1926	2782	1819 2782
1975	29.31	35.44	1747	2409	2043	2421	3492	2280 3492
1978	44.13	50.15	2500	3280	3113	3859	4579	3113 4579

N.B. The figures are not themselves complete because of the gaps in the Pay Research Unit's own records. Also some of the figures I quote for a given year were only partial because there were changes during the year. Wherever possible I have quoted figures for 1 January.

Source: the Civil Service Pay Research Unit except:

a Source: the Priestley Commission Report, p.78.

b Source: the Society of Civil Servants, Evidence to Priestley Commission 1954, p.238.

c Source: Halsey and Crewe, p.113.

d Source: Routh, p.70.

Higher executive officer		Senior executive officer[4]		Principal			Senior chief E O post-Fulton senior principal mid-upper grade	Assistant secretary		
B	M	B	T	B	M	T		B	M	T
							3500[c]			
1684	2005	2115	2580	2408	2911	3324	3745	3745	4280	4185
1740	2100	2220	2720	2475	2990	3425	3850	3850	4400	4950
1982	2392	2529	3099	2820	3407	3902	4390	4390	5015	5640
2150	2625	2775	3400	3250	3940	4400	5000	5000	5620	6300
2301	2809	2969	3638	3478	4216	4708	5350	5350	6260	7276
2445	2961	3129	3796	3635	4397	4908	5550	5550	6460	7476
2953	3585	3756	4542	4360	5216	5775	6300	6300	7141	7988
3711	4477	4671	5628	5416	6543	7115	8340	8260	9870	10570
4842	5718	5937	7032	6791	7552	8729	10152	10043	11302	12273

[†]Women only.

[‡]Figures for London only.

[1]Calculated at age 21.

[2]Higher clerical officer not included in these calculations.

[3]Did not calculate top of old AP grade because it was absorbed into HEO grade.

[4]Did not include CEO grade: post-Fulton merged with Principal.

APPENDIX 2 Salaries of scientific Civil Servants, 1954-78

Grade

Year	Chief scientific officer	Deputy chief scientific officer	Senior principal scientific officer	Principal scientific officer		Chief experimental officer (bottom of scale only)	Senior scientific officer	
				B	T		B	T
1958	3100-3350	2450- 2750	2050- 2350	1410	2000	1670	1160	1370
1959	3450-3750	2750- 3050						
1960	3800-4050							
1961				1716	2418	1976	1342	1654
1962				1785	2515	2055	1396	1720
1963	3863-4050	3275- 3600	2800- 3150	1839	2590	2172	1438	1772
1964	4625-4700	3975- 4300	3300- 3800	2100	2900	2237	1481	1825
1965	5000-5250	4175- 4625	3500- 4000	2174	3002	2484	1635	2082
1966			3745- 4286	2250	3107	2571	1744	2155
1967								
1968	5150	4465- 4950		2408	3324	2751	1866	2306
1969	5240-5500	4600- 5000	3850- 4400	2475	3425	2860	1925	2327
1970	5880-6000	5240- 5700	4390- 5015	2820	3902	3258	2193	2703
1971	6600-6750	5830- 6380	5000- 5620	3100	4100		2303	3255
1972	7930-8250	6607- 7450	5350- 6260	3317	4387	Merged with P S O	2464	3483
1973	8180-8500	6807- 7700	5550- 6460	3472	4575		2615	3640
1974	8780-9000	7629- 8457	6300- 7280	4227	5550		2798	3895
1975	10950	9764-10840	8260- 9388	5257	6874		3979	5511
1978	13047	11718-12492	10043-11300	6609	8461		5154	6898

Source: The Civil Service Pay Research Unit.

Occupation etc.

Senior experimental officer (bottom of scale only)	Higher scientific officer (originally experimental officer)		Scientific officer (New) (originally called senior scientific assistant)		Scientific officer (Old)		Assistant scientific officer (originally called scientific assistant)		Assistant experimental officer
	B	T	B	T	B	T	B*	T	
1310	945	1160	753	1007	615	1080	630	670	665
1508	1087	1336	811	1082	738	1222	650	788	801
1568	1130	1389	843	1125	768	1271	676	811	833
1615	1164	1431	868	1159	791	1309	696	855	858
1663	1199	1474	894	1269	815	1348	750	920	884
1910	1319	1675	995	1315	895	1521	776	952	983
1977	1365	1734	1031	1359	926	1574	803	985	1017
							803	985	1017
2115	1461	1855	1103	1454	991	1684	859	1054	1088
2220	1514	1910	1200	1560	1020	1740	910	1100	1150
2529	1725	2177	1367	1777	1162	1982	1037	1253	1311
	Now H S O		Now S O						
	1810	2350	1120	1900			1235	1359	
Merged with S S O	1946	2515	1206	2043			1328	1500	
	2076	2667	1318	2177			1440	1612	
	2221	2854	1435	2329			1547	1899	
	3095	4237	2038	3357			1950	2428	
	4101	5448	2839	4415			2731	3303	

* Minimum adult wage

APPENDIX 3 Salaries of selected occupations, 1930-78

Year	Manual men	Non-manual men	Administration and management	Occupation Scientists
1930	42/1d [†a]			
1931	45/0d [†d]			
1935	159[c] 44/9d [†d]		634[c]	
1938				
1940	57/4d [†a]			
1952	118/11d [†a]			
1954	125/5d [†a]			
1955	527[c]		1541[c]	
1959	663[c]			
1960			2034[c]	
1968	22.40*[†b]	27.80*[†b]	34.80*[†b]	38.00*[†b]
1970	26.20[†b]	35.70[†b]	48.70[†b]	39.50[†b]
1971	28.80[†b]	38.90[†b]	51.80[†b]	43.90[†b]
1972	32.10[†b]	43.40[†b]	56.50[†b]	49.40[†b]
1973	37.00[†b]	47.80[†b]	(91.80[†b])	50.30[†b]
1974	42.30[†b]	54.10[†b]	66.30[†b]	56.00[†b]
1975	54.00[†b]	67.90[†b]	79.40[†b]	72.10[†b]
1976	63.30[†b]	81.00[†b]	93.50[†b]	86.20[†b]
1978	78.40[†b]	99.90[†b]	116.80[†b]	105.50[†b]

* Median figure.

† Per week.

Clerk considerable responsibility	Clerk some responsibility	Clerk routine	Laboratory technician
440[e]		192[c]	186[c]
440[e]			
1480[e]		523[c]	420[c]
1850[e]		682[c]	536[c]
25.90*[†b]	20.60*[†b]	17.40*[†b]	23.50[†b]
31.20[†b]	24.00[†b]	20.20[†b]	27.40[†b]
34.00[†b]	26.10[†b]	22.30[†b]	31.60[†b]
37.90[†b]	29.40[†b]	24.20[†b]	34.80[†b]
41.70[†b]	34.90[†b]	30.70[†b]	38.60[†b]
49.80[†b]	44.40[†b]	36.20[†b]	41.70[†b]
60.00[†b]	53.00[†b]	45.20[†b]	56.70[†b]
72.70[†b]	63.50[†b]	56.60[†b]	68.10[†b]
84.30[†b]	79.40[†b]	67.50[†b]	81.70[†b]

a Source: 'The Royal Commission on the Civil Service: The Priestley Commission. Minutes of Evidence by the Ministry of Labour and National Service', p.1102.

b Source: 'The New Earnings Survey', 1968-78.

c Source: G. S. Bain, 'The Growth of White Collar Unionism', 1970, p.52.

d Source: A. Bowley, 'Wages and Income in the United Kingdom since 1860', 1937, p.51.

e Source: G. Routh, 'Occupation and Pay in Great Britain, 1906-1960', 1965, pp.78, 104.

NOTES

CHAPTER 1   INTRODUCTION

1   N. Birnbaum, 'The Crisis of Industrial Society', Oxford University Press, London, Oxford and New York, 1969.
2   A. Cockburn and R. Blackburn, 'Student Power: Problems, Diagnosis, Action', Penguin, Harmondsworth, 1969.
3   T. Hayden, 'Rebellion in Newark: Official Violence and Ghetto Response', Random House, New York, 1967.
4   M. Oppenheimer, 'Urban Guerilla', Penguin, Harmondsworth, 1969.
5   The events leading up to and the events of May/June 1968 are fairly well known so here I have only sketched in a brief historical outline.
    For full accounts of Paris 1968 see the following: P. Seale and M. McConville, 'The French Revolution 1968', Penguin, Harmondsworth, 1968; A. Schnapp and P. Vidal-Naquet (eds), 'The French Student Uprisings: November 1967 - June 1968', trans. M. Jolas, Beacon, Boston, 1971, pp.1-64; and D. Cohn-Bendit and G. Cohn-Bendit, 'Obsolete Communism: The Left Wing Alternative', trans. A. Pomerans, André Deutsch, London, 1968.
6   A. Willener, 'The Action Image of Society: On Cultural Politicization', trans. A.M. Sheridan Smith, Tavistock, London, 1970, p.130.
7   'The Times', 8 May 1968, p.11.
8   Seale et al., op. cit.
9   'The Times', 18 May 1968, p.1, and 20 May 1968, p.1.
10 Birnbaum, op. cit., p.viii.
11 A. Touraine, 'The Post Industrial Society: Tomorrow's Social History: Classes, Conflicts and Culture in the Programmed Society', trans. L.F.X. Mayhew, Wildwood House, London, 1971 (first published in France 1969), especially chapter 2; and B. Denitch, The New Left and the New Working Class, in J.D. Colfax and J.L. Roach (eds), 'Radical Sociology', Basic Books, New York and London, 1971, p.345.
12 Ibid.
13 Civil Service Department, 'Staff Relations in the Civil Service', HMSO, London, 1969, fourth edition, 1976 impression, p.26.

14 See, for example, 'Civil Servants and Change: A Joint State-
   ment by the National Whitley Council and the Wider Issues
   Review Team', London, 1975, pp.9-11, and 'Red Tape', vol.62 (8)
   July/August 1973, p.308.

CHAPTER 2 THE MIDDLE CLASS IN INDUSTRIAL SOCIETY: A CASE OF
PROLETARIANIZATION?

1 H. Speier, The Salaried Employee in Modern Society, 'Social
  Research', vol. 1, 1934, pp.111-33; L. Corey, 'The Crisis of
  the Middle Class', Covici Friede, New York, 1935; F.D.
  Klingender, 'The Condition of Clerical Labour in Britain',
  Martin Lawrence, London, 1935; C. Wright Mills, 'White Collar:
  The American Middle Classes', Oxford University Press, New
  York, 1951; D. Lockwood, 'The Blackcoated Worker', Allen &
  Unwin, London 1958.
2 This is not to be considered a definitive statement of Marx's
  position. For recent elaborate accounts of Marx's theory see
  the following: S. Avineri, 'The Social and Political Thought
  of Karl Marx', Cambridge University Press, Cambridge, 1968;
  I. Zeitlin, 'Marxism: A Re-Examination', D. Van Nostrand, New
  York and London, 1967; A. Giddens, 'The Class Structure of the
  Advanced Societies', Hutchinson, London, 1973; R. Dahrendorf,
  'Class and Class Conflict in an Industrial Society', Routledge
  & Kegan Paul, London, 1959. I attempt here merely to bring
  out the essential and basic features of Marx's position in
  order to highlight the major problem areas.
3 K. Marx, 'The Grundrisse', translated, edited and with an
  introduction by D. McClellan, Macmillan, London, 1971, revised
  Paladin edition 1973, pp.53-4.
4 K. Marx, 'A Contribution to the Critique of Political Economy',
  Lawrence & Wishart, London, 1971, Preface pp.19-21; and K.
  Marx and F. Engels, 'The German Ideology', edited and with an
  introduction by C.J. Arthur, Lawrence & Wishart, London, 1970,
  Part one.
5 K. Marx, 'Capital: A Critique of Political Economy', vol. 3,
  Foreign Languages Publishing House, Moscow, 1962, Lawrence &
  Wishart, London, 1962 (first published in London 1894),
  pp.862-3.
6 Ibid.
7 For example see: K. Marx, The Class Struggles in France 1848-
  1850, in K. Marx, 'Selected Works', vol. II, edited by V.
  Adoratsky, Lawrence & Wishart, London, 1942; and K. Marx, 'The
  Eighteenth Brumaire of Louis Bonaparte', Progress Publishers,
  Moscow, 1954.
      In other contexts Marx identifies numerous other classes.
  It can be argued that Marx's excursions into this mode of
  analysis does not significantly interfere with his overall view
  of long term social change, and indeed Marx's recognition of
  the complex nature of modern society is complementary to his
  ideas of social change. For an elaboration of this point see:
  Z. Jordan, 'Karl Marx: Economy, Class and Social Revolution',
  Nelson, London, 1971, pp.21-30; R. Aron, 'Main Currents in

Sociological Thought', vol. I, trans. R. Howard and H. Weaver,
Weidenfeld & Nicolson, London, 1968, Penguin edition pp.163-8;
and T.B. Bottomore, 'Classes in Modern Society', George Allen
& Unwin, London, 1965, chapter 2.

8   K. Marx and F. Engels, 'The Communist Manifesto', trans. S.
Moore, Penguin edition, London, 1967, pp.79-88.

9   See Zeitlin, op. cit., Section II.

10 K. Marx, 'Capital', vol. 3, op. cit., p.294.

11 Ibid.

12 Ibid. This section in 'Capital' is not really clear on the
point and Marx does not spell out exactly how the process of
proletarianization will occur. He posits a change in class
position but provides no evidence to back up his claim. Engels
in a footnote to this section thought that evidence could be
found in the numbers of highly trained German clerks who
offered their services in the City of London at a rate far
below the wages of a 'good machine'.

13 Marx & Engels, 'The Communist Manifesto', op. cit., pp.87-8.

14 Ibid., p.89.

15 Ibid., p.90.

16 K. Marx, 'The Poverty of Philosophy', Lawrence & Wishart,
London, n.d., trans. 1847 French edition, p.166.

17 Lockwood, op. cit., pp.14-15; Wright Mills, op. cit., pp.296-7.

18 Lockwood, op. cit., pp.212-13.

19 Giddens, op. cit., p.93.

20 Ibid.

21 Avineri, op. cit., p.121.

22 R. Hyman, 'Marxism and the Sociology of Trade Unionism', Pluto,
London, 1971, pp.8-11.

23 V.I. Lenin, 'What is to be Done? Burning Questions of our
Movement', Progress Publishers, Moscow, 1947 (1973 edition);
first published in Stuttgart, 1902.

24 R. Michels, 'Political Parties: A Sociological Study of the
Oligarchical Tendencies in Modern Democracy', Trans. Eden and
Cedar Paul, Free Press, Glencoe, Illinois, 1949.

25 Quoted by Hyman, op. cit.

26 Giddens, op. cit., p.93.

27 Giddens, op. cit., and M. Mann, 'Consciousness and Action among
the Western Working Class', Macmillan, London, 1973.

28 A.W. Gouldner, 'Patterns of Industrial Bureaucracy', Free Press,
New York, Collier Macmillan, London, 1954; A.W. Gouldner,
'Wildcat Strike: A Study of an Unofficial Strike', Routledge &
Kegan Paul, London, 1955.

29 H. Behrend, The Effort Bargain, 'Industrial and Labour Relations Review', vol. 10, 1957, pp.503-15; W. Baldamus, 'Efficiency and Effort: An Analysis of Industrial Administration',
Tavistock, London, 1961.

30 D.F. Wilson, 'Dockers: The Impact of Industrial Change',
Fontana/Collins, London, 1972.

31 N. Dennis, F. Henriques, and C. Slaughter, 'Coal is Our Life:
An Analysis of a Yorkshire Mining Community', Eyre & Spottiswoode, London, 1956.

32 J.H. Westergaard, The Rediscovery of the Cash Nexus: Some
Recent Interpretations of Trends in British Class Strucure, in

R. Miliband and J. Saville (eds), 'The Socialist Register,
1970', Merlin, London, 1970.

33 Mann, op. cit.

34 R.H. Hill, 'Sources of Variation in the Class Consciousness of
the British Working Class', unpublished PhD thesis, Brown
University, 1978.

35 Throughout this section I will present an ideal typical version
of the various positions. This will leave me open to the
charge that I am merely building straw men which I can then
attack. But this approach is, in my opinion, necessary because
in general the writers I consider shift position or it is not
clear to which position or what group of workers they are
addressing themselves.

36 Goldthorpe and Lockwood distinguish the economic, normative
and relational aspects of class to understand the opposite concept to proletarianization, viz. embourgeoisement. My categories of class, consciousness of class and political action
do not, however, rely on an action frame of reference to make
them comprehensible, as Goldthorpe and Lockwood's do. This
seems to be the crucial difference. I do not see any contradiction implied between their work and mine, but suggest mine
as an alternative means of understanding the problem: see J.H.
Goldthorpe and D. Lockwood, Affluence and the British Class
Structure, 'The Sociological Review', vol. 11, 1963, pp.133-63.
For a critique of the action frame of reference as developed
by Goldthorpe and Lockwood see G. MacKenzie, The 'Affluent
Worker' Study: An Evaluation and Critique, in F. Parkin (ed),
'The Social Analysis of Class Structure', Tavistock, London,
1974, pp.237-56.

37 In addition other writers have studied the status of white-
collar and non-manual workers; e.g. Lockwood, op. cit. I do
not deal with status at this point because I wish to contain
this discussion within an explicit Marxian framework. However,
below I explore changes in status in bureaucratized working
conditions within a Neo-Weberian framework, pp.74-86.

38 For varying accounts of this type of 'income proletarianiza-
tion' see the following: Corey, op. cit., especially chapters
7 and 10 and pp.248 and 254; Klingender, op. cit., pp.18-24;
J. Westergaard and H. Resler, 'Class in a Capitalist Society:
A Study of Contemporary Britain', Heinemann, London, 1975,
Penguin edition 1976, pp.72-83.

39 F. Parkin, 'Class, Inequality and the Political Order: Social
Stratification in Capitalist and Communist Societies',
MacGibbon & Kee, London, 1971, Paladin edition 1972, pp.25-6;
and R. Titmus, 'Income Distribution and Social Change: A Study
in Criticism', George Allen & Unwin, London, 1962.

40 R. Hamilton, The Income Difference between Skilled and White
Collar Workers, 'British Journal of Sociology', vol. 14, 1963,
pp.363-73.

41 Ibid. G. MacKenzie, The Economic Dimensions of Embourgeoisement,
'British Journal of Sociology', vol. 18, 1967, pp.29-44 takes
issue with many of Hamilton's claims.

42 G.S. Bain, 'The Growth of White Collar Unionism', Clarendon,
Oxford, 1970, chapter 5.

43 K. Marx, Die Moralisierende Kritik und die Kritische Moral,
    in Franz Mehring, (ed.), 'Aus dem Literarischen Nachlass von
    Karl Marx und Friedrich Engels', 3rd edition, Stuttgart, 1920,
    pp.466f. Quoted by R. Dahrendorf, op. cit., p.11.
44 The best exposition of this position is to be found in the work
    of Carchedi. See G. Carchedi, On the Economic Identification
    of the New Middle Class, in 'Economy and Society', vol. 4 (1),
    1975, pp.1-86; G. Carchedi, The Economic Identification of
    State Employees, 'Social Praxis', vol. 3 (1-2), 1976, pp.93-120
    For a general critique of Carchedi see T. Johnson, What is to
    be Known? The Structural Determination of Social Class,
    'Economy and Society', vol. 6 (2) 1977, pp.196-233.
45 For an analysis and explanation of Marx's labour theory of
    value see the following: A. Giddens, 'Capitalism and Modern
    Social Theory: An Analysis of the Writings of Marx, Durkheim
    and Max Weber', Cambridge at the University Press, 1971,
    pp.46-55; and R. Meek, 'Studies in the Labour Theory of Value',
    Lawrence & Wishart, London, 1956.
46 Marx, 'Capital', op. cit., pp.862-3; For example, Jordan, op.
    cit., p.26, and Dahrendorf, op. cit., pp.10-11 say that class
    is not to be defined by source of income, while Aron, op. cit.,
    p.161, says that it is.
47 Carchedi, On the Economic Identification of the New Middle
    Class, op. cit., says his definition is based on Lenin, pp.
    10-13; such a definition is questionable however since it is
    argued, notably by Jordan, op. cit. that Lenin's definition
    differs markedly from that of Marx, pp.24-6.
48 See particularly H. Speier, op. cit., p.120, and Parkin, op.
    cit., pp.51-3.
49 For example see D.V. Glass and J.R. Hall, Social Mobility in
    Great Britain: A Study of Inter Generational Changes in Status,
    in D.V. Glass, (ed.), 'Social Mobility in Britain', Routledge
    & Kegan Paul, London, 1954; and S.M. Lipset and H. Zetterberg,
    Social Mobility in Industrial Societies, in M. Lipset and R.
    Bendix, 'Social Mobility in Industrial Society', University of
    California Press, Berkeley and Los Angeles, 1957.
50 Parkin, op. cit., p.51.
51 F. Klingender, op. cit., chapter 1; Westergaard and Resler, op.
    cit., pp.88-106; Wright Mills, op. cit., pp.198-204; Lockwood,
    op. cit., pp.36-7, 122-5; A. Sturmthal, White Collar Unions: A
    Comparative Essay, in A. Sturmthal (ed.), 'White Collar Trade
    Unions: Contemporary Developments in Industrialized Societies',
    University of Illinois Press, Urbana, 1966; H. Braverman,
    Clerical Workers, 'Monthly Review', Summer 1974, vol. 26 (3),
    pp.48-109; H. Braverman, 'Labour and Monopoly Capital: The
    Degradation of Work in the Twentieth Century', Monthly Review
    Press, New York and London, 1974, pp.353-4; P. Bowen, V.
    Elsey and M. Shaw, The Attachment of White Collar Workers to
    Trade Unions, in 'Personnel Review', vol. 3 (3), Summer 1972,
    pp.22-3.
52 Speier, op. cit., pp.116-8; E.K. Glenn and R.L. Feldberg,
    Degraded and Deskilled: The Proletarianization of Clerical
    Work, 'Social Problems', vol. 25 (1), 1977, pp.52-64.
53 R.H. Hall, 'Occupations and the Social Structure', Prentice
    Hall, Englewood Cliffs, New Jersey, 1969.

54 The relationship between feminization and proletarianization
    is not always articulated; therefore in the following section
    I make explicit what I consider to be the characteristics of
    the relationship implied.
55 For a discussion of sociological sexism see A. Oakley, 'The
    Sociology of Housework', Martin Robertson, London, 1974, pp.
    1-28; and E. Garnsey, Womens' Work and Theories of Class
    Stratification, 'Sociology', vol. 12 (2), 1978, pp.223-43.
56 I will differentiate distinct position for heuristic purposes,
    while asking the reader to bear in mind that such clear cut
    statements are not necessarily to be found in the literature.
57 In fact the type of distinctions I make are commonplace in
    the literature on the sociology of work. See, for example,
    Hall, op. cit., pp.70-257.
58 See, for example, Wright Mills, op. cit., pp.291-2 for a dis-
    cussion of this.
59 See the accounts in Lockwood, op. cit., pp.19-35; Wright Mills,
    op. cit., pp.190-2.
60 Thus far the distinction I make closely follows the tradi-
    tional staff and line distinction. See W.E. Moore, 'Industrial
    Relations and the Social Order', Macmillan, New York, 1951,
    chapter 4.
61 For various accounts of this position see the following: D.
    Bell, The Measurement of Knowledge and Technology, in E.B.
    Sheldon and W.E. Moore (eds), 'Indicators of Social Change:
    Concepts and Measurement', Russell Sage Foundation, New York,
    1968; D. Bell, The Post Industrial Society: The Evolution of
    an Idea, 'Survey', vol. 17 (3), 1971, pp.102-68; D. Bell,
    Technocracy and Politics, 'Survey', vol. 17 (1), 1971, pp.1-24;
    D. Bell, Labour in the Post Industrial Society, 'Dissent',
    Winter, 1972, pp.163-89; A. Touraine, 'The Post Industrial
    Society: Tomorrow's Social History: Classes, Conflicts and
    Culture in the Programmed Society', trans. L.F.X. Mayhew,
    Wildwood House, London, 1971, first published in France, 1969;
    S. Mallet, 'The New Working Class', Spokesman, London, 1975,
    trans. A. and B. Shepherd, first published in France, 1963;
    E. Friedson, Professionalization and the Organization of Middle
    Class Labour in Post Industrial Society, in P. Halmos (ed.),
    Professionalization and Social Change, 'The Sociological
    Review Monograph', 20, 1973; R.D. Hopper, Cybernation, Margin-
    ality and Revolution, in I.L. Horowitz, 'The New Sociology',
    Oxford University Press, New York, 1964; B. Denitch, The New
    Left and the New Working Class, in J.D. Colfax and J.L. Roach
    (eds), 'Radical Sociology', Basic Books, New York, 1971. In
    fact Bell is probably the least extreme of these writers in
    the sense that he does not push the 'political' consequences
    of what he describes too far, so in part he will be absolved
    of some of the criticisms which I will level against these
    writers.
62 Those who suggest the use of this term are Touraine, op. cit.,
    and Bell, op. cit. This group of workers is sometimes referred
    to as a new working class, but the use of terms like this tends
    to be inconsistent and varies from one writer to another. I
    will thus where possible avoid the use of such terms.

63   Unfortunately the concept of power is not really defined
     adequately, nor why knowledge equals power. See T. Johnson,
     The Professions in the Class Structure, in R. Scase (ed.),
     'Industrial Society: Class Cleavage and Control', George Allen
     & Unwin, London, 1977.
64   See, for example, Touraine's conflation of the possible politi-
     cal consequences of technology, the actual events of May 1968,
     and the concept he terms post-industrial society - Touraine,
     op. cit.
65   As Mann, op. cit., clearly demonstrates.
66   Giddens, 'The Class Structure of the Advanced Societies', op.
     cit., pp.259-64.
67   R. Pahl and J. Winkler, The Economic Elite: Theory and Practice,
     in P. Stanworth and A. Giddens (eds), 'Elites and Power in
     British Society', Cambridge at the University Press, 1974; and
     R.P. Whalley, 'The Proletarianization of the Engineer?',
     unpublished paper.
68   J. Burnham, 'The Managerial Revolution: What is Happening in
     the World', John Day, New York, 1941; W.E. Moore, op. cit.,
     chapter 3; T. Caplow, 'The Sociology of Work', University of
     Minnesota Press, Minneapolis, 1954, chapters 5 and 6; Hall,
     op. cit., chapters 4 and 5; T.J. Johnson, 'Professions and
     Power', Macmillan, London, 1972. Although the separation of
     ownership and control and the extent of the managerial revolu-
     tion can itself be questioned at an empirical level, see, e.g.
     R. Miliband, 'The State in Capitalist Society', Weidenfeld &
     Nicolson, London, 1969, chapter 2; and Westergaard and Resler,
     op. cit., pp.154-68; and Pahl and Winkler, op. cit.
69   Denitch, op. cit.; M. Oppenheimer, The Proletarianization of
     the Professional, in P. Halmos (ed.), 'Professionalization and
     Social Change', The Sociological Review Monograph, 20, 1973.
     For a critique of Oppenheimer, see Johnson, The Professions in
     the Class Structure, op. cit.
70   K. Prandy, 'Professional Employees: A Study of Scientists and
     Engineers', Faber & Faber, London, 1965.
71   'The Times', 31 December, 1974, p.2.
72   'The Times', 18 June, 1976, p.4.
73   Braverman, 'Labour and Monopoly Capital', op. cit., pp.326-48.
74   Klingender, op. cit.; Wright Mills, op. cit.; Braverman,
     'Clerical Workers', op. cit.; Hopper, op. cit.; and Speier,
     op. cit.
75   The earliest writers on the phenomenon came indeed to such a
     conclusion: Speier, op. cit.; Corey, op. cit.; and Klingender,
     op. cit.
76   Lockwood, op. cit.
77   M. Crozier, 'The Bureaucratic Phenomenon', University of
     Chicago Press, Chicago, 1964, trans. the author, first pub-
     lished in France, Editions du Seuil, Paris, 1963; and M.
     Crozier, White Collar Unions: The Case of France, in A.
     Sturmthal (ed.), 'White Collar Trade Unions', University of
     Illinois Press, Urbana, 1966; and M. Crozier, 'The World of
     the Office Worker', University of Chicago Press, Chicago, 1971,
     trans. D. Landau, first published in France, 1965.
78   Such is the case in Britain, where until recently white-collar

workers were neither very well organized nor militant, as
Lockwood, op. cit., attests; there were however pockets which
were very highly organized. One such pocket was the Civil
Service. See L.D. White, 'Whitley Councils in the British
Civil Service: A Study of Conciliation and Arbitration',
University of Chicago Press, Chicago, 1933; B.V. Humphreys,
'Clerical Unions in the Civil Service', Blackwell & Mott,
London, 1958.

79 Giddens, 'The Class Structure of the Advanced Societies', op.
cit., p.193.

80 J.H. Goldthorpe, D. Lockwood, F. Bechhoffer and J. Platt,
'The Affluent Worker: Political Attitudes and Behaviour',
Cambridge University Press, Cambridge, 1968.

81 D. Lockwood, Sources of Variation in Working Class Images of
Society, 'Sociological Review', vol. 14, 1966, pp.249-67; and
J.H. Goldthorpe, Attitudes and Behaviour of Car Assembly
Workers: A Deviant Case and a Theoretical Critique, 'British
Journal of Sociology', vol. 17, 1966, pp.227-44.

82 I use the concepts of internal and external validity as elaborated by H.L. Zetterberg, 'On Theory and Verification in
Sociology', Bedminster Press, New Jersey, 1965, third edition;
and D.T. Campbell and J.C. Stanley, 'Experimental and Quasi-
Experimental Designs for Research', Rand McNally, Chicago,
1966.

83 Klingender, op. cit.; Wright Mills, op. cit.; Braverman, op.
cit.

84 K. Mannheim, Conservative Thought, in K. Mannheim, 'Essays on
Sociology and Social Psychology', edited by P. Kecskemeti,
Routledge & Kegan Paul, London, 1953, provides a paradigm for
understanding the possibilities in regard to political direction. In fact many of the earliest writers on this issue,
notably Corey, op. cit., Speier, op. cit., and Klingender, op.
cit., were all very well aware of the possibilities of a swing
in either direction. Admittedly they had before them the
evidence of Nazi Germany where clerks and other white-collar
workers had thronged to the Nazi cause. Much of the bombastic
tone of those three authors was actually directed at white-
collar workers with the purpose that if a trade union movement
could be built up based on proletarian consciousness then this
would be a sufficient bulwark against fascism. In more recent
writings the potential swing to left or right has been ignored
or forgotten although the configurations which Klingender,
Corey and Speier documented have not changed. See also
Blackcoated Unemployment, 'Spectator', 10 May, 1936, pp.653-4.

CHAPTER 3 OVERVIEW: THE GROWTH OF THE CIVIL SERVICE

1 In this chapter I do not attempt a detailed history of the
Civil Service, because although this topic is not covered
particularly well in the literature my main purpose is to make
a sociological study of the industrial behaviour of Civil
Servants and to see how this informs the general theoretical
problem of proletarianization. I consider in chapters 6 and 7

the specific effects of rationalization and bureaucratization of the Civil Service on the industrial behaviour of Civil Servants. The purpose of this chapter is merely to sketch a brief historical outline of the growth of the Civil Service, and to give a limited idea of the sorts of functions it undertakes.

2   E.N. Gladden, 'Civil Service or Bureaucracy?' Staples Press, London, 1956, p.31.

3   E. Russell-Smith, 'Modern Bureaucracy: The Home Civil Service', Longmans, London, 1974, p.9.

4   W.J.M. Mackenzie and J.W. Grove, 'Central Administration in Britain', Longmans Green, London, 1957, p.3.

5   G.A. Campbell, 'The Civil Service in Britain', Penguin, London, 1955, p.13.

6   Ibid., p.10.

7   Ibid., p.9.

8   See pp.74-86 where I discuss this in detail.

9   See M. Bruce, 'The Coming of the Welfare State', Batsford, London, 1968, 4th edition.

11   Ibid., pp.15-20.

12   F.M.G. Willson, 'The Organization of British Central Government 1914-64, edited by D.N. Chester, George Allen & Unwin, London, 1968, second edition, pp.19-23.

13   Ibid., p.25.

14   I. Varcoe, 'Organizing for Science in Britain: A Case Study', Oxford University Press, London, 1974, pp.9-43.

15   Willson, op. cit., pp.26-7.

16   Ibid., pp.30-2.

17   Ibid., p.33.

18   Civil Service Department, 'Civil Service Statistics 1977', HMSO, London, 1977, p.4.

19   'The Royal Commission on the Civil Service 1953-1955', (the Priestley Commission), HMSO, London, 1966, p.3; and 'The Royal Commission on the Civil Service 1929-1931' (the Tomlin Commission), HMSO, London, 1931.

20   For an up-to-date list of all government departments and ministries see 'The Civil Service Yearbook', HMSO, London, 1974-9.

21   'The Civil Service Vol. 1: Report of the Committee 1966-1968', (the Fulton Report), HMSO, London, 1968; for a discussion of the pre- and post-Fulton structure see Gladden, op. cit., pp. 38-46; J. Garrett, 'The Management of Government', Penguin, London, 1972, pp.7-57; The Civil Service National Whitley Council, 'Fulton: The Reshaping of the Civil Service: Developments During 1970', The Civil Service National Whitley Council 1971; 'The Third Report of the Civil Service Department', HMSO, London, 1974.

22   A.H. Halsey and I.M. Crewe, 'Social Survey of the Civil Service: The Civil Service, vol. 3 (1) Surveys and Investigations: Evidence submitted to the Committee under the Chairmanship of Lord Fulton 1966-68', HMSO, London, 1969, p.9.

23   Ibid.

CHAPTER 4 THE MARKET SITUATION OF CIVIL SERVANTS I: INCOME

1 A.L. Bowley, 'Wages and Income in the United Kingdom since
   1860', Cambridge University Press, Cambridge, 1937; G. Routh,
   'Occupation and Pay in Great Britain 1906-1960', Cambridge
   University Press, Cambridge, 1965; The Department of Employment, 'The New Earnings Survey' 1968 onwards, HMSO, London,
   1970-78.
2 I am particularly indebted to the Civil Service Pay Research
   Unit who allowed me access to their records from which I com-
   piled most of my information on Civil Service salaries. For a
   complete note on sources and a complete coverage of salaries
   both within the Civil Service and outside see Appendices 1, 2
   and 3 where I list all my sources and where the figures I use
   in this chapter are explained.
3 For varying accounts of this type of 'income proletarianization' see the following: L. Corey, 'The Crisis of the Middle
   Class', Covici Friede, New York, 1935, especially chapters 7
   and 10, and pp.248 and 254; F.D. Klingender, 'The Condition
   of Clerical Labour in Britain', Martin Lawrence, London, 1935,
   pp.18-24; J.H. Westergaard and H. Resler, 'Class in a Capitalist Society: A Study of Contemporary Britain', Heinemann,
   London, 1975, Penguin edition, 1976, pp.72-83.
4 See above, pp.12-13.
5 R. Hamilton, The Income Difference between Skilled and White
   Collar Workers, 'British Journal of Sociology', vol. 14, 1963,
   pp.363-73; G. Mackenzie, The Economic Dimensions of Embourgeoisement, 'British Journal of Sociology', vol. 18, 1967,
   pp.29-44.
6 Routh, op. cit.
7 For additional detailed examination of Civil Service salaries
   before 1955 see G. Routh, Civil Service Pay, 1875-1950,
   'Economica', vol. 21 (New Series), 1954, pp.201-23; and B.V.
   Humphreys, 'Clerical Unions in the Civil Service', Blackwell
   & Mott, London, 1958, pp.198-212.
8 About 75 per cent of this group have attended university,
   although the proportion of graduates increases in the higher
   grades; see A.H. Halsey, and I.M. Crewe, 'Social Survey of the
   Civil Service: The Civil Service vol. 3 (1) Evidence Submitted
   to the Committee under the Chairmanship of Lord Fulton
   1966-68', HMSO, London, 1969, p.60; and P. Sheriff, 'Career
   Patterns in the Higher Civil Service', HMSO, London, 1976,
   p.53.
9 See below, chapter 7.
10 See I. Varcoe, 'Organizing for Science in Britain: A Case
   Study', Oxford, Oxford University Press, London, 1974, p.36.
11 See below, p.82.
12 See below, p.64.
13 See above, pp.17-19.
14 Humphreys, op. cit., p.184.
15 Ibid., pp.190-2.
16 See below, p.64.
17 See below, pp.109-11.
18 See below, chapter 6.
19 See below, pp.70-2.

CHAPTER 5 THE MARKET SITUATION OF CIVIL SERVANTS II: SOCIAL ORIGINS

1 A.H. Halsey and I.M. Crewe, 'Social Survey of the Civil
   Service: The Civil Service: vol. 3 (1) Surveys and Investigations: Evidence Submitted to the Committee under the Chairmanship of Lord Fulton 1966-1968', HMSO, London, 1969.
2 A.L. Bowley, 'Wages and Income in the United Kingdom since
   1860', Cambridge at the University Press, 1937, pp.127-36: G.S.
   Bain, 'The Growth of the White Collar Unionism' Clarendon Press,
   Oxford, 1970, pp.11-20; R. Lumley, 'White Collar Unionism in
   Britain: A Survey of the Present Position', Methuen, London,
   1973; G.S. Bain and R. Price, Union Growth and Employment Trends
   in the United Kingdom 1964-70, 'British Journal of Industrial
   Relations', vol. 10, 1972, pp.336-81.
3 H. Braverman, Clerical Workers, in 'Monthly Review', Summer
   1974, vol. 26 (3), pp.48-109.
4 Bain, op. cit., p.11.
5 Ibid.
6 Ibid., p.13.
7 Ibid.
8 H. Speier, The Salaried Employee in Modern Society, 'Social
   Research', vol. 1, 1934, p.120; and F. Parkin, 'Class, Inequality and the Political Order: Social Stratification in Capitalist and Communist Societies', Paladin, London, 1972, pp.51-3.
9 H.E. Dale, 'The Higher Civil Service of Great Britain',
   Oxford University Press, Oxford, 1941; R.K. Kelsall, 'Higher
   Civil Servants in Britain from 1870 to the Present Day',
   Routledge & Kegan Paul, London, 1955; Halsey and Crewe, op.
   cit.; R.A. Chapman, Profile of a Profession: The Administrative Class of the Civil Service, in 'The Civil Service, vol. 3
   (2), Evidence Submitted to the Committee under the Chairmanship
   of Lord Fulton 1966-1968', HMSO, London, 1968: R.A. Chapman,
   'The Higher Civil Service in Britain', Constable, London, 1970;
   R.K. Kelsall, Recruitment to the Higher Civil Service: How Has
   the Pattern Changed?, in P. Stanworth and A. Giddens (eds),
   'Elites and Power in British Society', Cambridge University
   Press, Cambridge, 1974; and P. Sheriff, 'Career Patterns in
   the Higher Civil Service', HMSO, London, 1976.
10 Kelsall, 'Higher Civil Servants', op. cit., p.156.
11 Chapman, 'The Higher Civil Service', op. cit., p.122.
12 Halsey and Crewe, op. cit., p.51.
13 Ibid., p.53.
14 Ibid., pp.313-14.
15 Ibid., p.313.
16 Ibid., p.351.
17 Ibid., p.383.
18 Ibid., pp.123-4.
19 Ibid., p.159.
20 See, for example, J.R. Hall and D.V. Glass, Education and
   Social Mobility, in D.V. Glass (ed.), 'Social Mobility in
   Britain', Routledge & Kegan Paul, London, 1954; B. Jackson
   and D. Marsden, 'Education and the Working Class', Routledge
   & Kegan Paul, London, 1962; O. Banks, 'The Sociology of Education', Batsford, London, 1976, third edition.

21 F. Parkin, op. cit., pp.51-3; and H. Speier, op. cit., p.120.
22 Halsey and Crewe, op. cit., pp.81, 66.
23 Dale, op. cit.; J.P.W. Mallalieu, 'Passed to You Please:
    Britain's Red Tape Machine at War', Victor Gollancz, London,
    1942, Left Book Club edition; Kelsall, 'Higher Civil Servants
    in Britain', op. cit., p.126; C.H. Dodd, Recruitment to the
    Administrative Class 1960-1964, in 'Public Administration',
    volume 45 (1), 1967, pp.55-80; The Civil Service, vol. 1,
    Report of the Committee 1966-68' (the Fulton Report), HMSO,
    London, 1968; Halsey and Crewe, op. cit.; Chapman, op. cit.,
    p.4; J. Garrett, 'The Management of Government', Penguin,
    London, 1972; Kelsall, Recruitment to the Higher Civil Service,
    op. cit.; Sheriff, op. cit.
24 Halsey and Crewe, op. cit., p.70.
25 Ibid., p.79.
26 Ibid., p.79.
27 Ibid., p.66.
28 Ibid., p.69.
29 Ibid., pp.81-2; Dale, op. cit.; Kelsall, 'Higher Civil Servants
    in Britain', op. cit.; Dodd, op. cit.; Garrett, op. cit.;
    Sheriff, op. cit.
30 Halsey and Crewe, op. cit., p.91.
31 Ibid., p.25.
32 Ibid., p.315.
33 Ibid., p.354.
34 Ibid., p.387.
35 Ibid., p.317.
36 Ibid., pp.320-22.
37 Ibid., p.326.
38 Ibid., pp.354-5.
39 Ibid., p.358.
40 Ibid., pp.385-6.
41 Ibid., pp.159-67.
42 Ibid., p.126.
43 Ibid., p.129.
44 Ibid., p.162.
45 Ibid.
46 Ibid., p.124.
47 'The Civil Service Commission Annual Report 1975', Civil
    Service Commission, Basingstoke, 1976, p.12.
48 Halsey and Crewe, op. cit., pp.124-6.
49 Ibid., pp.159-62.
50 Ibid., p.49.
51 Ibid., p.122.
52 Ibid., p.155.
53 Ibid., p.311.
54 Ibid., p.349.
55 Ibid., p.382.
56 See above, chapter 3.
57 Braverman, op. cit., p.50.
58 P. Bowen, V. Elsey, M. Shaw, The Attachment of White Collar
    Workers to Trade Unions, 'Personnel Review', vol. 3 (3),
    Summer 1972, p.24.
59 Bain, op. cit., p.14.

60 Ibid., p.20.
61 Civil Service Department, 'Civil Service Statistics 1975', HMSO, London, 1975, p.12.
62 Ibid.
63 Halsey and Crewe, op. cit., p.52.
64 'Civil Service Statistics, 1975', op. cit., p.13 and Table 5.4.
65 Halsey and Crewe, op. cit., p.113; and 'Civil Service Statistics 1977', HMSO, London, 1977, pp.22-3.
66 Halsey and Crewe, op. cit., p.145; and 'Civil Service Statistics 1977', op. cit., pp.22-3.
67 Halsey and Crewe, op. cit., pp.304, 343 and 372; and 'Civil Service Statistics 1977', op. cit., pp.22-3.
68 A. Sturmthal, White Collar Unions: A Comparative Essay, in A. Sturmthal (ed.), 'White Collar Trade Unions: Contemporary Developments in Industrialized Societies', University of Illinois Press, Urbana and London, 1966.
69 'Civil Service Statistics 1977', op. cit., p.10.

CHAPTER 6   THE EXTENT OF BUREAUCRATIZATION AND MECHANIZATION IN THE CIVIL SERVICE

1 D. Bell, The Measurement of Knowledge and Technology, in E.B. Sheldon and W.E. Moore (Eds), 'Indicators of Social Change: Concepts and Measurements', Russell Sage Foundation, New York, 1968; D. Bell, Labour in the Post Industrial Society, 'Dissent', Winter 1972, pp.163-89; A. Touraine, 'The Post Industrial Society: Tomorrow's Social History: Classes, Conflicts and Culture in the Programmed Society', trans. L.F.X. Mayhew, Wildwood House, London, 1971, first published in France, 1969; E. Friedson, Professionalization and the Organization of Middle Class Labour in Post Industrial Society, in P. Halmos (ed.), 'Professionalization and Social Change: The Sociological Review Monograph 20', 1973; R.D. Hopper, Cybernation, Marginality and Revolution, in I.L. Horowitz (ed.), 'The New Sociology', Oxford University Press, New York, 1964; B. Denitch, The New Left and the New Working Class, in J.D. Colfax and J.L. Roach (eds), 'Radical Sociology', Basic Books, New York, 1971; M. Oppenheimer, The Proletarianization of the Professional, in P. Halmos (ed.), op. cit.; F.D. Klingender, 'The Condition of Clerical Labour in Britain', Martin Lawrence, London, 1935; H. Braverman, Clerical Workers, in 'Monthly Review', Summer 1974, vol. 26 (3), pp.48-109.
2 See above, pp.17-20.
3 See M. Albrow, 'Bureaucracy', Macmillan, London, 1970.
4 The two most readily available accounts by Weber are to be found in M. Weber, 'The Theory of Social and Economic Organization', trans. A.M. Henderson and T. Parsons, Free Press, New York, Collier Macmillan, London, 1947, pp.324-40; and M. Weber, 'From Max Weber: Essays in Sociology', trans., edited and with an introduction by H. Gerth and C. Wright Mills, Routledge & Kegan Paul, London, 1948, pp.196-244.
5 M. Weber, 'From Max Weber', op. cit., pp.180-95.
6 Albrow, op. cit., p.39.
7 Ibid.

8 M. Weber, 'The Theory of Social and Economic Organization', op. cit., p.152.
9 P.M. Blau and W.R. Scott, 'Formal Organizations: A Comparative Approach', Routledge & Kegan Paul, London, 1963, p.28.
10 Ibid.
11 M. Weber, 'The Theory of Social and Economic Organization', op. cit., p.328.
12 Ibid., pp.358, 361.
13 Ibid., pp.353, 362.
14 Ibid., pp.363-73.
15 Ibid., pp.341-58.
16 Blau and Scott, op. cit., p.30.
17 M. Weber, 'The Theory of Social and Economic Organization', op. cit., p.341.
18 Ibid.
19 Blau and Scott, op. cit., p.30.
20 Albrow, op. cit., p.43.
21 M. Weber, 'The Theory of Social and Economic Organization, op. cit., pp.330-32.
22 Ibid., pp.333-4. Weber's work has been subject to many criticisms. For a comprehensive discussion see Blau and Scott, op. cit., chapter two, Albrow, op. cit., chapters two and three; A. Etzioni, 'Modern Organizations', Prentice Hall, Englewood Cliffs, New Jersey, 1964, pp.50-7; R.K. Merton, A.P. Gray, B. Hockey and H. Selvin (eds), 'Reader in Bureaucracy', Free Press, New York, Collier Macmillan, London, 1952; N. Mouzelis, 'Organization and Bureaucracy: An Analysis of Modern Theories', Routledge & Kegan Paul, London, 1967.
23 M. Weber, 'From Max Weber', op. cit., pp.180-1. For another discussion of Weber's work in this context, see A. Giddens, 'Capitalism and Modern Social Theory: An Analysis of the Writings of Marx, Durkheim and Max Weber', Cambridge University Press, Cambridge, 1971, pp.163-8.
24 M. Weber, 'From Max Weber', op. cit., p.181.
25 Ibid.
26 Ibid., pp.182-3.
27 Ibid., pp.183-4.
28 Ibid., p.187.
29 Ibid.
30 Ibid., p.191.
31 Ibid., p.193.
32 Ibid., p.194.
33 D. Lockwood, 'The Blackcoated Worker', Unwin, London, 1958.
34 R.A. Chapman, 'The Higher Civil Service in Britain', Constable, London, 1970, p.9.
35 S.H. Northcote and C.E. Trevelyan, Report on the Organization of the Permanent Civil Service, reprinted in 'The Civil Service, vol. I: Report of the Committee 1966-1968', HMSO, London, 1968, pp.108-18.
36 It is argued that the new Prime Minister, Palmerston, only allowed action on this proposal after the scandals of the Crimean War had been revealed. See G.A. Campbell, 'The Civil Service in Britain', Penguin, London, 1955, p.38; and for general background see L. Woodward, 'The Age of Reform

1815-1870' (second edition), Clarendon Press, Oxford, 1962, pp.267-95.

37 Chapman, op. cit., p.32.

38 Indeed it is notable that this only occurred after a new Liberal administration had been put in power under the terms of the new franchise. This new franchise and its effects on the political parties effectively ended the need for patronage in the Civil Service as a method of exerting control over MPs and peers. Chapman, ibid., pp.46-7. For a discussion of the idea of open competition, see R.K. Kelsall, Intellectual Merit and Higher Civil Service Recruitment: The Rise and Fall of an Idea, 'History, Sociology and Education, the History of Education Society', Methuen, London, 1971.

39 For a detailed discussion of this, see J.B. Bourn, The Main Reports on the British Civil Service since the Northcote-Trevelyan Report, in 'The Civil Service, vol. 3 (2) Surveys and Investigations' (The Fulton Report), HMSO, London, 1968, pp.423-65.

40 E.N. Gladden, 'Civil Service or Bureaucracy?' Staples Press, London, 1956, pp.34-5.

41 Introductory Factual Memoranda, 'The Civil Service, vol. 4, Factual, Statistical and Explanatory Papers', Evidence submitted to the Committee under the chairmanship of Lord Fulton 1966-68, HMSO, London, 1968, p.15.

42 Ibid.

43 Ibid.

44 Ibid., p.5-16.

45 Gladden, op. cit., p.42.

46 See also S. Blume, 'Toward a Political Sociology of Science', Free Press, New York, Collier Macmillan, London, 1974, chapter 6; and I. Varcoe, 'Organizing for Science in Britain: A Case Study', Oxford University Press, London, 1974, chapter 6.

47 Carpenter Committee, 'Report of the Committee on the Staffs of Government Scientific Establishments', HMSO, London, 1931.

48 Barlow Committee on Scientific Staff, 1945. The report was published as an annexe to 'The Scientific Civil Service', Cmd 6679.

49 Introductory Factual Memoranda, op. cit., p.17.

50 J. Garrett, 'The Management of Government', Penguin, London, 1972, chapter 2 for a discussion of the detailed background to the appointment of this committee.

51 'The Civil Service, vol. 1', op. cit.

52 Ibid., paragraph 206.

53 Ibid., paras. 202 and 210.

54 Ibid., paras. 215-18.

55 The National Whitley Council, 'Fulton - The Reshaping of the Civil Service: Developments During 1970', HMSO, London, 1971, p.7.

56 See above, pp.26-7.

57 It is also worth noting that the whole problem of professional loss of autonomy might be something of a sociological red herring. See above, pp.19-20.

58 T.N. Profitt, Great Britain, in F.F. Ridley (ed.), 'Specialists and Generalists: A Comparative Study of the Professional

Civil Servant at Home and Abroad', George Allen & Unwin, London, 1968; F.F. Ridley, Specialists as Administrators, in 'State Service', February 1967, pp.31-8.

59 H.E. Dale, 'The Higher Civil Service of Great Britain', Oxford University Press, London, 1941, p.16.

60 The Institution of Professional Civil Servants, Comparative Career Values of Administrative, Works Group and Scientific Officer Classes, in 'The Civil Service, vol. 5 (1): Proposals and Opinions' (The Fulton Report), HMSO, London, 1968, pp.359-63 and 368-70.

61 Her Majesty's Treasury, Comparative Career Values of the Administrative, Works Group and Scientific Officer Classes, in 'The Civil Service, vol. 5 (1)', op. cit., pp.364-7.

62 J.P.W. Mallalieu, 'Passed to You Please: Britain's Red Tape Machine at War', Victor Gollancz, London, 1942, Left Book Club edition, p.82.

63 T. Balogh, The Apotheosis of the Dilettante, in H. Thomas (ed.), 'Crisis in the Civil Service', Antony Blond, London, 1968.

64 S. Brittan, 'The Treasury under the Tories 1951-1964', Penguin, Harmondsworth, 1964, p.29.

65 Ridley, op. cit.

66 The Ministry of Public Buildings and Works, Selected Memoranda to Fulton, in 'The Civil Service Vol. 4', op. cit., p.650.

67 Ibid.

68 Chapman, op. cit., p.89.

69 Ibid., p.92.

70 Reported in 'The Times', 12 May 1967, and quoted by Chapman, op. cit., p.93.

71 'The Times', 29 June 1968, quoted by Chapman, op. cit., p.93.

72 N. Walker, 'Morale in the Civil Service: A Study of the Desk Worker', Edinburgh at the University Press, 1961, p.66.

73 Ibid., pp.70, 73.

74 'Opinion', vol. 54, April, 1976, pp.112-3.

75 Wider Issues Review Team, 'Civil Servants and Change', Civil Service Department, London, 1975, pp.16-17.

76 H. Braverman, op. cit., pp.48-109; R.D. Hopper, op. cit.

77 B. Denitch, op. cit.

78 W. Silverman, The Economic and Social Effects of Automation in an Organization, 'American Behavioural Scientist', vol. 9 (10), 1966, pp.3-8.

79 R. Blauner, 'Alienation and Freedom: The Factory Worker and his Industry', University of Chicago Press, Chicago and London, 1964.

80 G. Friedman, 'The Anatomy of Work: The Implications of Specialization', trans. W. Rawson, Heinemann, London, 1961, first published in France, 1956.

81 J. Woodward, 'Industrial Organization: Theory and Practice', Oxford University Press, London, 1965.

82 F.D. Klingender, op. cit.; H.L. Wilensky, Work, Careers and Social Integration, 'International Social Science Journal', vol. 12, 1960, pp.534-74; E. Kassalow, White Collar Unions in the United States, in A. Sturmthal (ed.), 'White Collar Trade Unions: Contemporary Developments in Industrialized Societies',

University of Illinois Press, Urbana and London, 1966; J.H. Westergaard, Sociology: The Myth of Classlessness, in R. Blackburn (ed.), 'Ideology in Social Science', Fontana/Collins, London, 1972; A. Giddens, 'The Class Structure of the Advanced Societies', Hutchinson, London, 1973; C. Wright Mills, 'White Collar: The American Middle Classes', Oxford University Press, New York, 1951; D. Lockwood, op. cit.; Braverman, op. cit.
83 Wright Mills, op. cit.
84 Ibid.
85 Lockwood, op. cit.
86 H. Coughlin, What Automation Does, 'New Society', No.34, May 1963, pp.6-8.
87 Ibid., p.6.
88 R. Hall, 'Occupations and the Social Structure', Prentice Hall, New Jersey, 1969, chapter 11.
89 J.R. Dale, 'The Clerk in Industry', Liverpool University Press, Liverpool, 1962; see also Silverman, op. cit., for a detailed inventory of effects and an extensive bibliography of empirical studies on automation.
90 Her Majesty's Treasury, The Adequacy of the Provision of Office Machines in the Civil Service, 'The Civil Service, vol. 4', op. cit., p.644.
91 N. Hunt, E.K. Ferguson, J.L. Garrett, S.D. Walker, 'Report of a Management Consultancy Group: The Civil Service, vol. 2'. Evidence submitted to the committee under the chairmanship of Lord Fulton 1966-68, HMSO, London, 1968, p.35.
92 Garrett, op. cit., p.84.
93 Ibid., pp.84-6.
94 K. Owen, 'Computing in Central Government', Civil Service Department/HMSO, London, 1974, p.8.
95 Ibid.
96 Ibid., pp.2-3.

CHAPTER 7 THE INDUSTRIAL BEHAVIOUR OF CIVIL SERVANTS

1 This is not to be taken as a definitive history of Civil Service Unionism, two excellent studies have covered the early period of trade unionism in the Civil Service, viz. L.D. White, 'Whitley Councils in the British Civil Service: A Study of Conciliation and Arbitration', University of Chicago Press, Chicago, 1933; and B.V. Humphreys, 'Clerical Unions in the Civil Service', Blackwell & Mott, Oxford, 1958. I draw heavily on both these sources. My purpose is to distinguish the key elements in trade union growth and relate it to the theoretical context of the book.
2 See above, pp.78-82.
3 E.N. Gladden, 'Civil Service or Bureaucracy?', Staples Press, London, 1956, p.112.
4 Humphreys, op. cit., p.18.
5 Ibid., pp.20-31.
6 Ibid., p.20.
7 Ibid., pp.25-8.
8 Ibid., pp.33-4.

9 Ibid., p.34.
10 See above, pp.78-82.
11 White, op. cit., p.245.
12 Ibid.
13 Quoted by D. Houghton, Whitley Councils in the Civil Service, in W.A. Robson (ed.), 'The Civil Service in Britain and France', Hogarth Press, London, 1956, p.139.
14 B. Newman, 'Yours for Action', Herbert Jenkins, London, 1953, p.25.
15 Ibid.
16 D. Lockwood, 'The Blackcoated Worker', Unwin, London, 1958, p.168.
17 White, op. cit., chapter 12.
18 Quoted by Houghton, op. cit., pp.139-40.
19 Ibid., p.150.
20 W.J. Brown, 'So Far!', George Allen & Unwin, London, 1943, pp.51-2.
21 E.J. Hobsbawm, 'Labouring Men: Studies in the History of Labour', Weidenfeld & Nicolson, London, 1964, pp.272-303.
22 Humphreys, op. cit., pp.96-7.
23 Ibid., pp.80-2.
24 Brown, op. cit., p.80.
25 Ibid., p.81.
26 Humphreys, op. cit., pp.89-91.
27 Houghton, op. cit., pp.141-4 on which the following section is based.
28 Quoted by Houghton, ibid., p.141.
29 R.M. Blackburn, 'Union Character and Social Class', B.T. Batsford, London, 1967.
30 A.H. Halsey and I.M. Crewe, 'Social Surveys of the Civil Service, The Civil Service, vol. 3 (1), Surveys and Investigations: Evidence submitted to Committee under the Chairmanship of Lord Fulton', HMSO, London, 1969, pp.107, 109, 139, 169, 338, 367 and 393. Other sources put the figure on total membership of all Civil Service trades unions as high as 80 per cent. See 'Civil Service National Whitley Council (Staff Side)', n.d., p.1.
31 Civil Service Department, 'Staff Relations in the Civil Service', HMSO, London, 1971, p.2.
32 R.L. Hayward, 'Whitley Councils in the United Kingdom Civil Service: A Study in Staff Relations', Civil Service National Whitley Council (Staff Side), London, 1963, pp.2-3.
33 Civil and Public Services Association, 'A History of the Civil and Public Services Association'. Mimeographed copies available from the Civil and Public Services Association Library, and private communication.
34 Civil and Public Services Association, 'Civil and Public Services Association: Structure and Branch Organization', Mimeographed copies available from the Civil and Public Services Association Library.
35 'State Technology', vol. 1 (1), 1921, p.1.
36 Sources: 'State Service', vol. 43, 1963, p.42; 'State Service', vol. 53, 1973, p.170; V. Ellis, 'Some Sociological Dimensions of Unionization among Technical and Supervisory Employees', unpublished PhD thesis, University of Leeds, n.d.; and

'Institution of Professional Civil Servants. Annual Report
       1978', p.50.
37 Ellis, op. cit., p.50.
38 'State Service', vol. 53, 1973, p.170.
39 Ibid.
40 Ibid., p.174.
41 Ibid., p.182.
42 'The Society of Civil Servants Annual Report', 1970, p.7.
43 The Society of Civil and Public Servants, 'Report on Member-
       ship 1978', p.1.
44 The following section except where stated draws on Hayward,
       op. cit.
45 Civil Service Department, 1971, op. cit., p.11.
46 Ibid., pp.8-9.
47 J. Callaghan, 'Whitleyism: A Study of Joint Consultation in
       the Civil Service', Fabian Research Series No. 159, 1953.
48 A. Day, Negotiation and Joint Consultation in the Civil
       Service, 'Whitley Bulletin', vol. 33, 1953, p.100.
49 Hayward, op. cit., p.4.
50 Callaghan, op. cit., p.9.
51 Ibid., p.11.
52 G.A. Campbell, 'The Civil Service in Britain', Penguin,
       London, 1955, p.315.
53 Hayward, op. cit.
54 Ibid.
55 Civil Service Department, op. cit.; Hayward, op. cit.;
       Callaghan, op. cit.; Day, op. cit.; A. Winifrith, Negotiation
       and Joint Consultation in the Civil Service, 'Whitley Bulletin',
       vol. 33, 1953, pp.100-6.
56 See below, pp.119-21.
57 For a detailed account of this period and the clash over con-
       solidation and stabilization, see D. Houghton, An Appreciation
       of William Ewart Llewellyn OBE, 'Whitley Bulletin', vol. 33,
       1953, pp.116-18; and H. Parris, 'Staff Relations in the Civil
       Service: Fifty Years of Whitleyism', George Allen & Unwin,
       London, 1973, pp.89-92.
58 For a detailed account of the clashes and disputes see
       Humphreys, op. cit., and Parris, op. cit.
59 Day, op. cit., p.102.
60 Parris, op. cit., pp.35-6.
61 Day, op. cit.; Houghton, op. cit.; Parris, op. cit.;
       Humphreys, op. cit.
62 Day, op. cit., p.102.
63 See, for example, 'Opinion', May 1976, pp.140-3.
64 'Red Tape', vol. 62 (8), July/August 1973, p.308.
65 Ibid.
66 W.J.M. Mackenzie, and J.W. Grove, 'Central Administration in
       Britain', Longmans Green & Co, London and New York, 1957, p.141.
67 'Civil Service Opinion', vol. 38 (456), September 1961,
       pp.198-9.
68 'Red Tape', vol. 51, October 1961, p.6.
69 Ibid., November 1961, p.57.
70 Ibid., December 1961, p.85.
71 Ibid., January 1962, p.121.

72 Parris, op. cit., pp.97-101.
73 Ibid.
74 Ibid.
75 See above, pp.70-2.
76 A. Sturmthal, White Collar Unions: A Comparative Essay, in A. Sturmthal (ed.), 'White Collar Trade Unions: Contemporary Developments in Industrialized Societies', University of Illinois Press, Urbana and London, 1966.
77 See above, chapter 5.
78 'Red Tape', vol. 51, July-August 1962, p.354.
79 Ibid., vol. 52, June-July 1963, p.306.
80 Ibid., vol. 57 (8), May 1968, p.229.
81 Ibid., vol. 57, July-August 1968, pp.304-5, 319.
82 Ibid., vol. 58, December 1968, p.82.
83 'Civil Services Clerical Association, Strike Policy', CSCA, London, 1969; 'Red Tape', vol. 58, 1969, pp.165 and 316-17.
84 'Civil Service Opinion', vol. 47, 1969, p.181 and pp.336-9.
85 'Minutes of the Annual Conference of the Society of Civil Servants 1970', paragraphs 34 and 39.
86 'Civil Service Opinion', vol. 49, 1971, pp.18-19.
87 'Red Tape', vol. 59, February 1970, p.142.
88 Ibid.
89 Ibid., March 1970, p.165.
90 Ibid., p.200.
91 Ibid.
92 Civil Service Department, 'Third Report', HMSO, London, 1974, p.33.
93 'Red Tape', vol. 62 (4), January 1973, p.101.
94 'Civil Service Opinion', vol. 51, 1973, p.7.
95 'Red Tape', vol. 62 (5), February 1973, p.52.
96 Ibid., vol. 62 (6), March 1973, p.166.
97 'Civil Service Opinion', vol. 51, March 1973, p.73.
98 'Red Tape', vol. 62 (7), April 1973, p.200.
99 'The Times', 28 February 1973.
100 Ibid.
101 'Red Tape', vol. 62 (7), April 1973, p.201.
102 The Wider Issues Review Team, 'Civil Servants and Change', Civil Service Department, London, 1975, p.10.
103 N. Rothschild, The Organization and Management of Government Research and Development, in 'A Framework for Government Research and Development: A Green Paper', HMSO, London, 1971, Cmnd 4814.
104 See, for example, the letter columns of 'The Times' and the pages of the scientific periodicals 'Nature' and 'New Scientist' in the period December 1971 to February 1972.
105 'State Service', vol. 50, March 1970, pp.49-58.
106 Ibid., pp.105, 120.
107 Ibid., July 1970, p.170.
108 Ibid., vol. 51, March 1971, pp.65-6.
109 Ibid., April 1971, pp.97-8.
110 Ibid., June 1971, p.164.
111 Ibid., August 1971, p.229.
112 Ibid., pp.230, 241.
113 Ibid., p.289.

114 Ibid., vol. 52, September 1972, p.257.
115 Ibid., vol. 52, October 1972, p.289.
116 Ibid., vol. 53, February 1973, p.33.
117 Ibid., vol. 53, pp.35, 129, 225 and vol. 54, p.65.
118 Ibid., vol. 54, pp.65, 67 and 103.
119 For example, A. Touraine, 'The Post Industrial Society:
     Tomorrow's Social History: Class Conflicts and Culture in the
     Programmed Society', trans. L.F.X. Mayhew, Wildwood House,
     London, 1971.
120 See above, pp.17-19 where I discuss this position.
121 'Red Tape', vol. 67 (3), December 1977, pp.77-8, and vol. 67
     (4), January 1978, p.109.
122 'Red Tape', vol. 66 (11), September 1977, p.358.
123 'Opinion', (658), October 1978, p.7.
124 Ibid., (660), December 1978, pp.7-9.
125 'The Scotsman', 3 November 1978, p.1.
126 'SCPS Circular', 9 January 1979.
127 'Opinion', 661, January 1979, pp.8-9.
128 Ibid., 662, February 1979, p.4.
129 'SCPS Circular', 24 January 1979.
130 'The Scotsman', 25 January 1979, p.7; and 'Red Tape', vol. 68
     (7), May 1979, p.198.
131 'SCPS Circular', 29 January 1979.
132 'Red Tape', vol. 68 (5), February 1979, p.133, and vol. 68 (6),
     1979, p.165.
133 'Opinion', 662, February 1979, pp.4-5; 'The Scotsman', 7
     February 1979, p.1.
134 'The Scotsman', 20 February 1979, p.5.
135 Ibid., 23 February 1979, p.1.
136 SCPS and CPSA, 'Joint Letter to all Members of Parliament'.
137 'The Scotsman', 24 February 1979, pp.1 and 7.
138 'SCPS Circular', 24 February 1979.
139 'The Scotsman', 27 February 1979, p.5.
140 'SCPS Circular', 16 March 1979; 'The Scotsman', 5 March 1979,
     pp.1, 13; and CPSA 'Pay Fight Front Line', No. 5, p.1.
141 'SCPS Circular', 16 March 1979.
142 Ibid.
143 Quoted in 'The Scotsman', 17 March 1979, p.1.
144 'Opinion', campaign issue No. 4, March 1979, p.1.
145 'SCPS Circular', 26 March 1979.
146 'The Scotsman', 29 March 1979, pp.1, 7.
147 Ibid., 31 March 1979, pp.1, 6.
148 Ibid., and 'Opinion', campaign issue, No. 6, p.2.
149 'SCPS Circular', 3 April 1979.
150 'The Scotsman', 3 April 1979, p.1.
151 Ibid., 6 April 1979, p.9.
152 Ibid., 7 April 1979, p.1.
153 'SCPS Circular', April 1979.
154 'The Scotsman', 13 April 1979, p.9.
155 Ibid., 24 April 1979, p.8, 28 April 1979, p.7 and 3 May 1979,
     p.1.
156 Touraine, op. cit.
157 Lockwood, op. cit., p.168.
158 Ibid., pp.170-1.

177 Notes to Chapter 7

159 The story of the General Strike is fairly well known - thus I
    will only outline the major events leading up to it; for a
    more detailed consideration of the strike see the following:
    R.P. Arnot, 'The General Strike May 1926: Its Origins and
    History', Labour Research Department, 1926; C.L. Mowat,
    'Britain Between the Wars 1918-1940', Methuen, London, 1955;
    W.H. Crook, 'The General Strike: A Study of Labour's Tragic
    Weapon in Theory and Practice', Chapel Hill, The University
    of North Carolina, 1931; A. Mason, The Government and the
    General Strike 1926, 'The International Review of Social
    History', vol. XIV, 1969, pp.1-21.
160 Quoted by White, op. cit., p.282.
161 Quoted by White, op. cit., pp.297-8.
162 Lockwood, op. cit., p.176.
163 See, for example, 'Red Tape', vol. 51 (11), September 1962,
    p.337.
164 See, for example, Motion 841 at the 1963 CSCA conference when
    a move to disaffiliate was lost. 'Red Tape', vol. 52, p.350.
165 'Civil Service Opinion', vol. 48, November 1962.
166 Society of Civil Servants, Statement by the Executive Council
    on the Question of TUC Affiliation. A paper prepared for the
    1963 Conference p.2.
167 Ibid.
168 'Civil Service Opinion', vol. 41, November 1963, p.295.
169 Ibid., vol. 43, 1965, p.297.
170 Ibid., pp.297-8.
171 'The Society of Civil Servants Annual Report 1973', p.9.
172 'Civil Service Opinion', vol. 51, June 1973, p.212.
173 See, for example, 'State Service', vol. 42, 1967, pp.346-7.
174 Ibid., vol.43, January 1963, p.7.
175 Ibid., November 1963, pp.330-1.
176 Ibid., vol. 47, February 1967, pp.27,29; September 1967, p.214;
    vol. 49, March 1969, pp.59-60.
177 Ibid., vol. 53, November 1973, p.332; vol. 55, April 1975,
    p.110; and vol. 56, July 1976, pp.199-205.
178 'Civil Service Opinion', vol. 42, September 1964.
179 Ibid., vol. 48, July 1970, p.193.
180 'Red Tape', vol. 61 (5), February 1972, p.113; and 'The
    Society of Civil Servants Annual Report 1970', p.24.
181 'Red Tape', vol. 60, July-August 1971, pp.268-9; and vol. 61,
    July-August 1972, pp.296-8.
182 'State Service', vol. 56, December 1970, pp.337-9; vol. 52,
    July 1972, pp.196-206; and The Society of Civil Servants,
    'Minutes of the Annual Conference 1972', paragraph 108.
183 Lockwood, op. cit., pp.175-6.
184 Touraine, op. cit., chapter 3.
185 See A.W. Gouldner, 'Wildcat Strike', Routledge & Kegan Paul,
    London, 1955, who argues that this is a common phenomenon and
    a very important feature of all wage bargaining.
186 D. Lockwood, Sources of Variation in Working Class Images of
    Society, 'Sociological Review', vol. 14, 1966, pp.249-67.

CHAPTER 8 SUMMARY OF KEY PROBLEMS AND MAIN FINDINGS

1 See above, chapter 1.
2 See above, p.6.
3 See above, pp.6-11.
4 H. Speier, The Salaried Employee in Modern Society, 'Social Research', vol. 1, 1934, pp.111-33; L. Corey, 'The Crisis of the Middle Class', Covici Friede, New York, 1935; F.D. Klingender, 'The Condition of Clerical Labour in Britain', Martin Lawrence, London, 1935.
5 A. Touraine, 'The Post Industrial Society: Tomorrow's Social History: Classes, Conflicts and Culture in the Programmed Society', Wildwood, London, 1971; H. Braverman, Clerical Workers, 'Monthly Review', Summer 1974, vol. 26 (3), pp.48-109.
6 See above, pp.11-22.
7 See above, chapter 5.
8 See above, chapter 7.
9 See above chapters 2 and 4; and G. Carchedi, On the Economic Identification of the New Middle Class, 'Economy and Society', vol. 4 (1), 1975.
10 See above, chapter 5.
11 See above, chapter 7.
12 See above, chapter 6.
13 See above, chapter 7.
14 See above, chapter 7.
15 S. Blume and E. Chennels, Professional Civil Servants: A Study in the Sociology of Public Administration, 'Public Administration', vol. 53, Summer 1975.
16 See below, chapter 9.

CHAPTER 9 THEORETICAL ISSUES AND CONSIDERATIONS

1 See below where I relate my findings to the broader issue of overall changes in the class structure.
2 The model I have taken was originally devised by Gouldner in his studies of a mining complex in the USA. A.W. Gouldner, 'Patterns of Industrial Bureaucracy', Free Press, New York, Collier-Macmillan, London, 1954; and A.W. Gouldner, 'Wildcat Strike: A Study of an Unofficial Strike', Routledge & Kegan Paul, London, 1955.
3 R. Dahrendorf, 'Class and Class Conflict in an Industrial Society', Routledge & Kegan Paul, London, 1959.
4 M. Mann, 'Consciousness and Action among the Western Working Classes', Macmillan, London, 1973.
5 J.H. Westergaard, The Rediscovery of the Cash Nexus: Some Recent Interpretations of Trends in the British Class Structure, in R. Miliband and J. Saville (eds), 'Socialist Register 1970', Merlin, London, 1970.
6 A. Giddens, 'The Class Structure of the Advanced Societies', Hutchinson, London, 1973, p.193.
7 J.H. Goldthorpe and D. Lockwood, Affluence and the British Class Structure, 'Sociological Review', vol. 11, 1963, pp.133-63.

8 H. Behrend, The Effort Bargain, 'Industrial and Labour Relations Review', vol. 10, 1957, pp.503-15; W. Baldamus, 'Efficiency and Effort: An Analysis of Industrial Administration', Tavistock, London, 1961; D.F. Wilson, 'Dockers: The Impact of Industrial Change', Fontana/Collins, London, 1972; N. Dennis, F. Henriques, and C. Slaughter, 'Coal is Our Life: An Analysis of a Yorkshire Mining Community', Eyre & Spottiswoode, London, 1956; Westergaard, op. cit.; R.H. Hill, Sources of Variation in the Class Consciousness of the British Working Class, unpublished PhD thesis, Brown University, 1978.

9 P. Mathias, 'The First Industrial Nation: An Economic History of Britain 1700-1914', Methuen, London, 1969.

10 J.E.T. Eldridge, Industrial Relations and Industrial Capitalism, unpublished paper.

11 Mann, op. cit.

12 Eldridge, op. cit.

13 E.J. Hobsbawm, 'Labouring Men: Studies in the History of Labour', Weidenfeld & Nicolson, London, 1964, pp.250-343.

14 Mann, op. cit.

15 J. Ardagh, 'The New France', Penguin, London, 1973, second edition.

16 Ibid.

17 M. Crozier, White Collar Unions: The Case of France, in A. Sturmthal (ed.), 'White Collar Trade Unions', University of Illinois Press, Urbana, 1966.

18 Westergaard, op. cit.

19 See T.S. Kuhn, 'The Structure of Scientific Revolutions', University of Chicago Press, Chicago and London, 2nd edition 1970, for an elaboration of the idea of paradigm.

BIBLIOGRAPHY

ALBROW, M., 'Bureaucracy', Macmillan, London, 1970.

ALLEN, V.L., 'The Sociology of Industrial Relations: Studies in Method', Longman, London, 1971.

ARDAGH, J., 'The New France', Penguin, London, 1973, second edition.

ARMSTRONG, W., 'Professionals and Professionalism in the Civil Service: An Address prepared for the Oration at L.S.E., December 1969', London School of Economics, London, 1970.

ARMSTRONG, W., 'The Role and Character of the Civil Service', The Fifth Annual Lecture under the Thank Offering to Britain Fund, British Academy, Oxford University Press, London, 1970.

ARMSTRONG, W., 'Personnel Management in the Civil Service', A speech given to the Institute of Personnel Management October 1971, HMSO, London, 1971.

ARNOT, R.P., 'The General Strike May 1926: Its Origins and History', Labour Research Department, London, 1926.

ARON, R., 'Main Currents in Sociological Thought, vol. 1, Comte, Montesquieu, Marx, Tocqueville: The Sociologists and the Revolution of 1848', trans. R. Howard and H. Weaver, Weidenfeld & Nicolson, London, 1965; Pelican, London, 1968.

ASHTON, D.N. and FIELD, D., 'Young Workers: From School to Work', Hutchinson, London, 1976.

AVINERI, S., 'The Social and Political Thought of Karl Marx', Cambridge University Press, London, 1968.

BAIN, G.S., 'The Growth of White Collar Unionism', Clarendon Press, Oxford, 1970.

BAIN, C.S. and PRICE, R., Who is a White Collar Employee?, 'British Journal of Industrial Relations', vol. 10, 1972, pp.325-35.

BAIN, G.S. and PRICE, R., Union Growth and Employment Trends in the United Kingdom 1964-1970, 'British Journal of Industrial Relations', vol. 10, 1972, pp.336-81.

BALDAMUS, W., 'Efficiency and Effort: An Analysis of Industrial Administration', Tavistock, London, 1961.

BALOGH, T., The Apotheosis of the Dilettante, in H. Thomas (ed.), 'Crisis in the Civil Service', Antony Blond, London, 1968.

BANKS, J.A., 'Marxist Sociology in Action: A Sociological Critique of the Marxist Approach to Industrial Relations', Faber & Faber, London, 1970.

BANKS, O., 'The Sociology of Education', Batsford, London, 1976, third edition.

BARAN, P.A. and SWEEZY, P.M., 'Monopoly Capital: An Essay on the American Social and Economic Order', Monthly Review Press, New York, and London, 1966.

BARLOW, A. et al, Report of the Barlow Committee on Scientific Staffs, in 'The Scientific Civil Service: Reorganization and Recruitment during the Reconstruction Period', HMSO, London, 1945, Cmd 6679.

BECHHOFFER, F., ELLIOTT, B., RUSHFORTH, M. and BLAND, R., The Petits Bourgeois in the Class Structure: The Case of the Small Shopkeeper, in F. Parkin (ed.), 'The Social Analysis of Class Structure', Tavistock, London, 1974.

BEHREND, H., The Effort Bargain, 'Industrial and Labour Relations Review', vol. 10, 1957, pp.503-15.

BELL, D., The Measurement of Knowledge and Technology, in E.B. Sheldon and W.E. Moore (eds), 'Indicators of Social Change: Concepts and Measurement', Russell Sage Foundation, New York, 1968.

BELL, D., Technocracy and Politics, 'Survey', vol. 17 (1), 1971, pp.1-24.

BELL, D., The Post Industrial Society: The Evolution of an Idea, 'Survey', vol. 17 (3), 1971, pp.102-68.

BELL, D., Labour in the Post Industrial Society, 'Dissent', Winter, 1972, pp.163-89.

BENDIX, R., 'Higher Civil Servants in American Society: A Study of the Social Origins, the Careers and the Power Position of Higher Federal Administration', University of Colorado Press, Boulder, Colorado, 1949.

BENSMAN, J. and VIDICH, A.J., 'The New American Society: The Revolution of the Middle Class', Quadrangle Books, Chicago, 1971.

BERGER, P. (ed.), 'The Human Shape of Work: Studies in the Sociology of Occupations', Macmillan, New York; Collier-Macmillan, London, 1964.

BERGER, P., Some General Observations on the Problem of Work, in P. Berger, (ed.), 'The Human Shape of Work', op. cit., pp.211-41.

BERLIN, I., 'Karl Marx: His Life and Environment' (second edition), Oxford University Press, London, 1948.

BEYNON, R. and BLACKBURN, R., 'Perceptions of Work: Variations within a Factory', Cambridge at the University Press, 1972.

BIRNBAUM, N., 'The Crisis of Industrial Society', Oxford University Press, London, Oxford and New York, 1969.

BLACKBURN, R.M., 'Union Character and Social Class', B.T. Batsford, London, 1967.

BLALOCK, H.M., The Measurement Problem: A Gap between the Language of Theory and Research, in H.M. Blalock and A. Blalock (eds), 'Methodology in Social Research', McGraw Hill, New York, 1968.

BLAU, P.M. and SCOTT, W.R., 'Formal Organizations: A Comparative Approach', Introduction and additional biography by J.H. Smith, Routledge & Kegan Paul, London, 1963.

BLAUNER, R., 'Alienation and Freedom: The Factory Worker and his Industry', University of Chicago Press, Chicago and London, 1964.

BLUME, S., 'Toward a Political Sociology of Science', Free Press, New York, Collier Macmillan, London, 1974.

BLUME, S. and CHENNELS, E., Professional Civil Servants: A Study in the Sociology of Public Administration, 'Public Administration', vol. 53, Summer 1975.

BOOKER, C., 'The Neophiliacs: A Study of The Revolution in English Life in the Fifties and Sixties', Collins, London, 1969.

BOTTOMORE, T.B., Higher Civil Servants in France, in 'Transactions of the Second World Congress of Sociology', vol. II, 1954.

BOTTOMORE, T.B., 'Classes in Modern Society', George Allen & Unwin, London, 1965.

BOTTOMORE, T.B., 'Marxist Sociology', Macmillan, London, 1975.

BOURGEOIS, C.S., The Situational Perspectives of Premedical Students - Their Effect on Academic and Career Goals, An Exploratory Study, unpublished PhD thesis, Brown University, 1975.

BOURN, J.B., The Main Reports on the British Civil Service since the Northcote-Trevelyan Report, in 'The Civil Service, Vol. 3 (2), Surveys and Investigations', HMSO, London, 1968.

BOWEN, P., ELSEY, V., SHAW, M., The Attachment of White Collar Workers to Trade Unions, 'Personnel Review', vol. 3 (3), Summer 1972, pp.22-32.

BOWLEY, A.L. 'Wages and Income in the United Kingdom since 1860', Cambridge at the University Press, 1937.

BRAVERMAN, H., Clerical Workers, in 'Monthly Review', Summer 1974, vol. 26 (3), pp.48-109.

BRAVERMAN, H., 'Labour and Monopoly Capital: The Degradation of Work in the Twentieth Century', Monthly Review Press, New York and London, 1974.

BRITTAN, S., 'The Treasury under the Tories 1951-1964', Penguin, Harmondsworth, 1964.

BROWN, R., Women as Employees: Some comments on Research in Industrial Sociology, in D. Barker and S. Allen (eds), 'Dependence and Exploitation in Work and Marriage', Longman, London, 1976.

BROWN, W.J., 'So Far', George Allen & Unwin, London, 1943, with a preface by John Buchan.

BRUCE, M., 'The Coming of the Welfare State', Batsford, London, 1968, fourth edition.

BURNHAM, J., 'The Managerial Revolution: What is Happening in the World', John Day, New York, 1941.

BURNS, T., Cold Class War, in 'The New Statesman and Nation', 2 April 1956, pp.330-1.

CALLAGHAN, J., 'Whitleyism: A Study of Joint Consultation in the Civil Service', Fabian Research Series, no. 159, 1953.

CAMPBELL, D.T. and STANLEY, J.C., 'Experimental and Quasi-Experimental Designs for Research', Rand McNally, Chicago, 1966.

CAMPBELL, G.A., 'The Civil Service in Britain', Penguin, London, 1955.

CAPLOW, T., 'The Sociology of Work', University of Minnesota Press, Minneapolis, 1954.

CARCHEDI, G., On the Economic Identification of the New Middle Class, 'Economy and Society', vol. 4 (1), 1975, pp.1-86.

CARCHEDI, G., The Economic Identification of State Employees, 'Social Praxis', vol. 3, 1976, pp.93-120.

CARPENTER, H., 'Report of the Committee on the Staffs of Government Scientific Establishments (The Carpenter Committee)', HMSO, London, 1931.

CHAPMAN, B., 'British Government Observed: Some European Reflections', George Allen & Unwin, London, 1963.
CHAPMAN, R.A., Profile of a Profession: The Administrative Class of the Civil Service, in 'The Civil Service, vol. 3 (2) Surveys and Investigations: Evidence submitted to the Committee under the Chairmanship of Lord Fulton 1966-68', HMSO, London, 1968.
CHAPMAN, R.A., 'The Higher Civil Service in Britain', Constable, London, 1970.
CHINOY, E., 'Automobile Workers and the American Dream', Beacon Press, Boston, 1965; first published 1955 by Random House.
CHINOY, E., Manning the Machines: The Assembly Line Worker, in P. Berger (ed.), 'The Human Shape of Work', op. cit., pp.51-81.
CICOUREL, A.V., 'Method and Measurement in Sociology', Free Press Glencoe, London, 1964.
CIVIL AND PUBLIC SERVICES ASSOCIATION, 'A History of the Civil and Public Services Association, Mimeographed copies available from the CPSA Library.
CIVIL AND PUBLIC SERVICES ASSOCIATION, 'Civil and Public Services Association: Structure and Branch Organization', Mimeographed copies available from CPSA Library.
'The Civil Service: Volume 1: Report of the Committee' (The Fulton Report), HMSO, London, 1968.
'The Civil Service, Volume 2: Report of a Management Consultancy Group', HMSO, London, 1968.
'The Civil Service, Volume 3 (1): Surveys and Investigations: Social Survey of the Civil Service', HMSO, London, 1969.
'The Civil Service, Volume 3 (2): Surveys and Investigations', HMSO, London, 1969
'The Civil Service, Volume 4: Factual, Statistical and Explanatory Papers', HMSO, London, 1968.
'The Civil Service, Volume 5 (1): Proposals and Opinions', HMSO, London, 1968.
'The Civil Service, Volume 5 (2): Proposals and Opinions', HMSO, London, 1968.
'CIVIL SERVICE CLERICAL ASSOCIATION, Strike Policy', Civil Service Clerical Association, London, 1968.
'The Civil Service Commission, Annual Report 1975', Civil Service Commission, Basingstoke, 1976.
CIVIL SERVICE DEPARTMENT, 'Staff Relations in the Civil Service', HMSO, London, 1969, fourth edition.
CIVIL SERVICE DEPARTMENT, 'Third Report', HMSO, London, 1974.
CIVIL SERVICE DEPARTMENT, 'Civil Service Statistics, 1973', HMSO, London, 1973.
CIVIL SERVICE DEPARTMENT, 'Civil Service Statistics, 1974', HMSO, London, 1975.
CIVIL SERVICE DEPARTMENT, 'Civil Service Statistics, 1975', HMSO, London, 1975.
CIVIL SERVICE DEPARTMENT, 'Civil Service Statistics, 1977', HMSO, London, 1977.
CIVIL SERVICE DEPARTMENT, 'Civil Service Yearbook 1974', HMSO, London, 1974.
CIVIL SERVICE DEPARTMENT, 'Civil Service Yearbook 1975', HMSO, London, 1975.

CIVIL SERVICE NATIONAL WHITLEY COUNCIL, 'The Shape of the Post
Fulton Civil Service', CSNWC, London, March 1972.
COCKBURN, A. and BLACKBURN, R., 'Student Power: Problems, Diagnosis,
Action', Penguin, Harmondsworth, 1969.
COHN-BENDIT, D. and COHN-BENDIT, G., 'Obsolete Communism: The Left
Wing Alternative', trans. A. Pomerans, André Deutsch, London, 1968.
COREY, L., 'The Crisis of the Middle Class', Covici Friede, New
York, 1935.
COUGHLIN, H., What Automation Does, 'New Society', no. 34, May
1963, pp.6-8.
CROMPTON, R., Approaches to the study of White Collar Unionism,
'Sociology', vol. 10, 1976, pp.407-26.
CROMPTON, R. and GUBBAY, J., 'Economy and Class Structure',
Macmillan, London, 1977.
CROOK, W.H., 'The General Strike: A Study of Labour's Tragic
Weapon in Theory and Practice', Chapel Hill, North Carolina, 1931.
CROZIER, M., 'The Bureaucratic Phenomenon', University of Chicago
Press, 1965; Editions du Seuil, Paris, 1963.
CROZIER, M., White Collar Unions: The Case of France, in A.
Sturmthal (ed.), 'White Collar Trade Unions', University of
Illinois Press, Urbana, 1968.
CROZIER, M., 'The World of the Office Worker', trans. D. Landau,
University of Chicago Press, Chicago and London, 1971. First
published in France as 'Le Monde des Employes de Bureau', Editions
du Seuil, 1965.
DAHRENDORF, R., 'Class and Class Conflict in an Industrial
Society', Routledge & Kegan Paul, London, 1959. First published
in Germany, 1957.
DAHRENDORF, R. Recent Changes in the Class Structure of European
Societies, 'Daedalus', vol. 93 (1), Winter 1964, pp.225-70.
DALE, H.E., 'The Higher Civil Service of Great Britain', Oxford
University Press, Oxford, 1941.
DALE, J.R., 'The Clerk in Industry', Liverpool University Press,
Liverpool, 1962.
DAY, A., Negotiation and Joint Consultation in the Civil Service,
'Whitley Bulletin', vol. 33, 1953.
DENITCH, B., The New Left and the New Working Class, in J.D. Colfax
and J.L. Roach (eds), 'Radical Sociology', Basic Books, New York,
1971.
DENNIS, N., HENRIQUES, F. and SLAUGHTER, C., 'Coal is Our Life: An
Analysis of a Yorkshire Mining Community', Eyre & Spottiswoode,
London, 1956.
DEPARTMENT OF EMPLOYMENT, 'The New Earnings Survey 1968-78', HMSO,
London, 1970-78.
DEPARTMENT OF THE ENVIRONMENT, 'First Report on Research and
Development 1973', HMSO, London, 1973.
DEPARTMENT OF TRADE AND INDUSTRY, 'Report on Research and Develop-
ment 1972-73', HMSO, London, 1973.
DODD, C.H., Recruitment to the Administrative Class 1960-1964,
'Public Administration', vol. 45 (1), 1967, pp.55-80.
DURKHEIM, E., 'The Division of Labour in Society', trans. G.
Simpson, Free Press, New York; Collier Macmillan, London, 1933.

ELDRIDGE, J.E.T., 'Industrial Disputes: Essays in the Sociology of Industrial Relations', Routledge & Kegan Paul, London, 1968.
ELDRIDGE, J.E.T., 'Sociology and Industrial Life', Michael Joseph, London, 1971.
ELDRIDGE, J.E.T., Industrial Relations and Industrial Capitalism, unpublished paper.
ELLIS, V., Some Sociological Dimensions of Unionization among Technical and Supervisory Employees, unpublished PhD Thesis, University of Leeds, n.d.
ETZIONI, A., 'Modern Organizations', Prentice Hall, Englewood Cliffs, New Jersey, 1964.
EVAN, W.M., On the Margin: The Engineering Technician, in P. Berger (ed.), 'The Human Shape of Work', op. cit.
FLANDERS, A., Pay as an Incentive, in A. Flanders, 'Management and Unions: The Theory and Reform of Industrial Relations', Faber & Faber, London, 1970.
FLOUD, J., A Critique of Bell, 'Survey', vol. 17 (1), 1971, pp.25-36.
FRIEDMAN, G., 'The Anatomy of Work: The Implications of Specialization', trans. W. Rawson, Heinemann, London, 1961. First published as 'Le Travail en Miettes', Libraire Gallimard, 1956.
FRIEDSON, E., Professionalization and the Organization of Middle Class Labour in Post Industrial Society, in P. Halmos (ed.), Professionalization and Social Change, 'The Sociological Review Monograph 20', 1973.
FRY, G.K., 'Statesmen in Disguise: The Changing Role of the Administrative Class of the British Home Civil Service 1853-1966', Macmillan, London, 1969.
FULTON, J. et al., 'The Civil Service, vol. 1: Report of the Committee 1966-68 (The Fulton Report)', HMSO, London, 1968, Cmnd 3638.
FULTON, J., 'Afterthoughts on Administration', Thirty Third Haldane Memorial Lecture, delivered at Birkbeck College, London, May 1969.
GALBRAITH, J.K., 'The Affluent Society' (second edition), Hamish Hamilton, London, 1969.
GARNSEY, E., Women's Work and Theories of Class Stratification, 'Sociology', vol. 12 (2), 1978, pp.223-43.
GARRETT, J., 'The Management of Government', Penguin, London, 1972.
GIDDENS, A., 'Capitalism and Modern Social Theory: An Analysis of the Writings of Marx, Durkheim and Max Weber', Cambridge University Press, Cambridge, 1971.
GIDDENS, A., 'Politics and Sociology in the Thought of Max Weber', Macmillan, London, 1972.
GIDDENS, A., 'The Class Structure of the Advanced Societies', Hutchinson, London, 1973.
GIDDENS, A., Elites in the British Class Structure, in P. Stanworth and A. Giddens (eds), 'Elites and Power in British Society', Cambridge University Press, Cambridge, 1974.
GINSBURG, W., Review of Literature on Union Growth, Government and Structure, in 'A Review of Industrial Relations Research', no. 1, 1970, pp.207-60.
GLADDEN, E.N., 'Civil Service Staff Relationships', William Hodge, London, 1943.
GLADDEN, E.N., 'Civil Service or Bureaucracy?', Staples Press, London, 1956.

GLASER, B.G., 'Organizational Scientists: Their Professional
Careers', Bobbs-Merrill, Indianapolis and New York, 1964.
GLASER, B.G. and STRAUSS, A.L., 'The Discovery of Grounded Theory:
Strategies for Qualitative Research', Weidenfeld & Nicolson,
London, 1968.
GLASS, D.V., and HALL, J.R., Social Mobility in Britain: A Study
of Intergenerational Changes in Status, in D.V. Glass (ed.),
'Social Mobility in Britain', Routledge & Kegan Paul, London,
1954.
GLENN, E.K. and FELDBERG, R.L., Degraded and Deskilled: The Pro-
letarianization of Clerical Work, 'Social Problems', vol. 25 (1),
1977, pp.52-64.
GOLDSTEIN, B., Some Aspects of the Nature of Unionism among
Salaried Professionals in Industry, 'American Sociological Review',
vol. 20 (2), April 1955, pp.199-205.
GOLDSTEIN, B., The Perspective of Unionized Professionals, 'Social
Forces', vol. 37, 1958-9, pp.323-7.
GOLDTHORPE, J.H., Attitudes and Behaviour of Car Assembly Workers:
A Deviant Case and a Theoretical Critique, 'British Journal of
Sociology', vol. 17, 1966, pp.227-44.
GOLDTHORPE, J.H., Social Inequality and Social Integration in
Modern Britain, in D. Wedderburn (ed.), 'Poverty, Inequality and
Class Structure', Cambridge University Press, Cambridge, 1974.
GOLDTHORPE, J.H. and LOCKWOOD, D., Affluence and the British Class
Structure, 'The Sociological Review', vol. 11, 1963, pp.133-63.
GOLDTHORPE, J.H., LOCKWOOD, D., BECHHOFFER, F. and PLATT, J., 'The
Affluent Worker: Political Attitudes and Behaviour', Cambridge
University Press, Cambridge, 1968.
GOLDTHORPE, J.H., LOCKWOOD, D., BECHHOFFER, F. and PLATT, J., 'The
Affluent Worker in the Class Structure', Cambridge University
Press, Cambridge, 1969.
GOLDTHORPE, J.H., LOCKWOOD, D., BECHHOFFER, F. and PLATT, J., 'The
Affluent Worker: Industrial Attitudes and Behaviour', Cambridge
University Press, Cambridge, 1970.
GOULDNER, A.W., 'Patterns of Industrial Bureaucracy', Free Press,
New York; Macmillan, London, 1954.
GOULDNER, A.W., 'Wildcat Strike: A Study of an Unofficial Strike',
Routledge & Kegan Paul, London, 1955.
GRAY, R.Q., The Labour Aristocracy in the Victorian Class Structure,
in F. Parkin (ed.), 'The Social Analysis of Class Structure',
Tavistock, London, 1974.
GROSS, E., 'Work and Society', Thomas Y. Crowell Company, New
York, 1958.
HALL, J.R. and GLASS, D.V., Education and Social Mobility, in D.V.
Glass (ed.), 'Social Mobility in Britain', Routledge & Kegan Paul,
London, 1954.
HALL, R.M., 'Occupations and the Social Structure', Prentice Hall,
Englewood Cliffs, New Jersey, 1969.
HALSEY, A.H. and CREWE, I.M., 'Social Survey of the Civil Service:
The Civil Service, vol. 3 (1) Surveys and Investigations: Evidence
submitted to the Committee under the Chairmanship of Lord Fulton:
1966-68', HMSO, London, 1969.
HAMILTON, R., The Income Difference between Skilled and White
Collar Workers, 'British Journal of Sociology', vol. 14, 1963,
pp.363-73.

HARTWELL, R.M., 'The Causes of the Industrial Revolution in England', Methuen, London, 1967.

HAYDEN, T., 'Rebellion in Newark: Official Violence and Ghetto Response', Random House, New York, 1967.

HAYWARD, R.L., 'Whitley Councils in the United Kingdom Civil Service: A Study in Staff Relations', Civil Service National Whitley Council (Staff Side), London, 1963.

HILL, R.H., Sources of Variation in the Class Consciousness of the British Working Class, unpublished PhD thesis, Brown University, 1978.

HOBSBAWN, E.J., 'Labouring Men: Studies in the History of Labour', Weidenfeld & Nicolson, London, 1964 (1971 edition).

HOMANS, G.C., Status Among Clerical Workers, 'Human Organization', vol. 12, Spring 1953, pp.5-10.

HOPPER, R.D., Cybernation. Marginality and Revolution, in I.L. Horowitz (ed.), 'The New Sociology', Oxford University Press, New York, 1964.

HOUGHTON, D., An Appreciation of William Ewart Llewellyn OBE, 'Whitley Bulletin', vol. 33, 1953, pp.116-18.

HOUGHTON, D., Whitley Councils in the Civil Service, in W.A. Robson (ed.), 'The Civil Service in Britain and France', Hogarth Press, London, 1956.

HOUGHTON, D., The Going of Albert Day, 'Whitley Bulletin', vol. 36, April 1956, pp.52-4.

HUMPHREYS, B.V., 'Clerical Unions in the Civil Service', Blackwell & Mott, London, 1958.

HUNT, N., FERGUSON, E.K., GARRETT, J.L., WALKER, S.D., 'Report of a Management Consultancy Group: The Civil Service vol. 2: Evidence submitted to the Committee under the Chairmanship of Lord Fulton: 1966-68', HMSO, London, 1968.

HYMAN, R., 'Marxism and the Sociology of Trade Unionism', Pluto, London, 1971.

HYMAN, R., 'Strikes', Fontana/Collins, London, 1972.

HYMAN, R., Industrial Conflict in the Political Economy: Trends of the Sixties and Prospects for the Seventies, in R. Miliband and J. Saville (eds), 'Socialist Register', 1973, Merlin, London, 1974.

INGHAM, G.K., 'Strikes and Industrial Conflict: Britain and Scandinavia', Macmillan, London, 1974.

JACKSON, B. and MARSDEN, D., 'Education and the Working Class', Routledge & Kegan Paul, 1962; revised Penguin edition, London, 1966.

JOHNSON, T.J., 'Professions and Power', Macmillan, London, 1972.

JOHNSON, T.J., What is to be Known? The Structural Determination of Social Class, 'Economy and Society', vol. 6 (2), 1977, pp.196-233.

JOHNSON, T.J., The Professions in the Class Structure, in R. Scase (ed.), 'Industrial Society: Class Cleavage and Control', George Allen & Unwin, London, 1977.

JORDAN, Z.A. (ed. and introduction), 'Karl Marx: Economy, Class and Social Revolution', Nelson, London, 1971.

JOSLIN, W.R., 'Mortal Men', Camden Publishing Company, London, 1970.

KASSALOW, E., White Collar Unions in the United States, in A. Sturmthal (ed.), 'White Collar Trade Unions: Contemporary Developments in Industrialized Societies', University of Illinois Press, Urbana, 1966.

KELSALL, R.K., 'Higher Civil Servants in Britain from 1870 to the Present Day', Routledge & Kegan Paul, London, 1955.
KELSALL, R.K., Intellectual Merit and Higher Civil Service Recruitment: The Rise and Fall of an Idea, 'History Sociology and Education, The History of Education Society', Methuen, London, 1971.
KELSALL, R.K., Recruitment to the Higher Civil Service: How has the Pattern Changed?, in P. Stanworth and A. Giddens (eds), 'Elites and Power in British Society', Cambridge University Press, Cambridge, 1974.
KERLINGER, F.M., 'Foundations of Behavioural Research: Educational and Psychological Enquiry', Holt Rinehart & Winston, New York, 1969.
KLINGENDER, F.D., 'The Condition of Clerical Labour in Britain', Martin Lawrence, London, 1935.
KRISTY, N.F., Criteria of Occupational Success among Post Office Counter Clerks, unpublished PhD thesis,   London, 1952.
KUHN, T.S., 'The Structure of Scientific Revolutions' (second edition), University of Chicago Press, Chicago and London; first edition 1962, second edition 1970.
LAYDER, D.R., Occupational Careers in Contemporary Britain; With Special Reference to The Acting Profession, unpublished PhD thesis, University of London, 1976.
LEFEBVRE, H., 'The Sociology of Marx', trans. N. Guterman, Allen Lane, Penguin Press, London, 1968. First published in France, 1966.
LENIN, V.I., 'What is to be Done? Burning Questions of our Movement', Progress Publishers, Moscow, 1947. First published in Stuttgart.
LICHTEIM, G., 'Marxism: An Historical and Critical Study', Routledge & Kegan Paul, London, 1961.
LIPSET, S.M. and ZETTERBERG, H., Social Mobility in Industrial Societies, in S.M. Lipset and R. Bendix, 'Social Mobility in Industrial Society', University of California Press, Berkeley and Los Angeles, 1957.
LOCKWOOD, D., 'The Blackcoated Worker', Allen & Unwin, London, 1958.
LOCKWOOD, D., The New Working Class, 'European Journal of Sociology, Archives Européennes de Sociologie', vol. 1 (2), 1960, pp.248-59.
LOCKWOOD, D., Sources of Variation in Working Class Images of Society, 'Sociological Review', vol. 14, 1966, pp.249-67.
LUKACS, G., 'History and Class Consciousness: Studies in Marxist Dialectics', trans. R. Livingstone, Merlin Press, London, 1971.
LUKES, S., 'Power: A Radical View', Macmillan, London, 1974.
LUMLEY, R., 'White Collar Unionism in Britain: A Survey of the Present Position', Methuen, London, 1973.
MACKENZIE, G., The Economic Dimensions of Embourgeoisement, 'British Journal of Sociology', vol. 18, 1967, pp.29-44.
MACKENZIE, G., Class, 'New Society', 19 October 1972.
MACKENZIE, G., The 'Affluent Worker' Study: An Evaluation and Critique, in F. Parkin (ed.), 'The Social Analysis of Class Structure', Tavistock, London, 1974, pp.237-56.
MACKENZIE, W.J.M. and GROVE, J.W., 'Central Administration in Britain', Longmans, Green & Co., London and New York, 1957.
MCLELLAN, D., 'Marx's Grundrisse', Macmillan, London, 1971; Revised Paladin edition, 1973.

MCLELLAN, D., 'The Thought of Karl Marx: An Introduction',
Macmillan, London, 1971.
MCLELLAN, D., 'Marx', Fontana/Collins, London, 1975.
MALLALIEU, J.P.W., 'Passed to You Please: Britain's Red Tape
Machine at War', Victor Gollancz, London, 1942, Left Book Club
edition. With an introduction by H.J. Laski.
MALLET, S., 'The New Working Class', Spokesman, London, 1975.
Trans. A. and B. Shepherd. First published in France, 1963.
MANN, M., The Social Cohesion of Liberal Democracy, 'American
Sociological Review', vol. 35 (3), June 1970.
MANN, M., 'Consciousness and Action among the Western Working
Class', Macmillan, London, 1973.
MANNHEIM, K., Conservative Thought, in K. Mannheim, 'Essays on
Sociology and Social Psychology', edited P. Kecskemeti, Routledge
& Kegan Paul, London, 1953.
MARTINS, H., The Kuhnian Revolution and its Implications for
Sociology, in T.J. Nossiter, A.H. Hanson, S. Rokkan (eds),
'Imagination and Precision in the Social Sciences: Essays in
Memory of Peter Nettl', Faber & Faber, London, 1972.
MARX, K., Toward the Critique of Hegel's Philosophy of Law:
Introduction, in D. Easton and K. Guddat (editors and translators),
'Writings of the Young Marx on Philosophy and Society', Anchor
Books and Doubleday, New York, 1967.
MARX, K., 'The Economic and Philosophic Manuscripts of 1844',
Foreign Languages Publishing House, Moscow, 1961.
MARX, K., Theses on Feuerbach, in K. Marx and F. Engels, 'The
German Ideology (Part One)', edited and with an introduction by
C.J. Arthur, Lawrence & Wishart, London, 1970.
MARX, K., The Class Struggles in France 1848-1850, in 'K. Marx:
Selected Works Volume II', edited by V. Adoratsky, Lawrence &
Wishart, London, 1942.
MARX, K., 'The Eighteenth Brumaire of Louis Bonaparte', Progress
Publishers, Moscow, 1954.
MARX, K., 'The Poverty of Philosophy', Lawrence & Wishart, London,
n.d., fr. 1847 French edition.
MARX, K., 'A Contribution to the Critique of Political Economy',
Introduction by M. Dobb, Lawrence & Wishart, London, 1971.
MARX, K., Die Moralisierende Kritik und die Kritische Moral, in
F. Mehring (ed.), 'Aus dem Literarischen Nachlass von Karl Marx
und Friedrich Engels', third edition, Stuttgart, 1920.
MARX, K., 'Capital: A Critique of Political Economy', vol. 3,
Foreign Languages Publishing House, Moscow, 1962; Lawrence &
Wishart, London, 1962.
MARX, K., 'Grundrisse', (ed., trans. and introduction by D.
McLellan), Macmillan, London, 1971; revised Paladin edition, 1973.
MARX, K. and ENGELS, F., 'The Communist Manifesto', trans. S.
Moore. This edition first published in England 1888; Penguin
edition, London, 1967.
MARX, K. and ENGELS, F., 'The German Ideology (Part One)', edited
and with an introduction by C.J. Arthur, Lawrence & Wishart,
London, 1970.
MASON, A., The Government and the General Strike 1926, 'The
International Review of Social History', vol. XIV, 1969, pp.1-21.
MATHIAS, P., 'The First Industrial Nation: An Economic History of
Britain 1700-1914', Methuen, London, 1969.

MEEK, R., 'Studies in the Labour Theory of Value', Lawrence & Wishart, London, 1956.
MERTON, R.K., Bureaucratic Structure and Personality, 'Social Forces', vol. 18 (4), 1939-40, pp.560-8.
MERTON, R.K., GRAY, A.P., HOCKEY, B., and SELVIN, H., (eds), 'Reader in Bureaucracy', Free Press, New York, Collier Macmillan, London, 1952.
MICHELS, R., 'Political Parties: A Sociological Study of the Oligarchical Tendencies of Modern Democracy', trans. Eden and Cedar Paul, Free Press, Chicago, 1949.
MILIBAND, R., 'The State in Capitalist Society', Weidenfeld & Nicolson, London, 1969.
MINISTRY OF LABOUR AND NATIONAL SERVICE, 'Evidence to the Priestley Commission', 26th Day, 16 December 1954.
MOORE, W.E., 'Industrial Relations and the Social Order' (new edition), Macmillan, New York, 1951.
MOORE, W.E., 'The Professions: Roles and Rules', Russell Sage Foundation, New York, 1970.
MORSE, N.C., 'Satisfactions in the White Collar Job', Survey Research Center, University of Michigan, Ann Arbor, 1953.
MORSE, N.C. and WEISS, R.S., The Function and Meaning of Work and the Job, 'American Sociological Review', vol. 20 (2), April 1955, pp.191-8.
MOUZELIS, N., 'Organization and Bureaucracy: An Analysis of Modern Theories', Routledge & Kegan Paul, London, 1967.
MOWAT, C.L., 'Britain between the Wars', Methuen, London, 1955.
NATIONAL WHITLEY COUNCIL, 'Fulton - The Reshaping of the Civil Service: Developments during 1970', HMSO, London, March 1971.
NATIONAL WHITLEY COUNCIL, 'Civil Servants and Change: A Joint Statement by the National Whitley Council and the Wider Issues Review Team', London, 1975.
NEWMAN, B., 'Yours for Action', Herbert Jenkins, London, 1953.
NICOLAUS, M., Foreword, in K. Marx, 'Grundrisse', edited and trans. M. Nicolaus, Penguin Books, London, 1973.
NORTHCOTE, S.H. and TREVELYAN, C.E., Report on the Organization of the Permanent Civil Service, reprinted in 'The Civil Service vol. 1: Report of the Committee 1966-67' (The Fulton Report), HMSO, London, 1968.
OAKLEY, A., 'The Sociology of Housework', Martin Robertson, London, 1974.
'OPINION', vol. 35, 1958 - no. 662, February 1979 and special campaign issues 1979. The journal of the Society of Civil and Public Servants, formerly known as 'Civil Service Opinion'.
OPPENHEIMER, M., 'Urban Guerrilla', Penguin, Harmondsworth, 1970; Quadrangle, USA, 1969.
OPPENHEIMER, M., The Proletarianization of the Professional, in P. Halmos, 'Professionalization and Social Change', Sociological Review Monograph 20, 1973.
OWEN, K., 'Computing in Central Government', CSD/HMSO, London, 1974.
PAHL, R. and WINKLER, J., The Economic Elite: Theory and Practice, in P. Stanworth and A. Giddens (eds), 'Elites and Power in British Society', Cambridge at the University Press, 1974.
PARKIN, D., 'Class, Inequality and the Political Order: Social Stratification in Capitalist and Communist Societies', MacGibbon & Kee, London, 1971; Paladin edition, 1972.

PARKIN, F. (ed.), 'The Social Analysis of Class Structure',
Tavistock, London, 1974.
PARRIS, H., 'Staff Relations in the Civil Service: Fifty Years of
Whitleyism', George Allen & Unwin, London, 1973.
POPITZ, H., BAHRDT, H.P., JEURES, E.A. and KESTING, A., The
Worker's Image of Society, translated from Ver Such Einer Typologie,
by C. Ryan, in T. Burns (ed.), 'Industrial Man: Selected Readings',
Penguin, Harmondsworth, 1969.
PRANDY, M., 'Professional Employees: A Study of Scientists and
Engineers', Faber & Faber, London, 1965.
PREISS, J. and EHRLICH, H.J., 'An Examination of Role Theory: The
Case of the State Police', University of Nebraska Press, Lincoln,
Nebraska, 1966.
PRIESTLEY, R. et al., 'Royal Commission on the Civil Service 1953-
1955', (The Priestley Commission), HMSO, London, 1955, Cmd 9613,
1966 reprint.
PROFITT, T.H., Great Britain, in F.F. Ridley (ed.), 'Specialists
and Generalists: A Comparative Study of the Professional Civil
Servant at Home and Abroad', George Allen & Unwin, London, 1968.
'RED TAPE', vol. 1, 1911 - vol. 68, 1979. The journal of the Civil
and Public Services Association.
RIDLEY, F.F., Specialists as Administrators, 'State Service', vol. 47,
February 1967, pp.31-8.
RIDLEY, F.F. (ed.), 'Specialists and Generalists: A Comparative
Study of the Professional Civil Servant at Home and Abroad',
George Allen & Unwin, London, 1968.
ROBERTSON, J.H., 'Reform of British Central Government', Chatto &
Windus, London, 1971.
ROBSON, W.A. (ed.), 'The Civil Service in Britain and France',
Hogarth Press, London, 1956.
ROSTOW, W.W., 'The Stages of Economic Growth: A Non Communist
Manifesto', second edition, Cambridge University Press, Cambridge,
1971.
ROTHSCHILD, N. et al., The Organization and Management of Govern-
ment Research and Development, in 'A Framework for Government
Research and Development: A Green Paper', HMSO, London, 1971,
Cmnd 4814.
ROUTH, G., Civil Service Pay, 1875-1950, 'Economica', vol. 21 (New
Series), 1954, pp.201-23.
ROUTH, G., 'Occupation and Pay in Great Britain 1906-1960',
Cambridge University Press, Cambridge, 1965.
'ROYAL COMMISSION ON THE CIVIL SERVICE 1953-55', HMSO, London, 1955.
'ROYAL COMMISSION ON THE CIVIL SERVICE 1953-55'; Minutes of Evidence
taken before the Royal Commission', HMSO, London, 1955.
RUSSELL-SMITH, E., 'Modern Bureaucracy: The Home Civil Service',
Longmans, London, 1974.
SCASE, R., Conceptions of the Class Structure and Political Ideo-
logy. Some Observations on Attitudes in England and Sweden, in F.
Parkin (ed.), 'The Social Analysis of Class Structure', Tavistock,
London, 1974.
SCHNAPP, A. and VIDAL-NAQUET, P. (eds), 'The French Student Up-
risings: November 1967 - June 1968', trans. M. Jolas, Beacon,
Boston, 1971.
SEALE, P. and MCCONVILLE, M., 'The French Revolution 1968', Penguin,
Harmondsworth, 1968.

SEGERSTEDT, T.T., An Investigation of Class Consciousness among
Office Employees and Workers in Swedish Factories, in 'Transactions
of the Second World Congress of Sociology 1953', vol. II, 1954.
SHERIFF, P., 'Career Patterns in the Higher Civil Service', HMSO,
London, 1976.
SILVERMAN, W., The Economic and Social Effects of Automation in an
Organization, 'American Behavioural Scientist', vol. 9 (10), 1966,
pp.3-8.
SOCIETY OF CIVIL SERVANTS, 'Annual Report', 1970.
SOCIETY OF CIVIL SERVANTS, 'Annual Report', 1973.
SOCIETY OF CIVIL SERVANTS, 'Annual Report', 1974.
SOCIETY OF CIVIL SERVANTS, 'Minutes of Evidence taken before the
Royal Commission on the Civil Service', 8th Day, 25 May 1954 (wit-
nesses), p.238.
SOCIETY OF CIVIL AND PUBLIC SERVANTS, 'Report on Membership', 1978.
SPECTATOR, The, Blackcoated Unemployment, 'The Spectator', 10 May
1936, pp.653-4.
SPEIER, H., The Salaried Employee in Modern Society, 'Social
Research', vol. 1, 1934, pp.111-33.
STANLEY, D.T., 'The Higher Civil Service: An Evaluation of Federal
Personnel Practices', The Brookings Institution, Washington, 1964.
STANWORTH, P. and GIDDENS, A. (eds), 'Elites and Power in British
Society', Cambridge University Press, Cambridge, 1974.
'STATE SERVICE', vol. 34, 1954 - vol. 54, 1974. The journal of the
Institution of Professional Civil Servants, formerly known as
'State Technology'.
STEDMAN-JONES, G., The Meaning of the Student Revolt, in 'Student
Power: Problems, Diagnosis, Action', Penguin, Harmondsworth, 1969.
STURMTHAL, A., White Collar Unions: A Comparative Essay, in A.
Sturmthal (ed.), 'White Collar Trade Unions: Contemporary Develop-
ments in Industrialized Societies', University of Illinois Press,
Urbana and London, 1966.
SYKES, A.J.M., Some Differences in the Attitudes of Clerical and
Manual Workers, 'Sociological Review', vol. 13, 1965, pp.297-310.
TAYLOR, K.F., Opportunities in Management for Scientific Civil
Servants: A Consumer Survey, Behavioural Science Research Division,
Civil Service Department, Report No. 1, second distribution March
1972, unpublished.
TENNANT, M., 'Report of a Committee appointed to Review the Organ-
ization of the Scientific Civil Service' (The Tennant Report),
HMSO, London, 1965.
THOMAS, H. (ed.), 'Crisis in the Civil Service', Antony Blond,
London, 1968.
TITMUS, R.M., 'Income Distribution and Social Change: A Study in
Criticism', George Allen & Unwin, London, 1962.
TOMLIN, et al., 'The Royal Commission on the Civil Service' (The
Tomlin Commission), HMSO, London, 1931.
TOURAINE, A., 'The Post Industrial Society: Tomorrow's Social
History: Classes, Conflicts and Culture in the Programmed Society',
trans. D.F.X. Mayhew, Wildwood House, London, 1971. First published
in France, 1969.
TROW, M., Reflections on the Transition from Mass to Universal
Higher Education, 'Daedalus', vol. 99 (1), 1970, pp.1-42.
VARCOE, I., 'Organizing for Science in Britain: A Case Study',
Oxford University Press, London, 1974.

WALKER, C.R. and GUEST, R.H., 'The Man on the Assembly Line', Harvard University Press, Cambridge, Massachusetts, 1952.
WALKER, J. and MARRIOTT, R., A Study of Some Attitudes to Factory Work, 'Occupational Psychology', vol. 25, 1951, pp.181-91.
WALKER, N., 'Morale in the Civil Service: A Study of the Desk Worker', Edinburgh University Press, 1961.
WEBER, M., 'The Theory of Social and Economic Organization', trans. A.M. Henderson and T. Parsons, edited and with an introduction by T. Parsons, Free Press, New York; Collier Macmillan, London, 1947.
WEBER, M., 'From Max Weber: Essays in Sociology', edited and with an introduction by H. Gerth and C. Wright Mills, Routledge & Kegan Paul, London, 1948.
WEDDERBURN, D. and CROMPTON, R., 'Workers' Attitudes and Technology', Cambridge University Press, Cambridge, 1972.
WERSKEY, G., Making Socialists of Scientists: Whose Side is History on?, 'Radical Science Journal', 2/3, 1975, pp.13-49.
WESTERGAARD, J.H., The Rediscovery of the Cash Nexus: Some Recent Interpretations of Trends in British Class Structure, in R. Miliband and J. Saville (eds), 'Socialist Register 1970', Merlin, London, 1970.
WESTERGAARD, J.H., Sociology: The Myth of Classlessness, in R. Blackburn (ed.), 'Ideology in Social Science', Fontana/Collins, London, 1972.
WESTERGAARD, J.H. and RESLER, H., 'Class in a Capitalist Society: A Study of Contemporary Britain', Heinemann, London, 1975, Penguin edition, London, 1976.
WHALLEY, R.P., The Proletarianization of the Engineer: A Discussion of Some Preliminary Research Findings, unpublished, n.d.
WHITE, L.D., 'Whitley Councils in the British Civil Service: A Study of Conciliation and Arbitration', University of Chicago Press, Chicago, 1933.
WIDER ISSUES REVIEW TEAM, 'Civil Servants and Change', Civil Service Department, London, 1975.
WILENSKY, H.L., Work Careers and Social Integration, 'International Social Science Journal', vol. 12, 1960, pp.534-74.
WILLENER, A., 'The Action Image of Society: On Cultural Politicization', trans. A.M. Sheridan Smith, Tavistock, London, 1970.
WILLSON, F.M.G., 'The Organization of British Central Government 1914-64', edited by D.N. Chester, George Allen & Unwin, London, 1968, second edition.
WILSON, D.F., 'Dockers: The Impact of Industrial Change', Fontana Collins, London, 1972.
WINNIFRITH, A.J.D., Negotiation and Joint Consultation in the Civil Service, 'Whitley Bulletin', vol. 33, 1953, pp.100-6.
WOODWARD, J., 'Industrial Organization: Theory and Practice', Oxford University Press, London, 1965.
WOODWARD, L., 'The Age of Reform 1815-1870' (second edition), Clarendon Press, Oxford, 1962.
WRIGHT MILLS, C., Situated Actions and Vocabularies of Motive, in J.G. Mannis and B.N. Meltzer (eds), 'Symbolic Interaction: A Reader in Social Psychology', second edition, Allyn & Bacon Inc., Boston, 1972, first edition 1967, pp.393-404. Reprinted from 'American Sociological Review', vol. 5, December 1940.
WRIGHT MILLS, C., 'White Collar: The American Middle Classes', Oxford University Press, New York, 1951; Galaxy Books Edition 1956.

YOUNG, M., 'The Rise of the Meritocracy 1870-2033: An Essay on Education and Equality', Thames & Hudson, 1958; Penguin edition.
ZEITLIN, I., 'Marxism: A Re-Examination', D. Van Nostrand Co., New York and London, 1967.
ZETTERBERG, H.L., 'On Theory and Verification in Sociology', third edition, Bedminster Press, New Jersey, 1965.

INDEX

Accommodation, office, in the Civil Service, 84-6
Administrators, Civil Service, 43-6,59,60,62-4,65,65-6,68, 70,71,72,81,83,84,132,134, see also Mandarins and Civil Service Management
Admiralty, the, 93
Agriculture, Department of, 110, 115
Assistant Clerks Association, 93,95,119, see also Civil Service Clerical Association and Civil and Public Services Association
Association of Professional Executive Clerical and Computer Staff, 141
Association of Scientific Technical and Managerial Staff, 141
Association of Temporary Clerks and Writers, 92
Authority, 75-6,82
Automation, 20-2,86,88,89,90, 136,138

Baldwin, Stanley, 119
Boy Clerks Association, 93-4
Bureaucracy, 16-17,75
Bureaucratization, 13,16,17,20-2, 26,74-86,90,91,92,94,96,109, 111,119,124,125,135,138,139
Buxton, Stanley, 93

Carchedi's theory of proletar-

ianization, 13-14,35,133
Carpenter Committee, the, 81
Cash nexus, 138,140,141,143
Chamberlain, Austen, 96
Civil and Public Services Association, 97,98,109,114,115, 116,117,121,123, see also Civil Service Clerical Association and Assistant Clerks Association
Civil Servants: definition of, 27; educational backgrounds, 65-8,117; income, 35-43,43-57, 103,110,117,124,132,136,141; geographical origins, 68-9, 72; militancy, 4,58,72,136; social origins, 62-5,109,117, 124,125,136; work situations, 74-90,96,117,136,141; working conditions, 80,82,94,95,96, 107,117,135,136
Civil Service: development, 25-7,28-30,59-60,80-2,136; management, 43-6,88,91,93; organization, 88,141; regional distribution, 28-30; sex composition, 28,70-2,141; size, 26-31,28,29,141; structure, 28,59-60,80-2,92,135, 136,141
Civil Service Clerical Association, 97,106-7,108-9,121,123, 132; strike policy, 107, see also Assistant Clerks Association and Civil Servants Clerical Association

195

For Product Safety Concerns and Information please contact our EU representative GPSR@taylorandfrancis.com Taylor & Francis Verlag GmbH, Kaufingerstraße 24, 80331 München, Germany